COLLECTED POEMS

EDITED BY PETER FALLON

CIARAN CARSON

WAKE FOREST UNIVERSITY PRESS

Collected Poems

Published simultaneously in paperback
and in a clothbound edition
First North American edition published 2009

For permission to reproduce or
broadcast these poems, write to:
Wake Forest University Press
Post Office Box 7333
Winston-Salem, NC 27109

Cover design by Quemadura
Printed on acid-free, recycled paper
in the United States of America

LCCN 2008943056
ISBN 978-1-930630-45-1 (paperback)
ISBN 978-1-930630-46-8 (clothbound)

First published by Gallery Press
Wake Forest University Press
www.wfu.edu/wfupress

Publication of this book has
been aided by the generosity
of the Boyle Family Fund.

CONTENTS

The Irish for No

The Twelfth of Never

For All We Know

FROM

THE NEW ESTATE
AND OTHER POEMS

(1976, 1988)

The Insular Celts

Having left solid ground behind
In the hardness of their placenames,
They have sailed out for an island:

As along the top of a wood
Their boats have crossed the green ridges,
So has the pale sky overhead

Appeared as a milky surface,
A white plain where the speckled fish
Drift in lamb-white clouds of fleece.

They will come back to the warm earth
And call it by possessive names —
Thorned rose, love, woman and mother;

To hard hills of stone they will give
The words for breast; to meadowland,
The soft gutturals of rivers,

Tongues of water; to firm plains, flesh,
As one day we will discover
Their way of living in their death.

They entered their cold beds of soil
Not as graves, for this was the land
That they had fought for, loved, and killed

Each other for. They'd arrive again:
Death could be no horizon
But the shoreline of their island,

A coming and going, as flood
Comes after ebb. In the spirals
Of their brooches is seen the flight

Of one thing into the other:
As the wheel-ruts on a battle-
Plain have filled with silver water,

The confused circles of their wars,
Their cattle-raids, have worked themselves
To a laced pattern of old scars.

But their death, since it is no real
Death, will happen over again
And again, their bones will seem still

To fall in the hail beneath hooves
Of horses, their limbs will drift down
As the branches that trees have loosed.

We cannot yet say why or how
They could not take things as they were.
Someday we will learn of how

Their bronze swords took the shape of leaves,
How their gold spears are found in cornfields,
Their arrows are found in trees.

St Ciaran's Island

Since I have come to this island
The big world has receded.
All I have is this brooch
Set in a silver plain. The reeds

Of its shores bind me to accept
Water as my outer limit.
There are some things I cannot cross.
I know the loneliness in it;

Having tried to talk to men
Of God, I have talked to the trees
Of God's silence. He gave no sign,
But covered me in leaves,

And made the stars seem small spaces
Of light. I set these ornaments
Down, as illuminations
To my sacred texts, having meant

To lose the written word
In the appearances of art;
But the wind disordered me,
This island weather changed my heart.

Since I must forever be alone
With the green things of the world
I must learn to grow in silence,
And take things as they are:

Yet the trees are covering
For my head, and I have worked
The branches to this fine lace shell
I now inhabit. In the dark

It seems as if the island itself
Is muttering with the sound of water:
Soon my hut may be the only island.
It will not matter.

I will be myself alone.
Through the holes in the trellis
Falls thin rain. What drizzles
Slowly into my skull is this:

I will acclimatize.
My head will shrink in size.

O'Carolan's Complaint

The great tunes
I never played are lost
To monied patronage, the lit rooms
In grey façades

Whisper, fall silent
At their harmony and grace. I think
Of all the girls I might have loved
Instead of music —

One hand finding melody
As easily as the pulse of a heart,
The other making fluent gestures
Towards the purse of love.

My real performances
Never yet embraced an actual beauty —
Mere competence, my inward ear
And theirs heard better:

Like intervals of silence
Between the notes,
Their upturned faces wanting more,
The lives I never lived.

Casting the Bell

The glittering ore
Of chalices and plates — offerings
Of tin and copper, silverware
Sprinkled in shining motes —
Is made liquid by the hour.

Now the steady hush of the bellows
Draws breath; halts.
The sluice-gates of the furnace
Are sprung open; runnels of molten light
Stream into the cupped darkness,
Finding the mould of clay.

Silence, as the metal cools,
The shape, the hidden note, made
Irrevocable — the ear, the iron tongue,
The mouth, the sounding-bow of bronze
Ringing out unchanging noons;
The long procession of the days
Swelling and dwindling across
The listening parishes.

Interior with Weaver

All we can see of him
Are his arms, his shoulders,
And his head
Hunched away from the door:

See how light
From the door and windows
Has edged the tautness
Of his face,

The clenched fingers
Of the hand
Where he holds the cords,
And light

Lies along the loom
Shaping it out of the darkness,
Till the wooden beams
Seem to fill the room

And the cross-frame
Is repeated
In the bars of the window.
To see him seated

There, you'd think
His endless repetitions
Were those of the loneliness
Of human passion,

The pain that must
In the end give meaning
To the grass and trees
That blur outside the door.

Linen

From the photographs of bleach-greens
Mill-hands stare across the snowy acres.
In a frieze white as marble
Their lives are ravelled and unravelled —
Golden straw, bright thread, the iron looms
Are cast in tangled cordage.

The shapes of wheels and spindles shine
In darkness. When the weave is finished
Light will fall on linen simply, as it would
On glass, or silverware, or water,
Things needed for a wedding or a funeral;
We will be reconciled to those cold sheets.

An Early Bed

A bubble of damp
Jaundiced the scrolled flowers
On the candy-stripe wallpaper.
To pass the time
I counted the flawed petals,
Each flecked angrily with red,
Like father's face.

His voice unravelled from below
In disembodied phrases —
A child who struck his father,
He once told me, died
Soon afterwards;
But the disobedient hand
Would not be buried:

One white flower
In a grave of flowers, it struggled
Upwards through the clay
As if to fend off judgement.
I thought of dying out of spite,
My parents' faces worn
To a threadbare lace . . .

I held my breath
And tried to sink below the surface
Of myself, into somewhere else.
But my right hand stayed where it was,
The final speck of air
Blossoming above my finger.
I cried because I could not die.

This evening, re-papering
My room, those early failures

Came to light. Tissued layers
Peeled beneath the decorating knife
Like fronds of skin. Beneath,
Gauzed over with old paste,
I found the yellowed flowers again.

Twine

My father's postman sack
Hung on a nail behind the kitchen door,
Its yellow straps undone. I stuck my head inside
The canvas flap and breathed the gloom.

The smell of raffia and faded ink
Was like the smell of nothing. The twine lay in
My mother's bottom drawer, the undelivered
Letters were returned to sender.

I thought of being shut up under stairs.
Outside it was snowing, and my father's hands
Were blue with cold. Soon he would return,
His hands would warm me.

Christmas came. He worked all day.
His dinner would be kept hot in the oven.
There was the twine to tie the turkey's legs.
There was the tawse behind the kitchen door.

The Incredible Shrinking Man

The navy gaberdine was one size big
For me: the cuffs reached to my knuckle, but
My hands would grow. My mother put an extra
Eyelet in the belt, and changed the buttons round.

I watched my progress anxiously.
I looked in the mirror every morning. Still,
I didn't seem to grow. Was there something
Wrong with me? I ate lots of spinach.

Then I remembered the Incredible Shrinking Man.
He had been lying on the yacht. His wife
Had just gone down below when the electric
Cloud appeared — like a silver teapot, shining,

Like nothing on earth. It whistled over him
And ended suddenly as it began. Nothing
Seemed to have changed. His wife kissed him.
They both went down below.

The next morning he began to shrink.
His nylon shirt seemed strange, he thought
It was another man's. He complained
To the laundry, but they did nothing for him.

Inside a month he had to stand on a chair
To kiss his wife goodnight. Inside two,
He fought a spider with a darning needle.
The film ended as he climbed a blade of grass.

Within a year everything had changed.
Another baby came into the family; that made four
With me the eldest boy. My younger brother
Wore the threadbare gaberdine.

I looked at his face and then the baby's face.
They both looked different and yet the same.
The baby was shrivelled and very wise.
My brother's hands drooped in the mirror.

Rubbish

From the sick-room window, past
The leaning-sideways
Railway sleepers of the fence,
The swaying nettles,
You can just make out
The rusty fire of a crushed
Coke tin, the dotted glint of staples in
A wet cardboard box.

I could be sifting through
The tip at the bottom of Ganges Street.
Eggshells. Bricks. A broken hypodermic,
And one bit of plaster
Painted on one side
I seem to recognize from somewhere —

It is the off-white wall
I stared at as a child
As my mother picked my hair for nits.
The iron comb scraped out
A series of indefinite ticks
As they dropped on a double leaf
Of last week's *Irish News*.
I had a crick in my neck.

I thought that someone
On the last train might look up
And see me staring out beyond
The almost-useless strip
Between the railway
And the new industrial estate.

Engraving from a Child's Encyclopaedia

Here is a glacier carrying down stones,
A slow declension towards a terminal moraine.
Three tiny, human figures on a precipice
Carry alpenstocks, one pointing
At the snowy pyramid above, where the ice
Divides, and so on into unseen valleys,
And higher still, to silver, pewter-shadowed
Clouds, that carry messages of further snow.

You can clearly see the etched lines on the plate,
How many hours of trouble went in making this,
The walls, the towers, the minarets of ice
And cloud. The Alpine flowers — scratches that could be
Edelweiss, or grass — must have been obscured
By boredom; they were unimportant. You can see
The grand gesture of the guide ignores them;
He is concerned with higher things.

Some other life persists: the *roches moutonnées*,
For example, might perhaps be taken
For black sheep, resting furtively on pinnacles
Of ice after their long journey. One of the human
Figures is seated, looking towards them.
Is he counting them, is he asleep?
All three are lost in contemplation.
They seem a long way from home.

King's Lynn

East Winch, Holbeach,
Clenchwarton, Heacham:
They squelch and rasp like shingle,
Coarse-grained syllables
Disputing every inch
Back from the Wash.

The wind whorls
To a Van Gogh sky.
Estuaries silt up,
Lost in a choke of mud.
Fields mutate
To another branch of the sea.

A perennial art, this
Striving for form:
In miniature it is
The ebb and flow of tide
Sweeping clean; its inspiration
Dried up, receding daily.

And whelks bear
The sea's convolution,
Are ribbed and spiralled,
Realizing perfect beauty:
Delicate cages
Hooding flesh and water.

The Half-Moon Lake

It was here the boy entered the skylight
And was gone, into the reversed world
Of his dreams, hoping that life there might

Prove otherwise. Walking the tentative
Pane of ice there might have been that morning
He would have imagined himself to live

In one final image, the star-shaped hole
Approaching darkly, sudden as his
Disappearance from our lives. Or had his soul

Just then been frailed too taut
For human heart, had the white sheet
Already failed beneath him at the thought?

No one heard him go in silence,
Nor when they dragged for him, deep as a chance
Allowed, was there any trace.

Was the faultless mirror shattered
By the thin boy diving for the moon
Of his own face rising through the water?

They could not yet say why
He left so quickly, not leaving any word,
Or whether the glass existed purely

For his own forgetfulness. Deep
In the unseen water it is possible
He lies, with himself at last asleep.

It was for the other children that they feared.
It had been necessary that the Half-Moon Lake be
Filled in, and altogether disappear.

The Excursion

Here, the ascension — the Guidebook had foreseen it —
Became 'picturesque'. Even in our funicular
Car we could appreciate with what laboriousness
A traveller on foot might climb, assisted only
By an alpenstock, his wish to be alone —
To climb, to see the view his efforts yielded:

Silver crests on silver clouds, snowcaps almost
Airborne, precipitously vanishing
Through lower hazes, and underneath, far off,
A green field momentarily made clear
By sunlight; a white church like a delft church,
And cows like toy cows, leaden, grazing, slanted.

We turned to the place in the book to find the hamlet;
But over on the Lake a shower had suddenly
Developed, a rainbow glazed upon the air like aerosol,
Distracting us. We rubbed the windows on the car;
One of us took out a camera, too late. Just then
I almost wished we had not come —

I already thought of questions, constantly repeated:
What did you do? and *What was it like?* and searching
For the words; as if a traveller at dusk, perplexed
By snowy mountains, gorges and defiles,
Might chance upon his downward footprints
Once again, regretting them, and think of home.

The Holiday

At breakfast I remembered
The mutilated sheep we found yesterday.
The pus had thickened to a sour cream
In the pink-lipped wounds;

Their fixed stare recalled
The waitress's eyes, the frivelled lids
Still bleared with sleep, the net
Of veins running through the white.

The clouds beyond the window
Curdled suddenly; a whey-coloured skin
Had crawled and wrinkled
On the coffee. Going home to Belfast

We would find a house denied our presence,
The door handle cobwebbed —
The papers lying, unread, in the hall,
The milk turned sour on our doorstep.

The Bomb Disposal

Is it just like picking a lock
With the slow deliberation of a funeral,
Hesitating through a darkened nave
Until you find the answer?

Listening to the malevolent tick
Of its heart, can you read
The message of the threaded veins
Like print, its body's chart?

The city is a map of the city,
Its forbidden areas changing daily.
I find myself in a crowded taxi
Making deviations from the known route,

Ending in a cul-de-sac
Where everyone breaks out suddenly
In whispers, noting the boarded windows,
The drawn blinds.

Dunne

It was then I heard of the missing man.
The wireless spoke through a hiss of static —
Someone was being interviewed:
The missing man, the caller said, can be found
At Cullyhanna Parochial House.
That was all. Those were his very words.
I reached an avenue of darkened yews.
Somewhere footsteps on the gravel.

I then identified myself, and he
Embraced me, someone I had never seen
Before, but it was him all right, bearded
And dishevelled. There were tears in his eyes.
He knew nothing of the ransoms.
He did not know who they were. He knew nothing
Of his whereabouts. He did not even know
If he was in the South or North.

It seemed he was relieved from hiding in
Some outhouse filled with ploughs and harrows,
Rusted winnowings that jabbed and rasped
At him. He had felt like a beaten child.
When they hooded him with a balaklava
He thought the woolly blackness was like being
Shut up under stairs, without a hint of hope,
Stitches dropped that no one could knit back.

From Camlough, Silverbridge and Crossmaglen
The military were closing in. He was,
It seemed, the paste on the wallpaper, or
The wall, spunked out between the leaves, etched
At last into the memories of what might have been.
He was released. The three bullets they had given him
As souvenirs chinked in his pocket. He slipped
Through a hole in the security net.

All day long for seven days he had lain
On the broad of his back on the floor.
He could see nothing, but turned, again
And again, to an image of himself as a child
Hunched in bed, staring at the ceiling,
At the enigmatic pits and tics
That scored the blankness, and then, farther,
To the stars that brushed against the windowpane.

Fishes in a Chinese Restaurant

I wonder if they see me.
Fluttering like swallows
Behind a window, their wings
Take the invisible

Curtain of water
Heavily as silk, as air
Before a storm, for their
Own weathers move them only

Slowly, their mouths opening
And shutting like an eyelid.
The branches where they nest
Half asleep are those of

An ornamental garden;
Where they drift
Miniature trees
Flower as paint through water;

The thin bubbles
Rising in scales to the surface
Mime various bird-musics.
Suddenly I felt helpless

As if, seeing an accident
Outside, my mouth was pressed
To the glass, my hands uttered
Dialects of silence.

At the Windy Gap, 1910

It seems they all have met here at a crossroads
Quite by accident, and — bored with the 'Grand Atlantic'
Tour — agreed to have their pictures taken.
The three charabancs would be empty, only the ladies
Remain seated. They are very correct: frills and lace
Glint quietly in watery light; it is almost raining;
China cups shine dully in the twilight
On a wooden trestle. Two girls were selling tea
But now they too have turned away from what
They should be doing. They look towards us;
Their pinafores are lifted gently by the wind.

Two gentlemen with clerical collars look sideways
At the other gentlemen, and some of the other gentlemen
Smile seriously, looking at the camera.
A cyclist has wandered in at the edge of the picture;
He stands with his head bowed, scrutinized
By three men smoking cigarettes and laughing.
Only one man has his back turned towards us. Hidden
In the crowd, we see his bowler hat, the back
Of his expensive collar, and follow what we think
Might be his gaze across the valley to the mountain,
Then a further mountain, then the clouds.

No one casts a shadow, least of all this one
Who turns away from us, in shyness, or disinterest,
Or in contemplation. Does he watch the weather,
Or perhaps, if someone came to photograph hours
Later, would he still be there, the charabancs gone back
To where they came from, to the safe hotels?
Perhaps he came to look at poverty, the barren stone,
The rain clouds thickening, in a sepia wash
Above the darkened mountains, through the mountain gap
One patch of sunlight, and no one to be seen for miles.

Excerpts from a Tourist Handbook

Here, for the first time, the outside world can see
The faith and triumph of the God-fearing quarrymen
    of Blaenau Ffestiniog
Who honeycombed their mountains with 130 miles

Of tunnels linking hundreds of caverns — the caverns like
A series of cathedrals, the cathedrals like a series of caverns.

In the dressing-shed the God-fearing quarrymen of
    Blaenau Ffestiniog
Are splitting slate. Everywhere are reams of it —

Thin bluish-grey veneers, or darkened panes
Which roof the houses of five continents, the outside world.

Under the slates of the Blaenau Ffestiniog School
The God-fearing children of Blaenau Ffestiniog wrote
    on slates.

Arithmetic and Geography, the names of continents.

In 1917 the industry suffered a serious setback.
The Blaenau Ffestiniog District Memorial to the Dead
    is engraved
With a list of the names of 363 quarrymen who became
    soldiers.

One quarter of the skilled slate dressers of Blaenau Ffestiniog
Failed to return from the Sands of Sinai, or the Mud
    of Flanders.

Many slates remained unwritten-on.

For every ton of goods is 10 tons' waste.

The children of Blaenau Ffestiniog continued to write.

East of Cairo

One day I walked into the village compound
And found the headsman and his family watching television.
They were sitting in rickety bamboo chairs
And it was pouring rain, but no one seemed to mind.

It was one of those travelogues on French Cambodia.
A policeman was directing traffic. Temples,
Cows and awnings rippled in the sun. Maidens danced
Around with bangles on their arms. The usual stuff.

Why did these people sit here, watching this?
Could they not be themselves? It was then I decided
To leave Sarajasthan. I had come to the East, after all,
To find myself, and there was nothing there.

I now have plans to go to the holy city of Lhasa.
They say the only wheel there is a prayer-wheel.
And I hear that the Dalai Lama has a scheme
To separate the spirit from the body.

All day long, from high in his palace tower,
The god-king stares through Swiss binoculars
At three monks gliding on the river
On ice skates left them by the last explorer.

The Rosary Rally

It was the first of May.
The crowd spilled out from the Convent Field;
White flowers nodded on the tarred road.
Everyone was praying hard.

The World War was to come
If not tomorrow, then the next day, or the next;
From Nagasaki, Hiroshima,
The white cloud drifted nearer, nearer —
So quietly it would be there
Before you saw it coming.
It was the cloud of my dreams, thick
And noiseless, everywhere.

Decades of the Rosary passed.
We saw the troops march on the Red Square
Of Russia. My mother wiped her hands,
Then went to make the tea.
When everything was cleared away
We all knelt down. I tried to think of the words,
The lull before each Mystery.

All there was was the sound
Of coming rain, a light touch on the window,
Then the clouds, and the stars
Between the clouds.

The Alhambra

The picture-house was next door
To the laundry. I passed through clouds
Of boiling steam to a foyer
Marbled like the palaces of Pompeii.

There is a smoky avenue
Of light that leads to history — the Fall of Rome,
The death of Al Capone; the instant
Where the chariot wheels collide.

It is here I will kiss
A girl who will never be my wife, watching
The *Titanic* founder for the second time
Through cascades of broken ice.

I am washed back into daylight,
To the laundry — sea-foam on the lens,
Shirts and underwear revolving
In my struggle to escape the glass.

To Margaret

When we stop
Wishing you an easy death
Your pain will be forgotten.

I will remember
Honey, snuff and whiskey,
The copper bracelet on your wrist,

The clarity
Of the tainted water
You had sent from Lourdes.

Will it be like this,
A cold, sour taste, reminding me
Of disappointed cures?

Even the pearl
Forgets the suffering that made it
And acquires an unintended beauty.

Visiting the Dead

When she was found
Her tongue protruded from her gums;
Her face was knuckled,
Her hand clenched on the sheet.

Now her skin has eased out,
New-washed cloth in which the wrinkles fade
Beneath the iron's hiss.
They have laid her in clean linen.

We drink tea from her best china.
A knot of mourners unravels upstairs;
A maiden aunt descends, weeping softly
Into her starched handkerchief.

When they brought down the body
The coffin stuck in the crooked staircase.
We hesitated, awkward in our best suits,
Then rushed to help, and freed her.

Eaves

from the Welsh

Rain in summer —
It is the sound of a thousand cows
Being milked.

In winter
The eaves are heavy with ice,
Their snowy teats drip silence.

Moving In

For days there have been empty sounds
At the sound of our feet
On the bare boards. The last drift
Of shavings has been swept out.

I have painted the inside of the linen
Cupboard, and the off-white smell
Has spread even to the loft.
She says to do the kitchen

Gloss, for the condensation.
The bathroom will be tiled.
Between the floorboards in the roof-space
Fibreglass, for insulation.

For days she has appeared
As if behind transparencies of skin,
As various papers are held to the light.
We have unpacked, careful not to break.

Things are falling into place,
Though much remains unfilled —
I am feeling my way around
The eggshell finish of the walls,

Switching off those folds of light
Softer than snowflakes drifted
On the white sheets whiter than snow.
I will shift her body over

For my warmed place. As yet there is no heat.
The double glazing, there to keep out
Wind and ice, has kept cold in.
There is silence in the space between.

Our Country Cousins

On birthdays
Or your goings-away

To become black sheep
We'd sleep

In each other's
Houses then, mothers

Being sisters again,
Lying apart from their men;

Dressed in clothes of another kind,
We'd play blind

Man's buff,
The farmer wants a wife,

Knowing our real kin
To lie beneath the skin.

Our ones
Would be buried with your ones.

Someone, pretending an accident,
Wore bandages, sent

His partner with a knife in her head.
Another painted his body red.

Even your eggs were flecked with blood,
Your bread had the coarse grain of tweed.

Céilí

If there was a house with three girls in it
It only took three boys to make a dance.
You'd see a glimmer where McKeown's once was
And follow it till it became a house.
But maybe they'd have gone on, up the hill
To Loughran's, or made across the grazing,
Somewhere else. All those twistings and turnings,
Crossroads and dirt roads and skittery lanes:
You'd be glad to get in from the dark.

And when you did get in there'd be a power
Of *poitín*. A big tin creamery churn,
A ladle, those mugs with blue and white bars.
Oh, good and clear like the best of water.
The music would start up. This one ould boy
Would sit by the fire and rosin away,
Sawing and sawing till it fell like snow.
That *poitín* was quare stuff. At the end of
The night you might be fiddling with no bow.

When everyone was ready out would come
The tin of Tate and Lyle's Golden Syrup,
A spoon or a knife, a big farl of bread.
Some of those same boys wouldn't bother with
The way you were supposed to screw it up.
There might be courting going on outside,
Whisperings and cacklings in the barnyard;
A spider thread of gold-thin syrup
Trailed out across the glowing kitchen tiles
Into the night of promises, or broken promises.

Blues

Gallagher's corner shop
Had a brass snuff scales
And a pitted blue enamel sign
For *Gallaher's Blues*.

My uncle's moustache was ochre-
Stained, his mantel nicked
By cigarette burns, one terminating in
A worm of ash.

On Sunday afternoons
He'd slip out the half-morocco
Loose-leaf album from between
The Pelicans and Penguins:

There was the *Blue Mauritius*
That we both knew for a forgery,
Its delicate engraving
Hinged to one blank page.

He lay in the coffin, his face
A posthumous blue stubble.
The parlour was a gloom
Of nicotine and ivory —

I could hear his smoker's cough,
The clink of a half-ounce weight
On the scales; I wondered, once again,
About the missing *g* in *Gallaher*.

Great-Grandmother

She is about to collect the eggs
With which the family will break
Their fast. Her face is turned away from us
To show the plaited coils of her hair,
The folds and edgings of her crinoline,
Elaborations gone forever:

Here is the morning, interrupted
By the waiting eye, the sunlight broken by
The open shutters of the henhouse door,
The basket not yet filled with eggs.

Grandfather

For a moment it was twenty years ago
And I heard your voice, mumbling
About tea, the scarcity of milk; a gas flame
Swayed, the kettle hissed, and outside, through
A curtain, was a glint of drays and hearses
Over cobbles.

They were coming from the mill
Where you had spent your life in copperplate
Accounting for its yards of linen.
Two polished shoes on the rungs of a high stool,
You gave authority to wheels and ratchets
In receipts and bills-of-lading, hours declined
And weighed at every page;
The spindle and the thread.

It is not years ago but now
Though I can see you shaking out a handkerchief
With its bruise of snuff, or buttering
A piece of bread, then pausing, looking round
At me, your face as empty
As that clock on the mantelpiece:
A date, a name and two gold hands
That almost touch each other every hour.

Stitch

Again I sifted through
My mother's Quality Street
Chocolate-tin button-box:

Shingly mock
Tortoiseshell and mother-of-pearl,
Clouded amber plastic,

Beads of jet and jade;
Squeaky plaited leather knobs,
The synthetic horn

Of a duffel-coat toggle;
A spiky thistle brooch
With a broken catch.

And more, the shimmering
Shifting hourglass
Of everything mismatched . . .

As I poured them back in
A hailstorm drum-roll
Heralded a glimpse

Of what I had been
Looking for: not the twin
Of this lost button,

But something very like;
Near enough to do,
To speak

That moment when the thread
Was loosed, that look.
Lethargic Adam

In the Sistine Chapel,
I extend my dangling
Cuff to her:

She sews the button
Back, then snips
The thread.

Post

My fingers were bitten
By the flip-top
Of the plastic rubbish bin

As I tried to retrieve
Yesterday's *Irish News*
From the sodden tea leaves

And broken eggshells.
It brought me back
With a letterbox snap

To the Christmas break,
The canvas sack
And black armband

Of the casual worker:
Something dredged up
From the dead-letter box.

I was taken on
Because I was
My father's son.

So now he talks
Of how it's changed:
District codes,

His mnemonics
For the various streets
Of the Falls Road walks —

Bow-legged *Baker*
With a *Pound* of *English*
And *Scotch Nails* —

As at a funeral
He might recall those absent
Workmates who yesterday

Perused, like me,
The Deaths column
Of *The Irish News*.

To a Married Sister

Helping you to move in, unpacking,
I was proudly shown the bedroom. Patches
Of damp stained the walls a tea colour,
Like the sluggish tints of an old map.
Our mother would have said, 'A new bride
And a throughother house make a bad match.'

But you like dilapidation, the touch
Of somewhere that's been lived-in — the gloom
Of empty hallways, the shadow of the fanlight
Fading dimly, imperceptibly
Along the flowered paper; the hairline net
Of cracks on worn enamel; a tree-darkened room.

I left you cluttered with gifts — crockery,
Knives, the bedlinen still in its cellophane —
Watching you in that obscure privacy
Pick your way through the white delft
And golden straw to trace your new initials
On the spidered windowpane.

Your husband had talked of mending
Broken doors, the cheap furniture
That bore the accidents of others' lives,
That were there before you. A gold resin
Leaked from the slackened joints.
His new saw glittered like your wedding silver.

The Moon Parlour

Still no sign; she has quietly forgone
Our invitation. Our host is downcast, he gestures
As if dusting glass.

We handle his expensive china reverently,
Seeking gentle dislocations. My watch ticks
Slowly; pockmarks drizzle on the window.

Our illumination mists upon the lawn outside.

Tuaim Inbir

adapted from the Early Irish

More ingenious than a mansion,
My little house is lit
By trickeries of sun and moon.
The stars are all in scansion.

God is not aloof.
He has made this place for me
And lets his changing skies
As thatch to my roof.

Yet no rain falls.
Pointed spear-points are not feared.
It is all gifted with brightness
In my garden without garden walls.

Belleek

Waiting for dinner, or for tea,
The parlour is full of 'Character Pieces' —
The Tobacco Brewer, 'Jack at Sea',
The Prisoner of Love —
Miming with their crimped hands
The minute elaborations of the afternoon,
The crinkling of the table-linen.

Fingering the 'bound leaves and grasses'
Motif on the covered muffin dish, my hands —
Occurring also on the milk jug and the teapot —
Are touched by beauty, and by guilt.
Should I escape the spider's-web-on-thorn
Design upon the dinnerplates, finding satisfaction
In the heavy-duty earthenwares?

But the slop basin, the spitting mug
And the French bedpan (mentioned only
By the servants, or a bad patient) are also
Covered with that iridescent glaze.
Tints of rose and soured cream ebb and flow
Through replete evenings, approaching
The incontinence of early hours:

It is like those moments of sickness
When one stares at the gold-edged cloud
Suddenly visible at the breathed-on window,
Its milk and pearl that blooms and blooms
Into the lens of suffering — opening, unfurling
Till it dims back into nothingness,
The sky remembering its eggshell blue.

House Painting

The soft rot in the glazing bars
Appalled me. Nevertheless I painted
Over them. Dove-grey and white, I said
The colours over to myself.

I wash my hands when it is finished;
The turpentine clouds milkily.
I sniff my fingers all day, noticing
One fleck of white ingrained.

I want to touch again the stillness
Under eaves, the sooty emptiness
That gathered there invisibly, until
I brushed it off without a word.

Smithfield

I have forgotten something, I am
Going back. The wrought-iron flowers
Of the gate breathe open to
Sooty alcoves, the withered shelves
Of books. There is a light
That glints off tin and earthenware
Reminding me of touch, the beaded moulding
Of a picture-frame —

Here is a hand that beckons from
An empty doorway. Open the gilt clasp,
The book of strangers:
The families arranged with roses,
The brothers, the sister
In her First Communion frock, their hands
Like ornaments in mine beneath
The muffled ribs of gloves.

We are all walking to school
Past the face of a clock, linked
Together in the glass dark of the
Undertaker's window: one, two, three, four
Figures in the gilt lettering.
Soon it will be dusk, and all of us are sent
To find each other, though each
Of us is lost in a separate field:

Over the waving meadow, through
The trees, a gap of light sways
Like a face, a hand discovering itself
Among the branches and the inlets.
One of us has fallen in the river,
The stream of my mother's veil at the porch,
Sunlight on a brick wall smiling
With the child who is not there.

Soot

It was autumn. First, she shrouded
The furniture, then rolled back the carpet
As if for dancing; then moved
The ornaments from the mantelpiece,
Afraid his roughness might disturb
Their staid fragility.

He came; shyly, she let him in,
Feeling ill-at-ease in the newly-spacious
Room, her footsteps sounding hollow
On the boards. She watched him kneel
Before the hearth, and said something
About the weather. He did not answer,

Too busy with his work for speech.
The stem of yellow cane creaked upwards
Tentatively. After a while he asked
Her to go outside and look, and there,
Above the roof, she saw the frayed sunflower
Bloom triumphantly. She came back

And asked how much she owed him, grimacing
As she put the money in his soiled hand.
When he had gone a weightless hush
Lingered in the house for days. Slowly,
It settled; the fire burned cleanly;
Everything was spotless.

Hearing that soot was good for the soil
She threw it on the flowerbeds. She would watch
It crumble, dissolving in the rain,
Finding its way to lightless crevices,
Sleeping, till in spring it would emerge softly
As the ink-bruise in the pansy's heart.

Epitaph

after Dafydd Jones

Now I am bereft of answers
Your questions have gone astray —
Your roofs are open to the wind,
My roof is but cold clay.

The Lost Girl

after Robert ab Gwilym Ddu

An open window, the door unhinged,
Its lintel gleaming like a silver bone —

A cold moon rises
Over miles and miles of empty space.

I search through all her chambers,
In dark recesses
Hope to find her face.

The New Estate

Forget the corncrake's elegy. Rusty
Iambics that escaped your discipline
Of shorn lawns, it is sustained by nature.
It does not grieve for you, nor for itself.
You remember the rolled gold of cornfields,
Their rustling of tinsel in the wind,
A whole field quivering like blown silk?

A shiver now runs through the laurel hedge,
And washing flutters like the swaying lines
Of a new verse. The high fidelity
Music of the newly-wed obscures your
Dedication to a life of loving
Money. What could they be for, those marble
Toilet fixtures, the silence of waterbeds,
That book of poems you bought yesterday?

The Patchwork Quilt

It took me twenty years to make
That quilt. My mother had just died when I began.
It took my mind off things. How many nights
I don't know. The children all in bed,
I'd light the lamp. Scraps of John's old shirts,
A curtain, a flowered dress I wore one summer
Then forgot about. Squares and diamonds,
Calico and gingham, linen, cotton, anything
That came to hand. I snipped them all up.

I think at first I had a pattern
In my head, though maybe I think now
It changed. For when I look at it it's hard
To see where I began, or where I ended.
Then I recognize a bit of print, Janie's blouse
The day she fell in the river. But then again it looks
Like something else. There are so many
Lines, so many checks.

There were times I hated John.
He would sit there saying nothing.
I'd sew on and on, I could almost do it
With my eyes closed. I didn't want
To look at anything. John is stitched
Into that quilt. The thread went in
And out and on and on, the tree was rustling
At the window; the clock ticked, someone
Cried upstairs, and all the while the needle
Thin as thin between my thumb and finger.

I had meant it to be a present
For Janie's wedding, but she went before
I finished. Now I suppose it's mine.
Some day I'll take it out and put it on my bed.
That tree. Someone should trim it, it's been there
So long, you can hardly see in here.
The leaves can fall, all the different

Bits and pieces that were joined can join.
And I feel that cloth now
Spread on the table, or draped around my knees.
I am in the middle somewhere, working
My way out. The two boys are tugging
At me and a stitch goes wrong. I take it out
And start again, and it goes wrong again.
But sometimes I look back, the room is
Still; the thimble shines, the stitches
Shine in everything I've made.

THE IRISH FOR NO

(1987)

PART ONE

Dresden

Horse Boyle was called Horse Boyle because of his brother
    Mule;
Though why Mule was called Mule is anybody's guess.
    I stayed there once,
Or rather, I nearly stayed there once. But that's another story.
At any rate they lived in this decrepit caravan, not two miles
    out of Carrick,
Encroached upon by baroque pyramids of empty baked bean
    tins, rusts
And ochres, hints of autumn merging into twilight. Horse
    believed
They were as good as a watchdog, and to tell you the truth
You couldn't go near the place without something falling over:
A minor avalanche would ensue — more like a shop bell, really,

The old-fashioned ones on string, connected to the latch, I think,
And as you entered in, the bell would tinkle in the empty shop,
    a musk
Of soap and turf and sweets would hit you from the gloom.
    Tobacco.
Baling wire. Twine. And, of course, shelves and pyramids of tins.
An old woman would appear from the back — there was
    a sizzling pan in there,
Somewhere, a whiff of eggs and bacon — and ask you what
    you wanted;
Or rather, she wouldn't ask; she would talk about the weather.
    It had rained
That day, but it was looking better. They had just put in
    the spuds.
I had only come to pass the time of day, so I bought a token
    packet of Gold Leaf.

All this time the fry was frying away. Maybe she'd a daughter
    in there
Somewhere, though I hadn't heard the neighbours talk of it;
    if anybody knew,

It would be Horse. Horse kept his ears to the ground.
And he was a great man for current affairs; he owned the only
    TV in the place.
Come dusk he'd set off on his rounds, to tell the whole town-
    land the latest
Situation in the Middle East, a mortar bomb attack in
    Mullaghbawn —
The damn things never worked, of course — and so he'd tell
    the story
How in his young day it was very different. Take young Flynn,
    for instance,
Who was ordered to take this bus and smuggle some sticks
    of gelignite

Across the border, into Derry, when the RUC — or was it
    the RIC? —
Got wind of it. The bus was stopped, the peeler stepped on.
    Young Flynn
Took it like a man, of course: he owned up right away. He
    opened the bag
And produced the bomb, his rank and serial number. For all
    the world
Like a pound of sausages. Of course, the thing was, the peeler's
    bike
Had got a puncture, and he didn't know young Flynn from
    Adam. All he wanted
Was to get home for his tea. Flynn was in for seven years and
    learned to speak
The best of Irish. He had thirteen words for a cow in heat;
A word for the third thwart in a boat; the wake of a boat on
    the ebb tide.

He knew the extinct names of insects, flowers, why this place
    was called
Whatever: *Carrick*, for example, was a *rock*. He was damn right
    there —

As the man said, *When you buy meat you buy bones, when you
        buy land you buy stones.*
You'd be hard put to find a square foot in the whole bloody
        parish
That wasn't thick with flints and pebbles. To this day he could
        hear the grate
And scrape as the spade struck home, for it reminded him
        of broken bones:
Digging a graveyard, maybe — or better still, trying to dig
        a reclaimed tip
Of broken delft and crockery ware — you know that sound
        that sets your teeth on edge
When the chalk squeaks on the blackboard, or you shovel
        ashes from the stove?

Master McGinty — he'd be on about McGinty then, and
        discipline, the capitals
Of South America, Moore's *Melodies*, the Battle of Clontarf, and
*Tell me this, an educated man like you: What goes on four legs
        when it's young,
Two legs when it's grown up, and three legs when it's old?* I'd
        pretend
I didn't know. McGinty's leather strap would come up then,
        stuffed
With threepenny bits to give it weight and sting. Of course
        it never did him
Any harm: *You could take a horse to water but you couldn't
        make him drink.*
He himself was nearly going on to be a priest.
And many's the young cub left the school as wise as when he came.

Carrowkeel was where McGinty came from — *Narrow Quarter,*
        Flynn explained —
Back before the Troubles, a place that was so mean and crabbed,
Horse would have it, men were known to eat their dinner from
        a drawer.
Which they'd slide shut the minute you'd walk in.

He'd demonstrate this at the kitchen table, hunched and furtive,
    squinting
Out the window — past the teetering minarets of rust, down
    the hedge-dark aisle —
To where a stranger might appear, a passerby, or what was
    maybe worse,
Someone he knew. Someone who wanted something. Someone
    who was hungry.
Of course who should come tottering up the lane that instant
    but his brother

Mule. I forgot to mention they were twins. They were as like
    two —
No, not peas in a pod, for this is not the time nor the place
    to go into
Comparisons, and this is really Horse's story, Horse who —
    now I'm getting
Round to it — flew over Dresden in the war. He'd emigrated
    first, to
Manchester. Something to do with scrap — redundant mill
    machinery,
Giant flywheels, broken looms that would, eventually, be ships,
    or aeroplanes.
He said he wore his fingers to the bone.
And so, on impulse, he had joined the RAF. He became a rear
    gunner.
Of all the missions, Dresden broke his heart. It reminded him
    of china.

As he remembered it, long afterwards, he could hear, or almost
    hear,
Between the rapid desultory thunderclaps, a thousand tinkling
    echoes —
All across the map of Dresden, storerooms full of china
    shivered, teetered
And collapsed, an avalanche of porcelain, slushing and
    cascading: cherubs,

Shepherdesses, figurines of Hope and Peace and Victory, delicate
    bone fragments.
He recalled in particular a figure from his childhood, a milkmaid
Standing on the mantelpiece. Each night as they knelt down
    for the Rosary
His eyes would wander up to where she seemed to beckon
    to him, smiling,
Offering him, eternally, her pitcher of milk, her mouth of rose
    and cream.

One day, reaching up to hold her yet again, his fingers stumbled,
    and she fell.
He lifted down a biscuit tin, and opened it.
It breathed an antique incense: things like pencils, snuff, tobacco.
His war medals. A broken rosary. And there, the milkmaid's
    creamy hand, the outstretched
Pitcher of milk, all that survived. Outside, there was a scraping
And a tittering; I knew Mule's step by now, his careful drunken
    weaving
Through the tin-stacks. I might have stayed the night, but there's
    no time
To go back to that now; I could hardly, at any rate, pick up
    the thread.
I wandered out through the steeples of rust, the gate that was
    a broken bed.

Judgement

The tarred road simmered in a blue haze. The reservoir was dry.
The railway sleepers oozed with creosote. Not a cloud to be seen
  in the sky

We were sitting at the Camlough halt — Johnny Mickey and
  myself — waiting
For a train that never seemed to come. He was telling me this
  story
Of a Father Clarke, who wanted to do in his dog. A black and
  white terrier.
He says to the servant boy, *Take out that old bitch*, he says,
  and drown her.
Johnny Mickey said the servant boy was Quigley, and now
  that he remembered it,
He'd been arrested by a Sergeant Flynn, for having no bell
  on his bike.
Hardly a hanging crime, you might say. But he was fined fifteen
  shillings.

The prisoner left the courtroom and his step was long and slow
By day and night he did contrive to fill this sergeant's heart with
  woe

So there was this auction one day, and Quigley sneaks in
  the back.
A lot of crockery ware came up. Delft bowls. Willow-pattern.
  Chamberpots.
The bidding started at a shilling. Quigley lifts his finger. One-
  and-six.
Everyone pretending not to look at one another. Or to know
  each other.
Nods and winks. A folded *Dundalk Democrat*. Spectacles put
  on and off.
And so on, till he won the bid at fifteen shillings. *Name, please,*
Says the auctioneer. *Sergeant Flynn*, says Quigley, Forkhill
  Barracks.

For to uphold the letter of the law this sergeant was too willing
I took the law upon myself and fined him back his fifteen shillings

He rambled on a bit — how this Flynn's people on his mother's
    side
Were McErleans from County Derry, how you could never trust
A McErlean. When they hanged young McCorley on the bridge
    of Toome
It was a McErlean who set the whole thing up. That was in '98,
But some things never changed. You could trust a dog but not
    a cat.
It was something in their nature, and nature, as they say, will out.
The pot would always call the kettle black. He hummed a few
    lines.

Come tender-hearted Christians all attention pay to me
Till I relate and communicate these verses two or three
Concerning of a gallant youth was cut off in his bloom
And died upon the gallows tree near to the town of Toome

Which brought Johnny Mickey back to the priest and the terrier
    bitch.
Quigley, it transpired, had walked the country — Ballinliss and
    Aughaduff,
Slievenacapall, Carnavaddy — looking for a place to drown her.
It was the hottest summer in living memory. Not a cloud to be
    seen in the sky.
The Cully Water was a trickle. The Tullyallen and the
    Ummeracam were dry.
Not a breath of wind. Not so much water as would drown
    a rat. After three days
Quigley and the bitch came back. They were both half dead
    with thirst.

He looked her up he looked her down in his heart was ne'er a pang
I'll tell you what says Father Clarke if she won't be drowned she'll
*   hang*

Johnny Mickey said that priests had a great way with ropes
and knots.
It was one of the tricks that they learned in the seminary.
Something to do
With chasubles and albs. In less time than it takes to tell,
Father Flynn
Had rigged up a noose. They brought the bitch out to the
orchard
And strung her up from the crook of an apple tree. And who
was passing by
But the poet McCooey. He peeped through a hole in the hedge.
He spotted the two boys at their trade, and this is what he said:

A man with no bell on his bike a man with a single bed
It's hardly any wonder that you'd go off your head
Poor old bitch poor old friend you died without a bark
Sentenced by Johnny Quigley and hung by Father Clarke

Of course, said Johnny Mickey, *your man McCooey's long
since dead.*
A white plume of steam appeared around the bend. A long
lonesome blast.
The tracks began to shimmer and to hum. Our train was
coming in
And not a minute late. It shivered to a halt. We both got on.
We would pass the crazy map of a dried-up reservoir.
A water-tower.
We would watch the telegraph lines float up and down till
we arrived
At the other end; I would hand Mickey Quigley over to the
two attendants.

Farewell unto you sweet Drumaul if in you I had stayed
Among the Presbyterians I ne'er would have been betrayed
The gallows tree I ne'er would have seen had I remained there
For Dufferin you betrayed me McErlean you set the snare

84

Calvin Klein's Obsession

I raised my glass, and — solid, pungent, like the soot-encrusted
    brickwork
Of the Ulster Brewery — a smell of yeast and hops and malt
    swam up:
I sniff and sniff again, and try to think of what it is I am
    remembering:
I think that's how it goes, like Andy Warhol's calendar of
    perfumes,
Dribs and drabs left over to remind him of that season's smell.
Very personal, of course, as *Blue Grass* is for me the texture
    of a fur
Worn by this certain girl I haven't seen in years. Every time
    that *Blue Grass*
Hits me it is 1968. I'm walking with her through the smoggy
    early dusk
Of West Belfast: coal-smoke, hops, fur, the smell of stout and
    whiskey
Breathing out from somewhere. So it all comes back, or nearly all,
A long-forgotten kiss.

Never quite. Horses' dung is smoking on the cobbles.
    Cobblestones?
I must have gone back further than I thought, to brewers' drays
    and milk-carts,
Brylcreem, Phoenix beer. Or candy apples — rich hard dark-
    brown glaze
Impossible to bite at first, until you licked and licked and
    sucked a way
Into the soft core. A dark interior, where I'd also buy a twist
    of snuff
For my grandma. She'd put two pinches on a freckled fist, and
    sniff.
Then a sip of whiskey and, as always, *I'm not long for this world.*
My father would make a face: *A whingeing gate,* he'd say, *hangs*
    longest —
Hoping it was true, perhaps — a phrase he'd said so often he'd
    forgotten

When he said it last. That Gold Label whiskey — nearly like
    a perfume:
I go crazy because I want to smell them all so much,

Warhol's high-pitched New York whine comes on again, with
All those exhalations of the Thirties and the Forties: Guerlain's
Sous le Vent, Saravel's *White Christmas*, Corday's *Voyage à Paris*, or
Kathleen Mary Quinlan's *Rhythm*: bottles of bottle-green, bruise-
    blues
Darker than the pansies at the cemetery gate lodge, bottles
    of frosted glass
And palest lilac — *l'odeur de ton sein chaleureux* — a rush of musk
And incense, camphor, beckons from the back of the wardrobe;
    I'd slipped
Through the mirror in a dream. *Opium* by Yves St Laurent? More
    than likely,
What my mother used to call a guilty conscience, or something
    that I ate:
Cheese and chopped dill pickle on wheaten farls, looking, if
    I thought of it,
Like Boots' Buttermilk and Clover soap —

Slipping and slipping from my grasp, clunking softly downwards
    through
The greying water; I have drowsed off into something else. The
    ornate fish
And frog and water-lily motif on the bathroom wallpaper reminds
    me
How in fact I'd stripped it off some months ago. It was April,
    a time
Of fits and starts; fresh leaves blustered at the window, strips and
    fronds
Of fish and water lilies sloughed off round my feet. A Frank
    Ifield song
From 1963, I think, kept coming back to me: *I remember you —
    you're the one*

Who made my dreams come true — just a few — kisses ago.
    I'm taking
One step forward, two steps back, trying to establish what it was
    about her
That made me fall in love with her, if that's what it was; *infatuation*
Was a vogue word then —

It meant it wasn't all quite real. Like looking at my derelict
    back garden,
Its scraggy ranks of docks and nettles, thistles, but thinking
There was something else, flicking idly through the pages of
    a catalogue:
Flowered violets and whites, or grey and silver foliage,
    suggesting
Thunderclouds and snowstorms, rivers, fountains; artemesias
    and lilies,
Phlox, gentians, scillas, snowdrops, crocuses; and thymes and
    camomiles
Erupted from the paving-cracks, billowing from half-forgotten
    corners;
An avalanche of jasmine and wisteria broke through. Or, the
    perfume
Of *Blue Grass*, bittersweet, which is, just at this moment, just
    a memory.
How often did she wear it, anyway? I must look her up again
    some day.
And can it still be bought?

For there are memories that have no name; you don't know
    what to ask for.
The merest touch of sunshine, a sudden breeze, might summon
    up
A corner of your life you'd thought, till then, you'd never
    occupied.
Her mother, for example, owned this second-hand shop, which
    is where

The fur coat came from, anonymous with shades of someone
    else. Rummaging
Through piles of coats and dresses I'd come across a thing
    that until then
I'd never wanted: a white linen Fifties jacket with no back vent,
Just that bit out of fashion, it was fashionable, or maybe, as
    they say,
It was just the thing I had been looking for. So, a box of worn
    shoes
Might bring me back to 1952, teetering across the kitchen floor
In my mother's high heels —

Not that I wanted to be her; easing off the lid of her powder
    compact,
Breathing in the flesh-coloured dust, was just a way of feeling
    her presence.
And so I have this image of an assignation, where it all comes
    back,
Or nearly all, a long-forgotten kiss: subdued lighting, musak —
    no, a live
Piano — tinkling in its endless loop; there is candlelight and
    Cointreau,
Whispered nothings, as Kathleen Mary Quinlan's *Rhythm*
    meets, across
A discreet table, Calvin Klein's *Obsession*. He has prospered
    since
He saw her last. There is talk of all the years that separated
    them, whatever
Separated them at first. There is talk of money, phrased
    as talk of
Something else, of how there are some things that can't be
    bought.
Or maybe it's the name you buy, and not the thing itself.

Whatever Sleep It Is

The leg was giving me a problem, interfering, somehow, with
the total
Composition — I didn't know, at this stage, if he'd be a walker
or a skier.
Certainly, a faraway look in his eyes suggested mountain
scenery, the light
Falling gradually, then pouring as an avalanche across a great
divide:
Cuckoo clocks and cowbells, everything as full of holes as
a Swiss cheese.
And I wanted to give him a leather jacket — leather is
'interesting' though
Sometimes it's easy and sometimes not, depending on the time
of day, the light,
The consistency of this particular tube of burnt sienna. So
if it doesn't work
It might be tweed. But then the air of mystery might vanish,
this spy
Or pilot whose whereabouts have yet to be established —

At any rate, I painted out the leg, and put in this flight of stairs
instead.
It seemed to me it should lead to a skylight, so dusty as to
be opaque,
Cobwebbed, opening with a slow reluctant creak — the see-saw
of a donkey —
On to clouds and bits of sky. A gusty March day, maybe, with
a touch of rain
Ticking on the glass. Someone keeps asking me why I hold
my hand like that,
But it's not to keep off the light — it's more to do with how
you often
Don't remember what a hand looks like. So you paint your
own, and give it
To this character who might, indeed, be you, but with a life
you haven't

Worked out yet. The sleeve of your jacket ticked with sky-blue,
        Chinese white.
I think the story is starting to take shape:

It usually takes three days, four days, and you can reckon
        on a week
Before it's finished. On the seventh day I'd go out on the town
        and celebrate,
And then come back and look at it again: sometimes I'd say yes,
        sometimes no.
On day five, for instance, the skylight acquired a broken pane,
        and someone
Had to be responsible: I thought of a message wrapped around
        a stone.
What was being said, and why? Could it be that the character
        I'd painted out
By now was lurking out there? Perhaps he is in love with
        this girl
Hunched in the attic, where the light-source now becomes
        a candle
Stuck in a Chianti bottle, a love that tells itself by paper, stone,
        scissors.
And the donkey keeps coming back,

Its too-big head lolling over a five-barred gate that opens out
        on to
An orchard: there is, in fact, a bowl of apples at her elbow that
        she seems
To be ignoring. It is there to concentrate the light, I think —
        flecks
And smuts of amber, yellow, russet, green, each fruit swirled
        into a fist,
The navel clenched between the finger and the thumb.
        Meanwhile Mr Natural,
As we'll call him, has climbed on to the roof and, with his feet
        lodged

In the guttering, is staring through the hole at her. *The pane of*
of glass
I skimmed this morning from the drinking trough, he whispers
to himself,
Melted, and I let it fall and break. Early frost: the stars are
blazing
Now like snowflakes — stem end and blossom end

Swelling and dimming over the black Alp of the roof. It is
an October
Sort of March, the apples ripened out of season; and now that
the ink-dark sky
Lightens into sapphire, I see it is an angel, not a man, who has
Descended, looking faintly puzzled at the poor response
of the girl
To whatever important announcement he has just made. She
is, in fact, asleep,
Oblivious also to the clink and hum of the electric milk float
Which has just pulled up outside. And the milkman looks up,
momentarily
Amazed at curtains, wings, gusting from the attic window.
He rubs his eyes;
He is still drowsy with these six days out of seven. Tomorrow
yawns ahead
With routine promises; tomorrow, after all, he will be free.

PART TWO

Belfast Confetti

Suddenly as the riot squad moved in it was raining exclamation
    marks,
Nuts, bolts, nails, car-keys. A fount of broken type. And
    the explosion
Itself — an asterisk on the map. This hyphenated line, a burst
    of rapid fire . . .
I was trying to complete a sentence in my head, but it kept
    stuttering,
All the alleyways and side streets blocked with stops and
    colons.

I know this labyrinth so well — Balaklava, Raglan, Inkerman,
    Odessa Street —
Why can't I escape? Every move is punctuated. Crimea Street.
    Dead end again.
A Saracen, Kremlin-2 mesh. Makrolon face-shields. Walkie-
    talkies. What is
My name? Where am I coming from? Where am I going?
    A fusillade of question marks.

Clearance

The Royal Avenue Hotel collapses under the breaker's
     pendulum:
Zig-zag stairwells, chimney-flues, and a Thirties mural
Of an elegantly-dressed couple doing what seems to be
     the Tango, in Wedgewood
Blue and white — happy days! Suddenly more sky
Than there used to be. A breeze springs up from nowhere —

There, through a gap in the rubble, a greengrocer's shop
I'd never noticed until now. Or had I passed it yesterday?
     Everything —
Yellow, green and purple — is fresh as paint. Rain glistens
     on the aubergines
And peppers; even from this distance the potatoes smell
     of earth.

Linear B

Threading rapidly between crowds on Royal Avenue, reading
Simultaneously, and writing in this black notebook, peering
    through
A cracked lens fixed with Sellotape, his *rendezvous* is not
    quite *vous*.
But from years of watching I know the zig-zags circle:
He has been the same place many times, never standing still.

One day I clicked with his staccato walk, and glimpsed
    the open notebook:
Squiggles, dashes, question marks, dense as the Rosetta Stone.
His good eye glittered at me: it was either nonsense, or
    a formula — for
Perpetual motion, the scaffolding of shopping lists, or
    the collapsing city.

Night Patrol

Jerking his head spasmodically as he is penetrated by invisible
    gunfire,
The private wakes to a frieze of pull-outs from *Contact* and
    Men Only.
Sellotape and Blu-Tack. The antiquated plumbing is stuttering
    that he
Is not in Balkan Street or Hooker Street, but in a bunk bed
In the Grand Central Hotel: a room that is a room knocked
    into other rooms.

But the whole Victorian creamy façade has been tossed off
To show the inner-city tubing: cables, sewers, a snarl
    of Portakabins,
Soft-porn shops and carry-outs. A Telstar Taxis depot that
    is a hole
In a breeze-block wall, a wire grille and a voice-box uttering
    gobbledygook.

August 1969

As the huge façade of Greeves's Mill is washed in a Niagara
of flame
The riot fizzles out. Still smouldering as the troops march
in, this welcome,
Singing, dancing on the streets. Confetti drifts across the city:
Charred receipts and bills-of-lading, contracts, dockets, pay-
slips.
The weave is set: a melt of bobbins, spindles, shuttles.

Happy days, my mother claims, the mill-girls chattering,
linking arms.
But then it all changed when I met your father. The flicker
of a smile.
It lights again on this creased photograph, a weekend
honeymoon.
She is crossing the Liffey, the indelible ink of *Dublin
September 1944.*

Campaign

They had questioned him for hours. Who exactly was he?
  And when
He told them, they questioned him again. When they accepted
  who he was, as
Someone not involved, they pulled out his fingernails. Then
They took him to a waste-ground somewhere near The
  Horseshoe Bend, and told him
What he was. They shot him nine times.

A dark umbilicus of smoke was rising from a heap of burning
  tyres.
The bad smell he smelt was the smell of himself. Broken glass
  and knotted Durex.
The knuckles of a face in a nylon stocking. I used to see him
  in The Gladstone Bar,
Drawing pints for strangers, his almost-perfect fingers flecked
  with scum.

Smithfield Market

Sidelong to the arcade, the glassed-in April cloud — fleeting,
    pewter-edged —
Gets lost in shadowed aisles and inlets, branching into
    passages, into cul-de-sacs,
Stalls, compartments, alcoves. Everything unstitched,
    unravelled — mouldy fabric,
Rusted heaps of nuts and bolts, electrical spare parts:
    the ammunition dump
In miniature. Maggots seethe between the ribs and
    corrugations.

Since everything went up in smoke, no entrances, no exits.
But as the charred beams hissed and flickered I glimpsed
    a map of Belfast
In the ruins: obliterated streets, the faint impression of a key.
Something many-toothed, elaborate, stirred briefly in
    the labyrinth.

Army

The duck patrol is waddling down the odd-numbers side
    of Raglan Street,
The bass-ackwards private at the rear trying not to think
    of a third eye
Being drilled in the back of his head. 55. They stop.
    The head
Peers round, then leaps the gap of Balaklava Street. He waves
    the body over
One by one. 49. Cape Street. A gable wall. Garnet Street.
    A gable wall.

Frere Street. 47. 45½. Milan Street. A grocer's shop.
They stop. They check their guns. 13. Milton Street. An iron
    lamp-post.
No. 1. Ormond Street. *Two ducks in front of a duck and two
    ducks*
Behind a duck, how many ducks? Five? *No. Three.* This is not
    the end.

33333

I was trying to explain to the invisible man behind the wire-
grilled
One-way mirror and squawk-box exactly where it was
I wanted to go, except
I didn't know myself — a number in the Holy Land, Damascus
Street or Cairo?
At any rate in about x amount of minutes, where x is a small
number,
I found myself in the synthetic leopard-skin bucket-seat of
a Ford Zephyr

Gunning through a mesh of ramps, diversions, one-way
systems. We shoot out
Under the glare of the sodium lights along the blank brick wall
of the Gasworks
And I start to ease back: I know this place like the back
of my hand, except
My hand is cut off at the wrist. We stop at an open door
I never knew existed.

Two Winos

Most days you will find this pair reclining on the waste ground
Between Electric Street and Hemp Street, sharing a bottle
    of Drawbridge
British Wine. They stare at isolated clouds, or puffs of steam
    which leak out
From the broken pipes and vents at the back of the Franklin
    Laundry . . .
They converse in snarls and giggles, and they understand each
    other perfectly.

Just now they have entered the giggling phase, though what
    there is
To laugh at, who knows. Unless it was this momentary ray
    of sunlight
That glanced across their patch of crushed coke, broken glass
    and cinders;
And the bottle which had seemed half-empty until then is now
    half-full.

Cocktails

Bombing at about ninety miles an hour with the exhaust
    skittering
The skid-marked pitted tarmac of Kennedy Way, they hit
    the ramp and sailed
Clean over the red-and-white guillotine of the check-point
    and landed
On the M1 flyover, then disappeared before the Brits knew
    what hit them. So
The story went: we were in the Whip & Saddle bar of the
    Europa.

There was talk of someone who was shot nine times and lived,
    and someone else
Had the inside info on the Romper Room. We were trying
    to remember the facts
Behind the Black & Decker case, when someone ordered
    another drink and we entered
The realm of Jabberwocks and Angels' Wings, Widows'
    Kisses, Corpse Revivers.

Travellers

On the waste ground that was Market Street and Verner
  Street, wandering trouserless
Through his personal map — junked refrigerators, cars and
  cookers, anchored
Caravans — the small boy trips over an extended tow-bar,
  picks himself up, giggles
And pisses on a smouldering mound of Pampers. *Sic transit
  gloria mundi* —
This is the exact site, now that I recall it, of Murdock's stables,
  past tense.

Murdock himself moved out to the Flying Horse estate some
  years ago. He wanted
To end his days among friends; there were Murdocks in
  the local graveyard.
The long umbilicus of dung between his backyard and
  Downpatrick faded. Belfast
Tore itself apart and patched things up again. Like this. Like
  his extended family.

Box

I can't sleep as long as I see this man with a cardboard box
    perched
On his head — no hands, his body bent into the *S* or *Z*
    of a snake-charmer's
Rope. HP Sauce, Heinz Baked Beans or Crosse & Blackwell's
    Cock-a-Leekie?
Hen-stepping out of a pea-soup fog, he makes a shift for
    Cornmarket
And pops up again in Smithfield: has he discarded this box
    for another?

In all these years don't ask me what was in there: that would
    take
A bird's-eye view. But I get a whiff of homelessness, a scaldy
    fallen
From a nest into another nest, a cross between a toothbrush
    and a razor.
Open-mouthed, almost sleeping now. A smell of meths and
    cardboard.

Snowball

All the signs: beehive hair-do, white handbag, white stilettos,
   split skirt.
An Audi Quattro sidles up in first gear past the loading-bay of
   Tomb Street
GPO — a litter of white plastic cord, a broken whiskey bottle —
Then revs away towards the Albert Clock. The heels click off —
   another
Blind date? Like a fishnet stocking, everything is full of holes . . .

Arse-about-face, night-shift and the Christmas rush, perfume
   oozing from
Crushed packets — *Blue Grass, Obsession* — and once, in a
   forgotten pigeon-hole,
I woke up to this card stamped 9 August 1910: *Meet me usual
   place & time*
Tomorrow — What I have to tell you might not wait — Yours —
Forever — B.

The Exiles' Club

Every Thursday in the upstairs lounge of The Wollongong Bar
    they make
Themselves at home with Red Heart Stout, Park Drive
    cigarettes and Dunville's whiskey,
A slightly-mouldy batch of soda farls. Eventually they get
    down to business.
After years they have reconstructed the whole of the Falls Road,
    and now
Are working on the backstreets: Lemon, Peel and Omar,
    Balaklava, Alma.

They just about keep up with the news of bombings and
    demolition, and are
Struggling with the finer details: the names and dates carved out
On the back bench of the Leavers' Class in Slate Street School;
    the Nemo Café menu;
The effects of the 1941 Blitz, the entire contents of Paddy
    Lavery's pawnshop.

Slate Street School

Back again. Day one. Fingers blue with cold. I joined
    the lengthening queue.
Roll-call. Then inside: chalk dust and iced milk, the smell
    of watered ink.
Roods, perches, acres, ounces, pounds, tons weighed
    imponderably in the darkening
Air. We had chanted the twelve-times table for the twelfth
    or thirteenth time
When it began to snow. Chalky numerals shimmered down;
    we crowded to the window —

*These are the countless souls of purgatory, whose numbers
    constantly diminish*
*And increase; each flake as it brushes to the ground is yet
    another soul released.*
And I am the avenging Archangel, stooping over mills and
    factories and barracks.
I will bury the dark city of Belfast forever under snow: inches,
    feet, yards, chains, miles.

PART THREE

The Irish for No

Was it a vision, or a waking dream? I heard her voice before I saw
What looked like the balcony scene in *Romeo and Juliet*, except
    Romeo
Seemed to have shinned up a pipe and was inside arguing with
    her. The casements
Were wide open and I could see some Japanese-style wall-
    hangings, the dangling
Quotation marks of a yin-yang mobile. *It's got nothing,* she was
    snarling, *nothing*
To do with politics, and, before the bamboo curtain came down,
    That goes for you too!

It was time to turn into the dog's-leg short cut from Chlorine
    Gardens
Into Cloreen Park, where you might see an *Ulster Says No*
    scrawled on the side
Of the power-block — which immediately reminds me of
    The Eglantine Inn
Just on the corner: on the missing *h* of Cloreen, you might say.
    We were debating,
Bacchus and the pards and me, how to render *The Ulster Bank —*
    the Bank
That Likes to Say Yes into Irish, and whether eglantine was alien
    to Ireland.
I cannot see what flowers are at my feet, when *yes* is the verb
    repeated,
Not exactly yes, but phatic nods and whispers. *The Bank That*
    Answers All
Your Questions, maybe? That Greek portico of Mourne granite,
    dazzling
With promises and feldspar, mirrors you in the Delphic black
    of its windows.

And the bruised pansies of the funeral parlour are dying
    in reversed gold letters,
The long sigh of the afternoon is not yet complete on
    the promontory where the victim,

A corporal in the UDR from Lisbellaw, was last seen having
    driven over half
Of Ulster, a legally-held gun was found and the incidence
    of stress came up
On the headland which shadows Larne Harbour and the black
    pitch of warehouses.
There is a melancholy blast of diesel, a puff of smoke which
    might be black or white.
So the harbour slips away to perilous seas as things remain
    unsolved; we listen
To the *ex cathedra* of the fog-horn, and *drink and leave
    the world unseen* —

What's all this to the Belfast businessman who drilled
Thirteen holes in his head with a Black & Decker? It was just
    a normal morning
When they came. The tennis court shone with dew or frost,
    a little before dawn.
The border, it seemed, was not yet crossed: the Milky Way
    trailed snowy brambles,
The stars clustered thick as blackberries. They opened the door
    into the dark:
The murmurous haunt of flies on summer eves. Empty jam-jars.
Mish-mash. Hotch-potch. And now you rub your eyes and get
    acquainted with the light
A dust of something reminiscent drowses over the garage smell
    of creosote,
The concrete: blue clouds in porcelain, a paintbrush steeped
    in a chipped cup;
Staples hyphenate a wet cardboard box as the upturned can
    of oil still spills
And the unfed cat toys with the yin-yang of a tennis ball,
    debating whether *yes* is *no.*

Serial

As the Guinness-like chiaroscuro of the cat settled into
    the quickthorn hedge
I had a feeling I'd been there before: in a black taxi, for
    example, when this bullet
Drilled an invisible bee-line through the open window and
    knocked a chip
Off the Scotch sandstone façade of the Falls Road Library.
    Everybody ducked
To miss the already-dead split-second; the obvious soldier
    relaxed back into
His Guinness-and-tan uniform, since to hear the shot is to
    know you are alive.

It is this lapse of time which gives the film its serial quality:
    the next
Episode is about the giant statue of the newly-renovated
    Carson, verdigris becoming
Bronze. It is suggested that it might be camouflage — as
    glossed on
In the SF novels of W D Flackes, particularly in his novel,
    The X
People. And so in the words of another commentator,
    the future is only today
Fading into the past — drawing, perhaps, a retrospective dotted
    line on the map

For from here the border makes a peninsula of the South,
    especially in the shallows
Of Lough Erne, where so much land is so much water anyway.
    And, since the Ormsby
Room in Lakeland still remains un-named, they are thinking
    of calling it
Something else: not a name, but the name of a place. Blacklion,
    for instance.
The Blacklion Room has a certain sort of armorial flavour
    which would suit

The tourist junkets, the loops and spirals of an Irish dancing
    costume.
Waterfowlers in ulsters, mackintoshes, flak jackets, tank-tops,
    wade in
Through the rushes and ignore the German fishermen trapped
    in the caves of Boho.
The water-level is neither here nor there: as they say, *it's making
    up its mind*
To rain, the grey brainy mass of the clouds becoming cabbages,
    since a foot patrol
Has just gone over to the other side: you can identify them
    by the black markings
On their cheeks, the fact that it is winter and the hedges are bare.

These errors of reading are not the only difference between
    us and them
Though the shibboleths are *lingua franca*, since German became
    current.
As for Irish, it was too identifiable as foreign: a museum where
    the stuffed
Wolfhound was just as native as the Shell tiger — I am hunting
    with a telephoto
Fish-eye, shooting, as they say, some footage. The crackly static
Of the portable still gives some news, though, in between
    the magazines:

I am hearing a lot, for example, of this campaign to save
    the English frog.
Refrigerators stocked with spawn are humming quietly in wait;
    the light
Goes off with a click as you shut the door. The freezing dark
    suggests
That they are dying anyway, perplexed by their bi-focal vision,
    as next week,
Or the last week, are the same, and nothing can be justified
As the independent eye of the chameleon sees blue as green.

Asylum

The first indication was this repeated tic, the latch jigging and
    clicking
As he rehearsed the possibility of entering, or opening. Maybe
It was a knock, a question; Uncle John was not all there. Yet
    he had
His father's eyes, his mother's nose; and I myself, according
    to my mother,
Had his mouth. I would imagine speaking for him sometimes.
    He had
A second cousin's hands, or a cousin's twice removed, an uncle's
    way of walking:
In other words, he was himself. So he might walk in this very
    minute, or turn
His back on us to contemplate the yellow brick edgings
    of the bricked-in
Windows of the mill wall opposite. He seemed to see things
    that we didn't
See: cloud-shadow eddying and swirling round a manhole;
    the bits of grit
That glittered at the edges; individual as dirt, the dog-leg walk
    of a dog
As it followed its nose from one side of the street to the other.
    His ears
Might prick to the clatter of an empty tin kicked down an entry,
Diminishing the yelps of children as their skipping rope became
    a blur,
Then slowed and stopped, then whipped back up again,
    the up-hill down-dale
Quickening pulse of a cardiograph. We watched him hover
    and dilate
In the frosted glass. Someone would get up; he would retreat.
    An electric
Yellow bakery van hummed by; he sniffed the air. A car
    backfired.

Like the fast-forward or the rewind button, everything is going
   far too
Fast, though we might know precisely, having heard it all
   before for real,
What is going on, like that climactic moment of a rounded,
   oratorical
Gesture, practised in the mirror till it seemed completely
   unfamiliar:
The hyped-up, ninety-to-the-dozen commentary that illustrates,
   in retrospect,
The split second when a goal is scored; the laid-back, bit-by-bit
   analysis
As we take in every slowed-down motion of the replay. We are
   looking
For a piece we know is there, amongst the clutter and the glug
   of bottles,
Whispering, the chink of loose change, the unfamiliar voices that
   are us
And cloud our hearing. The repeated melancholic parp
   of a car-horn
Eventually has heralded the moment: now we know what's
   coming next, the voice
Hoarsened by the second-generation tape, the echo of a nearly-
   empty dusty
Concert hall, illuminated, we imagine, by the voice, one shaft
   of fitful sunlight
That retreated almost instantly to a nimbo-cumulus — gold-
   edged, slate-blue,
Glimmering between its cup and lip — imponderably weighing
   on the skylight.
A yellow bakery van hums by. There is a lull, and then a car
   backfires.

It's getting nearer now, that out-of-focus look he had: a wall-eye
With its yellowed white, the confused rainbow of the iris weeping
   unpredictably.

The tortoiseshell frame had one missing lens. Why they were
   bi-focals
I don't know; he didn't read. Spinning yarns was more his line,
   always something
Off the top of his head. Or he might sing a song: perhaps
   I'm going down the town
And I know who's going with me. I have a wee boy of my own,
   and his name is —
Here he'd mention my name, which was almost my name; half
   of it, at least,
Was right. All this while he champed, between gulps of tea, two
   thick buttered
Doorsteps of a Peter Pan loaf, and cast his eye on the yellowed
   pages
Of an *Old Moore's Almanac* for 1948, the year, in fact, that
   I was born.
Storms this month, I see; *hurricanes and thunder . . .* the almanac
   was upside down,
But sure enough, just then, above the smoke-stack of the mill
   on up the street,
I caught a dark umbilicus of cloud, a momentary flash. Rain
   pattered on the window.
A yellow bakery van went by; he sniffed the ozone. A car
   backfired.

You can tell that this was all some time ago, although it does
   repeat itself.
On this particular day, my other uncle, Pat, had just come
   in from work.
He plunked two loaves down on the table. A doughy-sour
   inveterate smell
Breathed out from him, and as he lifted off the white cloud
   of his cap, it sparked off
The authoritative onset of this other, needle-in-the-haystack
   day that I
Began with. That ratchety delay with which the clock is poised,
   conjugating

All its tensed-up coils and springs: rain pattered on the window. An electric
Yellow bakery van whirred off. A car backfired. Someone seemed to get up very
Slowly. A dog was barking. The car backfired again. Everything was getting faster

And the door bursts open. He is babbling, stammering, contractions
Getting nearer, nearer, all the blips run into one another till they are
A wave, a wall: *They said to push, she pushed, they said to shut her mouth,*
She pushed, they said to keep her head down, and she pushed once more —
The wave has almost broken — *more, they said*: a lock of hair, a bald patch,
Hair again. Flecks of blood and foam. He cannot get it all out fast enough.

Afterwards, a lull. He sits up and he takes a cup of tea, a slice of toast.
He is himself again, though I can see myself in him. *I remember very well*, he says,
When you were born; oh yes, thunder, hurricanes; and as I see the bruised
Posthumous violet of his face I hear him talk about the shape of this particular
Cloud he saw last week, or this dog he'd noticed last week, which he'd imitate,
Panting, slabbering and heaving as it lolled about the margins of the new estate —
Nettles, yellow chickweed, piss-the-beds — sniffing, wagging, following itself
Back through that remembered day of complex perfume, a trail of moments

Dislocated, then located. This dog. That bitch. There is a
    long-forgotten
Whimper, a groan of joy as it discovers home: a creosoted
    hutch, a bowl,
The acrid spoor of something that was human.

Patchwork

It was only just this minute that I noticed the perfectly
    triangular
Barbed wire rip in the sleeve of my shirt, and wondered where
    I'd got it.
I'd crossed no fences that I knew about. Then it struck me:
    an almost identical
Tear in my new white Sunday shirt, when I was six. My mother,
    after her initial
Nagging, stitched it up. But you can never make a perfect job
    on tears like that.
Eventually she cut it up for handkerchiefs: six neatly-hemmed
    squares.
Snags of greyish wool remind me of the mountain that we
    climbed that day —
Nearly at the summit, we could see the map of Belfast. My
    father stopped
For a cigarette and pointed out the landmarks: Gallaher's
    tobacco factory,
Clonard Monastery, the invisible speck of our house, lost
    in all the rows
And terraces and furrows, like this one sheep that's strayed
    into the rags
And bandages that flock the holy well. A little stack of ball-
    point pens,
Some broken spectacles, a walking stick, two hearing-aids:
    prayers
Repeated and repeated until granted.
                        So when I saw, last week,
    the crucifix
Earring dangling from the right ear of this young Charismatic
Christian fiddle-player, I could not help but think of beads,
    beads
Told over and over — like my father's rosary of olive stones from
Mount Olive, I think, that he had thumbed and fingered so
    much the decades
Missed a pip or two. The cross itself was ebony and silver, just
    like

This young girl's, that swung and tinkled like a thurible. She was playing
    playing
'The Teetotaller'. Someone had to buy a drink just then, of course:
    a pint of Harp,
Four pints of stout, two Paddy whiskies, and a bottle
    of Lucozade — the baby
Version, not the ones you get in hospital, wrapped in crackling
    see-through
Cellophane. You remember how you held it to the light, and
    light shone through?
The opposite of Polaroids, really, the world filmed in dazzling
    sunshine:
A quite unremarkable day of mist and drizzle. The rainy hush
    of traffic,
Muted car-horns, a dog making a dog-leg walk across a zebra
    crossing . . .
As the lights changed from red to green and back to red again
I fingered the eighteen stitches in the puckered mouth
    of my appendicectomy.

The doctor's waiting room, now that I remember it, had a print
    of *The Angelus*
Above the fireplace; sometimes, waiting for the buzzer, I'd hear
    the Angelus
Itself boom out from St Peter's. With only two or three
    deliberate steps
I could escape into the frame, unnoticed by the peasant and his
    wife. I'd vanish
Into sepia. The last shivering bell would die on the wind.
I was in the surgery. Stainless steel and hypodermics glinted
    on the shelves.
Now I saw my mother: the needle shone between her thumb
    and finger, stitching,
Darning, mending: the woolly callous on a sock, the unravelled
    jumper
That became a scarf. I held my arms at arms' length as she
    wound and wound:

The tick-tack of the knitting needles made a cable-knit pullover.
Come Christmas morning I would wear it, with a new white
    shirt unpinned
From its cardboard stiffener.
                    I shivered at the touch of cold
    white linen —
A mild shock, as if, when almost sleeping, you'd dreamt you'd
    fallen
Suddenly, and realized now you were awake: the curtains fluttered
In the breeze across the open window, exactly as they had before.
    Everything
Was back to normal. Outside, the noise of children playing:
    a tin can kicked
Across a tarred road, the whip-whop of a skipping rope, singing —
*Poor Toby is dead and he lies in his grave, lies in his grave, lies
    in his grave* . . .
So, the nicotine-stained bone buttons on my father's melodeon
    clicked
And ticked as he wheezed his way through *Oft in the Stilly Night*
    — or,
For that matter, *Nearer My God to Thee*, which he'd play
    on Sundays, just before
He went to see my granny, after Mass. Sometimes she'd be sick
    — *Another*
Clean shirt'll do me — and we'd climb the narrow stair to where
    she lay, buried
Beneath the patchwork quilt.
                    It took me twenty years to make
    that quilt —
I'm speaking for her now — and, *Your father's stitched into*
    that quilt,
Your uncles and your aunts. She'd take a sip from the baby Power's
On the bedside table. *Anything that came to hand, a bit of cotton*
    print,
A poplin tie: I snipped them all up. I could see her working
    in the gloom,

The shadow of the quilt draped round her knees. A needle
    shone between
Her thumb and finger. Minutes, hours of stitches threaded
    patiently; my father
Tugged at her, a stitch went wrong; she started up again. *You
    drink your tea*
Just like your father: two sups and a gulp: and so I'd see a mirror
    image
Raise the cup and take two sips, and swallow, or place my cup
    exactly on
The brown ring stain on the white damask tablecloth.
                                                    Davy's
        gone to England,
Rosie to America; who'll be next, I don't know. Yet they all
    came back.
I'd hardly know them now. The last time I saw them all together
    was
The funeral. As the Rosary was said I noticed how my father
    handled the invisible
Bead on the last decade: a gesture he'd repeat again at the
    graveside.
A shower of hail: far away, up on the mountain, a cloud of sheep
    had scattered
In the Hatchet Field. *The stitches show in everything I've made,*
    she'd say —
The quilt was meant for someone's wedding, but it never got
    that far.
And some one of us has it now, though who exactly I don't
    know.

BELFAST CONFETTI

(1989)

do m'athair, Liam Mac Carráin
for my father, William Carson

Turn Again

There is a map of the city which shows the bridge that was
    never built.
A map which shows the bridge that collapsed; the streets that
    never existed.
Ireland's Entry, Elbow Lane, Weigh-House Lane, Back Lane,
    Stone-Cutter's Entry —
Today's plan is already yesterday's — the streets that were there
    are gone.
And the shape of the jails cannot be shown for security reasons.

The linen backing is falling apart — the Falls Road hangs
    by a thread.
When someone asks me where I live, I remember where I used
    to live.
Someone asks me for directions, and I think again. I turn into
A side street to try to throw off my shadow, and history
    is changed.

PART ONE

Not to find one's way about in a city
is of little interest ... But to lose one's
way in a city, as one loses one's way in
a forest, requires practice ... I learned this
art late in life: it fulfilled the dreams
whose first traces were the labyrinths on
the blotters of my exercise books.
                              — Walter Benjamin,
                        A Berlin Childhood Around
                            the Turn of the Century

Loaf

I chewed it over, this whiff I got just now, but trying to pin
    down
That aroma — yeast, salt, flour, water — is like writing on
    the waxed sleeve
That it's wrapped in: the nib keeps skidding off. Or the ink
    won't take. Blue-black
Quink is what I used then. I liked the in-between-ness of it,
    neither
One thing nor the other. A Conway Stewart fountain-pen,
    blue-ish green
Mock tortoiseshell . . . the lever sticking sometimes in the quick
    of my thumb,
I'd fill her up: a contented slurp like the bread you use to sup up
Soup. McWatters' pan loaf, some said, was like blotting paper:
    I thought of
Leonardo's diary, or a mirror code ending with, *Eat this*.
Well, some people *like* blotting paper. I used to eat chalk
    myself. Raw
Flour, oatmeal. Paper. A vitamin deficiency? The corners of
My books weren't dog-eared, they were chewed. But neatly
    chewed, like the thumb-index
Of a dictionary. I ate my way from *A* to *Z*, the list of weights
And measures. So now I'm in McWatters' flour-loft. Grains,
    pecks and bushels:

So much raw material. *I* was raw. This was a summer job, not
    real
Work. Myself and this other skiver, we mostly talked of this
    and that —
Cigarettes and whiskey — between whatever it was we were
    supposed
To do. Joe reckoned that Jameson's Three Swallows was hard
    to beat
Though you could make a case for their Robin Redbreast
    or Power's Gold Label.
One had the edge the others didn't, though you couldn't quite
    describe it.

Like Gallaher's Greens: dry, smoky, biting. He had this bebop
        hairstyle —
Bee-bap, as they say in Belfast, a golden fuzz pricked up from
        the scalp —
And he'd done time at one time or another for some petty crime.
        Theft?
Jiggery-pokery. Night-shifts. The kind of fly moves that get you
        caught.
And as it happened, he was between times just then, like me
        between terms.

It seemed the Health Inspectors were due in a while, so we were
        given
Galvanized buckets, sponges, those mops with the head
        of an albino
Golliwog. The place breathed gunge and grease, the steamy
        damp of baking bread.
So as I say, we talked: football, drink, girls, horses, though
        I didn't know
Much on any of these scores. They were clouds on the blue
        of the future.
Walking the slippery catwalk from one bake-room to the next —
        like Dante's
Inferno, the midnight glare of ovens, a repeated doughy slap
Of moulds being filled — we'd think of the cool of the loo
        or a lunchtime pint.
The bitter edge of Guinness would cut through the bread and
        oxtail soup
Till bread and soup and stout became all one. We would talk
        with our mouths full.

Then back to Ajax and Domestos, the Augean pandemonium.
Or sorting out spoiled loaves for pig-feed — waxed wrappers
        in one bag, sliced pan
In the other; the pigs, it seemed, were particular. At other times,
Stacking up empty flour-sacks: cloudy caesurae floating one
        on top

Of one another, the print so faded we could barely read the text;
That choked-up weave meant nothing much but passing time.
    Expanding moments,
Watching dough rise, the stretch marks lost in the enormous
    puff-ball — *Is this*
The snow that was so bright last year?
                         We worked slowly through
    the levels, till
We found ourselves at last in No. 2 loft, high above the racket.
My last week. As for him, he didn't know. Muffled by forgotten
    drifts
Of flour, I was thinking of the future, he was buried in the past.
This move he'd worked, this girl he'd known. Everything stored
    away in cells.
Pent-up honey talk oozed out of him, while I sang, *Que sera sera.*

He asked if I'd remember him. We wrote our names on the
    snowed-up panes.
The date, the names of girls, hearts and arrows. We made up
    affairs between
The bakers and the packers — bread and paper — then we wiped
    it all clean.
The glass shone for the first time in years. We were staring out
    the window
At the end of summer. Aeroplanes flew by at intervals, going
    elsewhere:
Tiny specks, the white lines of their past already fuzzing
    up the blue.

Plains and mountains, skies
all up to their eyes in snow:
nothing to be seen.

— Joso

Snow

A white dot flicked back and forth across the bay window: not
A table-tennis ball, but 'ping-pong', since this is happening
    in another era,
The extended leaves of the dining-table — scratched mahogany
    veneer —
Suggesting many such encounters, or time passing: the celluloid
    diminuendo
As it bounces off into a corner and ticks to an incorrigible stop.
I pick it up days later, trying to get that pallor right: it's neither
    ivory
Nor milk. Chalk is better; and there's a hint of pearl, translucent
Lurking just behind opaque. I broke open the husk so many times
And always found it empty; the pith was a wordless bubble.

Though there's nothing in the thing itself, bits of it come back
    unbidden,
Playing in the archaic dusk till the white blip became invisible.
Just as, the other day, I felt the tacky pimples of a ping-pong bat
When the bank clerk counted out my money with her rubber
    thimble, and knew
The black was bleeding into red. Her face was snow and roses
    just behind
The bullet-proof glass: I couldn't touch her if I tried. I crumpled
    up the chit —
No use in keeping what you haven't got — and took a stroll
    to Ross's auction.
There was this Thirties scuffed leather sofa I wanted to make
    a bid for.
Gestures, prices: soundlessly collateral in the murmuring room.

I won't say what I paid for it: anything's too much when you
    have nothing.
But in the dark recesses underneath the cushions I found myself
    kneeling
As decades of the Rosary dragged by, the slack of years ago
    hauled up

Bead by bead; and with them, all the haberdashery of loss —
    cuff buttons,
Broken ballpoint pens and fluff, old pennies, pins and needles,
    and yes,
A ping-pong ball. I cupped it in my hands like a crystal, seeing
    not
The future, but a shadowed parlour just before the blinds are
    drawn. Someone
Has put up two trestles. Handshakes all round, nods and
    whispers.
Roses are brought in and, suddenly, white confetti seethes
    against the window.

As a scarecrow blows
over: the first whispering
of the autumn wind.

— Kyoruku

All the Better to See You With

No soft pink or peach scheme for Rose-Marie O'Hara when
    she married:
Since her favourite colour was red she was determined on
    a vivid red theme —
The bridesmaids were in scarlet lace and satin, armed with
    bouquets
Of vermilion roses; the friend's 'black taxi' which they
    borrowed for the bridal car
Was crimson lake. Into which they'd dive before the day was
    out. The invitations
Were, of course, red letters. My hands were shaking as I slit
    the envelope
And glimpsed the copperplate. My name. His and hers. All
    brought together
In a florid moment, a dashed-off sketch of what would happen,
    like this fox
I caught once in the corner of my eye, disappearing in a brambly
    thicket, its elongated brush
Hovering for an instant like a brush-stroke;
The kind of random mark that might be usefully retained for
    just that air
Of neither-here-nor-thereness. Coming in the act of going.

Some might have swamped the canvas in this red extravaganza,
    but convention
Was deferred to in her own ensemble: ivory organza, a tiered
    affair
With ruched bodice and hooped skirts, millefeuilles petticoats,
    and underneath
The trailing hem, if you could only lift it, red stilettos —
Such pretty shoes for dancing in, I don't think — which were,
    it seemed,
A bit too tight for comfort. Teetering up the knife-edge
    of the aisle,
Did she even then regret this? Whispers ran around her and
    jostled her dress.
Which she'd discard before the day was out.

134

Now the soles of the groom's feet are presented to me, hers are
    hidden
Still. She might have stepped into a muddied pool up to her
    ankles,
Or they are deep in the lacy avalanche. Thinking of *her cheeks
    like roses*
Or *like blood dropped on snow*, I would have climbed the
    Matterhorn for her,
Stood on my head, or run like a fox before hounds — through
    the copper beeches,
Glowing, bursting into thickets like the last coal stirred
    in the fire
Of his red hair. I'd blow and blow and try to stir it up again.
    Though still
I couldn't quite believe it. Like the wrong-sized foot
Stuck into this glass slipper, she was the glass and he was
    the foot.
Her own feet, lopped off, waltzed away into the forest.
How could I unravel all those brambles, tangles, nettles, thorns?
    I pulled
At jagged things, and more kept coming up in that erratic spiky
    hand
Of hers. Billets-doux, excuses, lies. Or a line or two that gave
    some hope . . .
I'd twist it inside out, this coil that led me on and on, and brings
    me back
To the red bud of his buttonhole, a shower of red confetti.
Or to this scenario of her as Wolf, and me as Little Red Riding
    Hood
Being gobbled up. *Many's the strawberry grows in the salt sea,*
    as the song
Would have it, *and many's the ship sails in the forest:* it's time
    for the fox
To go to earth. I painted a picture of myself curled up, the brush
Like a knife between my teeth. A few careless dribbles,
    incarnadine upon my wrist.

The newly-weds were found in a wood. His face was pock-
  marked by a fever
Of stilettos. Her belly was unstitched. Tomato ketchup flicked
  on her portrait.
Everything dissolves: the white spirit clouds with rust and
  cinnabar.

I know the wild geese
ate my barley — yesterday?
Today? Where did they go?

— Yasui

Ambition

*I did not allow myself to think of ultimate escape . . . one step
at a time was enough.*
> — John Buchan, *Mr Standfast*

Now I've climbed this far it's time to look back. But smoke
    obscures
The panorama from the Mountain Loney spring. The city and
    the mountain are on fire.
My mouth's still stinging from the cold sharp shock of water —
    a winter taste
In summer — but my father's wandered off somewhere. I can't
    seem to find him.
We'd been smoking 'coffin nails', and he'd been talking of his
    time inside, how
Matches were that scarce you'd have to split them four ways
    with your thumbnail;
And seven cigarette ends made a cigarette. *Keep a thing for
    seven years,*
You'll always find a use for it, he follows in the same breath . . .
    it reminds me
Of the saint who, when he had his head cut off, picked up his
    head and walked
With it for seven miles. And the wise man said, *The distance
    doesn't matter,*
It's the first step that was difficult.

Any journey's like that — *the first step of your life,* my father
    interrupts —
Though often you take one step forward, two steps back. For
    if time is a road
It's fraught with ramps and dog-legs, switchbacks and spaghetti;
    here and there,
The dual carriageway becomes a one-track, backward mind.
    And bits of the landscape
Keep recurring: it seems as if I've watched the same suburban
    tennis match

For hours, and heard, at ever less-surprising intervals,
  the applause of pigeons
Bursting from a loft. Or the issue is not yet decided,
  as the desultory handclaps
Turn to rain. The window that my nose is pressed against
  is breathed-on, giving
Everything a sfumato air. I keep drawing faces on it, or
  practising my signature.

And if time is a road, then you're checked again and again
By a mobile checkpoint. One soldier holds a gun to your head.
  Another soldier
Asks you questions, and another checks the information
  on the head computer.
Your name. Your brothers' names. Your father's name. His
  occupation. As if
The one they're looking for is not you, but it might be you.
  Looks like you
Or smells like you. And suddenly, the posthumous aroma
  of an empty canvas
Postman's sack — twine, ink, dead letters — wafts out from
  the soldiers'
Sodden khaki. It's obvious they're bored: one of them is watch-
  ing Wimbledon
On one of those postage-stamp-sized TV screens. *Of course,
  the proper shot,*
An unseen talking head intones, *should have been the lob.*
  He's using words like
Angled, volley, smash and *strategy.* Someone is *fighting a losing
  battle.*
Isn't that the way, that someone tells you what you should have
  done, when
You've just done the opposite? *Did you give the orders for this
  man's death?*
On the contrary, the accused replies, as if he'd ordered birth
  or resurrection.

Though *one nail drives out another*, as my father says.
And my father should have known better than to tamper with
    Her Majesty's
Royal Mail — or was it His, then? His humour was to take
    an Irish ha'penny
With the harp on the flip side, and frank a letter with it. Some
    people didn't
See the joke; they'd always thought him a Republican. He was
    reported,
Laid off for a month. Which is why he never got promoted.
    So one story goes.
The other is a war-time one, where he's supposed to go to
    England
For a training course, but doesn't, seeing he doesn't want to get
    conscripted.
My mother's version is he lacked ambition. He was too content
    to stay
In one place. He liked things as they were . . . *perfect touch,
    perfect timing, perfect*
Accuracy: the commentary has just nudged me back a little,
    as I manage
To take in the action replay. There's a tiny puff of chalk,
    as the ball skids off
The line, like someone might be firing in slow motion, far away:
    that otherwise
Unnoticeable faint cloud on the summer blue, which makes
    the sky around it
All the more intense and fragile.

It's nearer to a winter blue. A zig-zag track of footsteps is
    imprinted
On the frosted tennis court: it looks as if the Disappeared One
    rose before
First light, and stalked from one side of the wire cage to the
    other, off

Into the glinting laurels. No armed wing has yet proclaimed
   responsibility:
One hand washes the other, says my father, *as sure as one
   funeral makes many.*
For the present is a tit-for-tat campaign, exchanging *now* for
   then,
The Christmas post of Christmas Past, the black armband
   of the temporary man;
The insignia have mourned already for this casual preserve.
   Threading
Through the early morning suburbs and the monkey-puzzle
   trees, a smell of coffee lingers,
Imprisoned in the air like wisps of orange peel in marmalade;
   and sleigh-bell music
Tinkles on the radio, like ice cubes in a summer drink. I think
   I'm starting, now,
To know the street map with my feet, just like my father.

God never shuts one door, said my father, *but he opens up
   another*; and then,
I walked the iron catwalk naked in the freezing cold: he's back
   into his time
As internee, the humiliation of the weekly bath. It was seven
   weeks before
He was released: it was his younger brother they were after
   all the time.
God never opens one door, but he shuts another: my uncle was
   inside for seven years.
At his funeral they said how much I looked like him: I've got
   his smoker's cough,
At any rate. And now my father's told to cut down on the
   cigarettes he smokes
Them three or four puffs at a time. Stubs them out and lights
   them, seven times.
I found him yesterday a hundred yards ahead of me, struggling,
   as the blazing

Summer hauled him one step at a time into a freezing furnace.
　　And with each step
He aged. As I closed in on him, he coughed. I coughed.
　　He stopped and turned,
Made two steps back towards me, and I took one step forward.

To Lord Toba's hall
five or six horsemen blow in:
storm-wind of the fall.

— Buson

Queen's Gambit

A Remote Handling Equipment (Tracked) Explosive Ordnance
    Disposal unit — *Wheelbarrow*,
For short — is whirring and ticking towards the Ford Sierra
    parked in Tomb Street,

Its robotic arm extended indirectly towards this close-up
    of a soldier. He's wearing
An M69 flak jacket, Dr Marten boots and non-regulation
    skiing gloves.

Another soldier, armed with Self-loading Rifle, squats beneath
    a spray-gunned
Flourish of graffiti: *The Provos Are Fighting For You. Remember
    It. Brits Out.*

Now they're seen together leaning against the façade
    of a chemist's shop,
Admiring — so it would appear — the cardboard ad for
    Wilkinson Sword razor blades.

So much, they're now in the interior: a gauzy, pinkish smell
    of soap and sticking-
Plaster, through which they spit word-bubbles at the white-
    coated girl assistant.

Much of this is unintelligible, blotted out by stars and asterisks
Just as the street outside is splattered with bits of corrugated iron
    and confetti.

Her slightly antiseptic perfume is a reminiscent *je-ne-sais-quoi*
Glimpsed through Pear's Soap, an orange-sepia zest of coal-tar —

It's that moiré light from the bathroom window, or a body seen
    behind
The shower curtain, holding a champagne telephone — the
    colour, not the drink,

144

Though it gives off a perceptible hiss. And the continuous
    background
Rumble is a string of *M*s and *R*s, expanding and contracting

To reveal the windswept starry night, through which
    a helicopter trawls
Its searchlight. Out there, on the ground, there's a spoor of
    army boots;

Dogs are following their noses, and terrorists are contemplating
Terror, a glittering, tilted view of mercury, while the assistant
    slithers

Into something more comfortable: jeans, a combat jacket, Doc
    Marten boots;
Then weighs the confidential dumb-bell of the telephone. She
    pushes buttons:

Zero Eight Double Zero. Then the number of the Beast,
    the number of the Beast
Turned upside down: Six Six Six, Nine Nine Nine . . .

The ambient light of yesterday is amplified by talk of might-
    have-beens,
Making 69 — the year — look like quotation marks, comment-
    ators commentating on

The flash-point of the current Trouble, though there's any
    God's amount
Of Nines and Sixes: 1916, 1690, The Nine Hundred Years'
    War, whatever.

Or maybe we can go back to the Year Dot, the nebulous
    expanding brain-wave
Of the Big Bang, releasing us and It and everything into oblivion;

It's so hard to remember, and so easy to forget the casualty list —
Like the names on a school desk, carved into one another till
   they're indecipherable.

It's that frottage effect again: the paper that you're scribbling
   on is grained
And blackened, till the pencil-lead snaps off, in a valley
   of the broken alphabet

And the streets are a bad photostat grey: the ink comes off
   on your hand.
With so many foldings and unfoldings, whole segments
   of the map have fallen off.

It's not unlike the missing reel in the film, the blank screen
   jittering
With numerals and flak, till the picture jumps back — a bit
   out of sync,

As soldiers A and B and others of the lettered regiment discuss
   the mission
In their disembodied voices. Only the crackly Pye Pocketfone
   sounds real,

A bee-in-the-biscuit-tin buzzing number codes and decibels.
   They're in the belly
Of a Saracen called 'Felix', the cartoon cat they've taken
   as a mascot:

It's all the go, here, changing something into something else,
   like rhyming
Kampuchea with Cambodia. It's why Mickey Mouse wears
   those little white gloves —

Claws are too much like a mouse. And if the animals are trying
   to be people,

146

Vice versa is the case as well. Take 'Mad Dog' Reilly, for
  example, who

This instant is proceeding to the rendezvous. A gunman,
  he isn't yet; the rod
Is stashed elsewhere, somewhere in a mental block of dog-leg
  turns and cul-de-sacs.

He sniffs his hand, an antiseptic tang that momentarily brings
  back
The creak of a starched coat crushed against his double-
  breasted gaberdine.

After the recorded message the bleep announces a magnetic
  silence
Towards which she's drawn as conspirator, as towards
  a confessional, whispering

What she knows into the wire-grilled darkness: names, dates,
  places;
More especially, a future venue, Tomb Street GPO.

She wants the slate wiped clean, Flash or Ajax cutting a bright
  swathe
Through a murky kitchen floor, transforming it into a gleaming
  checkerboard.

Tiles of black and white on which the regiments of pawns move
  ponderously,
Bishops take diagonals, and the Queen sees dazzling lines
  of power.

Or, putting it another way, Operation 'Mad Dog', as it's known
  now,

Is the sketch that's taking shape on the Army HQ blackboard, chalky ghosts

Behind the present, showing what was contemplated and rubbed out, Plan A
Becoming X or Y; interlocked, curved arrows of the mortgaged future.

The raffia waste-paper bin is full of crumpled drafts and cigarette butts,
And ash has seeped through to the carpet. There's a smell of peeled oranges.

But the Unknown Factor, somewhat like the Unknown Soldier, has yet to take
The witness box. As someone spills a cup of tea on a discarded *Irish News*

A minor item bleeds through from another page, blurring the main story.
It's difficult to pick up without the whole thing coming apart in your hands,

But basically it invokes this bunch of cowboys who, unbeknownst to us all,
Have jumped on board a Ford Sierra, bound for You-Know-Where.

They're Ordinary Criminals: you know them by the dollar signs that shiver
In their eyes, a notion that they're going to hit the jackpot of the GPO.

Unbeknownst to themselves they'll be picked up in the amplified light
Of a Telescope Starlight II Night Observation Device (NOD)
— *Noddy*, for short,

But not before the stoolie-pigeon spool is reeled back;
    amplified,
Its querulous troughs and peaks map out a different curve
    of probability.

         ~

My newly-lowered ears in the barber's mirror were starting
    to take on a furtive look.
A prison cut — my face seemed Born Again — but then,
    I'd asked for *short.*

And I've this problem, talking to a man whose mouth is
    a reflection.
I tend to think the words will come out backwards, so I'm
    saying nothing.

And then, says he — he's staring straight into my eyes,
    the scissors poised —
It seems they think they're just about to nail your man O'Reilly

*When a bunch of hoods pulls up in a Ford Sierra and jumps out
    with the sawn-off*
*Shotguns, plastic masks they must have got in Elliot's — Mickey
    Mouse, Donald Duck*

*And Pluto — too much watching TV, if you ask me — so of
    course the Brits let go*
With everything. He snips at my right ear. *But now hear this:*

*This Post Office van bombs out from Tomb Street loading bay,
    its side door open,*
*And they've got this effing Gatling gun or something going full
    blast —*

*Dot, dot, dot, dot — and the Brits are all shot up — could you
    move your head a bit —*

Right — so the Mad Dog, he jumps in the back and him and
the boys are off like a shot.

So what do you think? It looks to me it was a set-up job, though
who exactly
Was set up, God only knows. You can see it for yourself — they've
been checking out

That Ford Sierra for the past two hours, just as soon as it was
light.
Seems they think the Disney characters were in on it. If you ask me,

With these confidential telephones, you never know who's doing
who, or why.
Better to keep your mouth shut, that's what I say. Haircut OK, sir?

He held a mirror to my neck. I nodded. He shook out the cloth,
and curls
And snippets writhed like commas on the chessboard tiles. Now
that I could see

Myself without the hair and beard, I looked like someone else.
He brushed
My shoulders, and I left him to a row of empty mirrors, sweep-
ing up

The fallen swathes. Turning into Tomb Street, I began to feel
a new man.
Perfume breathed from somewhere, opening avenues of love,
or something déjà vu.

These are wild slow days,
echoes trickling in from all
around Kyoto.

— Buson

PART TWO

. . . that the Mastive dogs belonginge to Butchers,
Tanners, and other Inhabitants dwelling in this
Corporation and the suburbs and ffields thereunto
belonginge, have Barbarously ffallen upon horses
in Carrs, upon the Street, and also horses out of
carrs, And have violently Torne and abused them,
That some of them have been in hazard to die, And
also ffallen upon severall cattell bothe upon the
Streets and in the ffields. Inso much that severall
catell are mightily abused, and some of them killed
to the great loss of many of the poore Inhabitants
of this Corporacon. And also that the said Dogs
have ffallen upon severall men and boyes upon the
Streets and Lanes of this Towne and suburbs
thereunto belonginge, and have pult them to the
Ground, Torne their cloathes and Torne some of their
ffleshe and eaten the same Insoemuch that many
Inhabitants ffeare their lives to walk the streets
or laines either by night or day for the said
dogs and Bitches . . .

Ordinance of the Corporation of Belfast,
25th July 1678

Gate

Passing *Terminus* boutique the other day I see it's got a bit
    of flak:
The *T* and the *r* are missing, leaving *e minus*, and a sign saying,
    MONSTER
CLOSING DOWN SALE. It opened about six months back, selling
    odd-job-lots,
Ends of ranges. Before that it was Burton's, where I bought
    my wedding suit.
Which I only wear for funerals now. *Gone for a Burton*,
    as the saying goes.

The stopped clock of *The Belfast Telegraph* seems to indicate
    the time
Of the explosion — or was that last week's? Difficult to keep
    track:
Everything's a bit askew, like the twisted pickets of the security
    gate, the wreaths
That approximate the spot where I'm told the night patrol went
    through.

Last Orders

Squeeze the buzzer on the steel mesh gate like a trigger, but
It's someone else who has you in their sights. *Click*. It opens.
  Like electronic
Russian roulette, since you never know for sure who's who,
  or what
You're walking into. I, for instance, could be anybody. Though
  I'm told
Taig's written on my face. See me, would *I* trust appearances?

Inside a sudden lull. The barman lolls his head at us. We order
  Harp —
Seems safe enough, everybody drinks it. As someone looks
  daggers at us
From the Bushmills mirror, a penny drops: how simple it
  would be for someone
Like ourselves to walk in and blow the whole place, and
  ourselves, to Kingdom Come.

Farset

Trying to get back to that river, this river I am about to explore, I imagine or remember peering between the rusted iron bars that lined one side of the alleyway behind St Gall's School at the bottom of Waterville Street, gazing down at the dark exhausted water, my cheeks pressed against the cold iron. It is only years later I will find its name. For now I take it in with a child's rapt boredom. Muck. Water. A bottomless bucket. The undercarriage of a pram. A rusted spring mattress. The river, the stream, the sewer trickles from a black mouth and disappears down a black hole. It is this which gives Belfast its name.

> *The utmost obscurity and perplexity, however, attend the derivation of the name . . . the name of* Bealafarsad, *which means, according to some, hurdleford town, while others have translated it, the mouth of the pool. Either of these explanations might receive some corroboration from local facts, but as it is a matter of complete hypothesis, there seems to be further room for further speculation.*

So says George Benn, writing in the 1820s. Dubourdieu, writing some years earlier, claims that Belfast *is supposed to have derived its present name from Bela Fearsad, which signifies a town at the mouth of a river, expressive of the circumstances, in which it stood.* Ward, Lock & Co.'s *Guide to Northern Ireland*, a hundred-odd years later, has yet another version: *While the bell in Belfast's civic coat of arms is a feeble pun, the word 'fast' refers to the 'farset', or sand-bank (also the now-covered-in High Street river). 'Bel' in Celtic means 'ford', i.e. Bel-feirste, the 'bel' or 'ford' of the 'farset'.*

In all this watery confusion one thing seems certain: that *Belfast* is a corruption of the Irish *Béal Feirste. Béal* is easy. It means a mouth, or the mouth of a river; an opening; an approach. Benn's informant seems to have mistaken it for *baile*, a town, thereby arriving at an English equivalent of the modern Irish name for Dublin, *Baile Átha Cliath*, which is precisely *hurdleford town*. But it is this *feirste* in which meaning founders, this genitive of *fearsad*, the Irish word for . . .

The Rev Dineen glosses it as a shaft; a spindle; the ulna of the arm; a club; the spindle of an axle; a bar or bank of sand at low water; a deep narrow channel on a strand at low tide; a pit or pool of water; a verse, a poem. The dictionaries of Edward O'Reilly and Thomas de Vere Conys agree substantially, though O'Reilly has the strange *wallet*, which turns up again in Duelly's Scottish Gaelic dictionary; and he has the nice adjective *fearsach*, *full of little ridges in the sand*, one of those illuminations glimpsed at dawn's low tide, where seeming *terra firma* mimics the ridges of the sea: I remember seeing this precisely in the remote Gaeltacht of *Rann na Feirste*, or Ranafast in Donegal. Not to mention *Béal Feirste*, or Belfarset in County Mayo, where I have never been.

But let us take the simple approach, and imagine that *fearsad* is a sandbank, formed by the confluence of the river of that name — the Farset — and the Lagan. So Belfast is the *approach to the sandbank*, or the *mouth of the Farset*; or the *approach to the ford*, since historically there was a ford at that point, and St George's Church in High Street, below which the Farset runs, reputedly stands on the site of the *Chapel by the Ford*. Or let us suppose, with the Jesuit McCionnaith's English-Irish dictionary, that *fearsad* stands for *axis*, as in the expression, *Bíonn an domhan ag casadh ar a fhearsaid féin*, *the world revolves on its own axis*: one imagines this, not as a scientific observation, but as a stock response to another's elaborate and banal anecdote. And my father tells me that the Axis forces in the Second World War were indeed known as *Lucht na Feirste*, or the Axis People (not to be confused with the X People of the eponymous SF novel dreamed up by Belfast's ex-political-correspondent of the BBC, W D Flackes). Or more fancifully, we could take Dineen's *poem* and let Belfast be the *mouth of the poem* — surely Farset is related to the Latin turn in the furrow known as *versus*? And strangely, by a conspiracy of history and accident and geography, the river Farset, this hidden stream, is all these things: it is the axis of the opposed Catholic Falls Road and the Protestant Shankill, as we follow it through the old Shankill Graveyard — now a municipal park — till it disappears beneath the Shankill Road and surfaces in Bombay Street (burned down in the '68 Troubles), sidles along the back of Cupar Street, following almost precisely the line of the Peace Line, this thirty-foot-high wall of graffiticized corrugated iron, the interface, the deadline, lost in what survives of Belfast's industrial Venice — for water, after all, was power — a maze of dams, reservoirs, sluices, sinks, footbridges that I remember in my dreams as walled-in by Titanic mills, gouts of steam breaking intermittently through the grit and smog, as it sinks and surfaces finally in Millfield and then is lost in its final culvert under High Street. It remembers spindles, arms, the songs of millgirls. It remembers nothing: no one steps in the same river twice. Or, as some wag has it, no one steps in the same river once.

Hairline Crack

It could have been or might have been. Everything Provisional
    and Sticky,
Daily splits and splinters at the drop of a hat or a principle —
The right hand wouldn't even know it was the right hand;
    some would claim it
As the left. If only this, if only that, if only pigs could fly.
Someone decides, hawk or dove. Ambushes are sprung. Velvet
    fist. Iron glove.

It was on the stroke of midnight by the luminous dial
    of the clock
When this woman, caught in crossfire, stooped for the dash-
    board cigarette lighter.
In that instant, a bullet neatly parted her permanent wave.
    So now
She tells the story, how a cigarette made all the odds. Between
    life. And death.

Bloody Hand

Your man, says the Man, *will walk into the bar like this —*
    here his fingers
Mimic a pair of legs, one stiff at the knee — *so you'll know exactly*
What to do. He sticks a finger to his head. Pretend it's child's
    play —
The hand might be a horse's mouth, a rabbit or a dog. Five
    handclaps.
Walls have ears: the shadows you throw are the shadows you
    try to throw off.

I snuffed out the candle between finger and thumb. Was
    it the left hand
Hacked off at the wrist and thrown to the shores of Ulster?
    Did Ulster
Exist? Or the Right Hand of God, saying *Stop* to this and
    No to that?
My thumb is the hammer of a gun. The thumb goes up. The
    thumb goes down.

Schoolboys and Idlers of Pompeii

On an almost-blank wall where East 4th — or was it East 6th? — Street intersects Avenue A in the area called Alphabet City in New York, New York, is this graffito in three-foot-high black letters, saying BELFAST, with the cross-stroke of the T extended into an arrow pointing east, to Belfast. I have a photograph to prove this, but it's lost. In New York no one that I ask seems to know the meaning of this careful scrawl, whether it's a gang, the code-word of a gang, a fashion, a club, or the name of the city where I was born; but the latter seems unlikely, though Alphabet City — barricaded liquor stores, secretive tobacco shops and elaborate Russian Orthodox churches — resembles Belfast, its roads pocked and skid-marked, littered with broken glass and crushed beer cans.

And on the back wall of Gallaher's tobacco factory in North Queen Street in Belfast there has recently appeared this New York underground graffiti mural — coded, articulated, multi-coloured spray-gunned alphabet — pointing west by style and implication.

At times it seems that every inch of Belfast has been written-on, erased, and written-on again: messages, curses, political imperatives, but mostly names, or nicknames — Robbo, Mackers, Scoot, Fra — sometimes litanized obsessively on every brick of a gable wall, as high as the hand will reach, and sometimes higher, these snakes and ladders cancelling each other out in their bid to be remembered. *Remember 1690. Remember 1916.* Most of all, *Remember me. I was here.*

Remembering is one of the main functions of the Falls Road Club which meets on the first Thursday of every month in The Woolongong Bar in Adelaide, Australia. Exiled here since the emigrations of the Fifties and the early Sixties, these Kennedys and McErleans and Hugheses begin with small talk of the present, but are soon immersed in history, reconstructing a city on the other side of the world, detailing streets and shops and houses which for the most part only exist now in the memory. Or ghosts which exist only in the memory: someone is telling the story of the policeman who was shot dead outside the National Bank at the corner of Balaklava Street in 1922; but the story does not concern the policeman; rather, it is about the tin can which was heard that night rolling down Balaklava Street into Raglan Street, and which was heard again for years after, whenever there was trouble in the offing; thousands heard it, no one saw it. Someone else produces a week-old copy of *The Irish News* which gives another slant to the story: the tin can has not been heard since the streets concerned were demolished; this is hardly surprising, since even ghosts must have somewhere to live. Someone else again ventures the notion that the ghost is only a by-product of the elaborate version of hide-and-seek known as *kick-the-tin*, and they all start to remember more, their favourite hidey-holes in entries and alleyways and backyards, till they are lost in the comforting dusk and smog and drizzle of the Lower Falls, playing: games of imitation, games of chance, of luck, of initiation; the agglomerate tag or *tig* called *chain-tig*. Or they recall the names carved on the desks of Slate Street School, the taste of school milk in winter, the aura of plasticine and chalk dust as they chant the twelve-times table for the twelfth or thirteenth time. Fortified by expensively-imported Red Heart Guinness and Gallaher's Blues, they talk on, trying to get back — before the Blitz, the avalanche, the Troubles — the drinker interrupted between cup and lip — winding back the clock . . .

The walls where they inscribed their names have been pulled down, but somewhere they survive. *Graffito*, says the dictionary, *a mural scribbling or drawing, as by schoolboys and idlers at Pompeii, Rome, and other ancient cities . . .*

Running back the film of the mind's eye, the alphabet soup of demolition sorts itself into phrases, names, buildings, as if, on the last day, not only bodies are resurrected whole and perfect, but each brick, each stone, finds its proper place again:

the spire of St Malachy's Church, which was *removed, with advantage, for the tolling of the great bell in it interfered with the satisfactory maturing of the whiskey in Messrs Dunville's adjacent distillery . . .*

the seven arches of the Long Bridge which fell in, *weakened by the passage of Schomberg's heavy cannon on their way to the Battle of the Boyne* . . .

the Great Salt Water Bridge, which still exists, *for it was not taken down when the Boyne Bridge was built, but was simply incorporated into the new structure and completely enveloped by it* . . .

bridges within bridges, the music in bad whiskey, the demolished air-raid shelters used as infill for the reclaimed land of Belfast Lough — who will sort out the chaos? Where does land begin, and water end? Or memory falter, and imagination take hold?

Barfly

Maybe you can figure it, why The Crown and Shamrock
  and The Rose and Crown
Are at opposite ends of the town. Politics? The odds change.
The borders move.
Or they're asked to. A nod's as good as a wink. For example,
  in The Arkle Inn
This night I'm getting it from the horse's mouth, when these
  two punters walk in,
Produce these rods, and punctuate the lunchtime menu: there's
  confetti everywhere.

Which, I take it, was a message. Or an audio-visual aid. At any
  rate, I buzzed off.
For, like the menu, everything's chalked up, and every now
  and then, wiped clean.
So now, I am a hyphen, flitting here and there: between The
  First and Last —
The Gamble — The Rendezvous — The Cellars — The Crow's
  Nest — The Elephant — The Fly.

Jump Leads

As the eggbeater spy in the sky flickered overhead, the TV
    developed a facial tic
Or as it turned out, the protesters had handcuffed them-
    selves to the studio lights.
Muffled off-camera, shouts of *No.* As I tried to lip-read
    the talking head
An arms cache came up, magazines laid out like a tray
    of wedding rings.
The bomb-disposal expert whose face was in shadow for
    security reasons

Had started very young by taking a torch apart at Christmas
    to see what made it tick.
Everything went dark. The killers escaped in a red Fiesta
    according to sources.
Talking, said the Bishop, is better than killing. Just before
    the Weather
The victim is his wedding photograph. He's been spattered
    with confetti.

Question Time

A native of Belfast, writes George Benn in his 1823 history of the city, *who had been brought up in one of the best streets which it contained, lately came over from America, after nearly a life-long absence, to visit the home of his youth. He could hardly find it. An immense place of business occupied its site, and he compared Belfast to an American town, so great was its progress in his absence, and so unexampled the growth of its population.*

That disorientation, that disappointed hunger for a familiar place, will be experienced all the more keenly by today's returning native; more than that, even the little piggy who stayed at home will sometimes feel lost. *I know this place like the back of my hand* — except who really knows how many hairs there are, how many freckles? A wound, a suture, an excision will remind us of the physical, of what *was* there — as the song has it, *you'll never miss your mother till she's buried beneath the clay.* For Belfast is changing daily: one day the massive Victorian façade of the Grand Central Hotel, latterly an army barracks, is *there,* dominating the whole of Royal Avenue; the next day it is gone, and a fresh breeze sweeps through the gap, from Black Mountain, across derelict terraces, hole-in-the-wall one-horse taxi operations, Portakabins, waste ground, to take the eye back up towards the mountain and the piled-up clouds.

The junk is sinking back into the sleech and muck. Pizza parlours, massage parlours, night-clubs, drinking-clubs, antique shops, designer studios momentarily populate the wilderness and the blitz sites; they too will vanish in the morning. Everything will be revised. The fly-specked gloom of The Elephant Bar is now a Winemark; Mooney's Bar is a denim shop; The Gladstone has disappeared. The tangle of streets that was the Pound Loney is the Divis Flats Complex, which is also falling apart, its high-rise Sixties optimism sliding back into the rubble and erasure. Maps and street directories are suspect.

No, don't trust maps, for they avoid the moment: ramps, barricades, diversions, Peace Lines. Though if there is an ideal map, which shows this city as it is, it may exist in the eye of that helicopter ratcheting overhead, its searchlight fingering and scanning the micro-chip deviations: the surge of funerals and parades, swelling and accelerating, time-lapsed, sucked back into nothingness by the rewind button; the wired-up alleyways and entries; someone walking his dog when the façade of Gass's Bicycle Shop erupts in an avalanche of glass and metal forks and tubing, rubber, rat-trap pedals, toe-clips and repair kits. Or it may exist in photographs — this one, for example, of Raglan Street, showing

> . . . a sight that was to become only too common to a generation of British soldiers as rioters stone 'A' Company, 2nd Battalion, The Queen's Regiment, during the savage Lower Falls riots of 3-5 July 1970 which left five civilians dead and eighteen military casualties . . .

But the caption is inaccurate: the camera has caught only one rioter in the act, his stone a dark blip in the drizzly air. The others, these would-be or has-been or may-be rioters, have momentarily become spectators, as their protagonist does his David-and-Goliath act; some might be talking about the weather, which seems unusually grey for July, or maybe this is a bad print; some others are looking down Bosnia Street at what is happening or might happen next. The left-hand frame of the photograph only allows us the 'nia' of Roumania Street, so I don't know what's going on there, but I'm trying to remember — was I there that night, on this street littered with half-bricks, broken glass, a battered saucepan and a bucket? In this fragment of a map, here is the lamp-post where I swung as a child, there is Smyth's corner shop; I can almost see myself in the half-gloom and the din. From here — No. 100 — I would turn into Leeson Street, on up to the Falls Road, across to Clonard Street on my way to St Gall's Primary School; at least, that was how I was told to go, and generally I did, but remember, *Never go by Cupar Street*, my father would warn me, and I knew this was a necessary pro-hibition without asking why, for Cupar Street was one of those areas where the Falls and Shankill joined together as unhappy Siamese twins, one sporadically and mechanically beating the other round the head, where the Cullens, Finnegans and Reillys merged with Todds and Camerons and Wallaces. One day I did come home by Cupar Street, egged on by a fellow pupil. Nothing happened, and we felt the thrill of Indian scouts penetrating the British lines, the high of invisibility. We did it again; it became addictive, this perilous sin of disobedience and disappearance. We crept along in the dark shadow of the Falls Flax Spinning Mill, becoming bolder day by day in our deceit. For who knew what we were, who could tell? The forays ended when we were stopped one day by four boys about our own age. One of them had fashioned two little charity-type flags from paper and pins: he held a Union Jack in one hand, a tricolour in the other. He eyed us slyly, knowingly: *See them flags?* We nodded nervously. *Well, which of them would youse say was the best?* He had us cornered. If we chose the Union Jack, we were guilty of cowardice and treason — and he would know we were lying anyway; if we chose the tricolour, we would get a hiding. So we ran the gauntlet, escaping with a few bruises into the unspoken force-field of the Catholic end of the street. My father knew something was up when I got home; I broke down under questioning, and got a real hiding. I had learned some kind of lesson. So I thought.

I was reminded of this today when I went out for what I imagined was a harmless spin on the bike. A showery day, blowing warm and cold — past the west side of Girdwood Barracks along Clifton Park Avenue — a few inhabited houses in a row of derelicts backing on to Crumlin Road Jail — up the Shankill; I come to the Shankill Road Library on the corner of Mountjoy Street (the name of yet another jail), remembering how I used to go here as a child in search of Biggles books because I had exhausted the entire Biggles stock of the Falls Library — I was older then, and was allowed to go, I think — how was it, across Cupar Street, up Sugarfield Street? I see the green cupola of Clonard Monastery towering high, almost directly above me, it seems, and I realize again with a familiar shock how little separates the Shankill and the Falls, how in the Troubles of '68 or '69 it was rumoured that this monastery tower was a sniper's nest — so yes, I think, why not re-trace the route of all those years ago, 1959 or 1960. I turn idly down Mountjoy Street, Azamor Street, Sugarfield Street. Dead end. Here is the Peace Line, a thirty-foot-high wall scrawled with graffiti, mounted with drab corrugated iron; Centurion Street; Battenberg Street; dead end again. Where I remember rows of houses, factories, there is recent wasteland, broken bricks, chick-weed, chain-link fencing. Eventually I find a new road I never knew existed — or is it an old street deprived of all its landmarks? — which leads into the Springfield Road. Familiar territory now, well, almost, for going down the Kashmir Road into Bombay Street — burned out in '68, some new houses there — I come to the other side of the Peace Line, which now backs on to St Gall's School — still there, graffiticized, wire mesh on the windows, but still the same, almost; the massive granite bulk of Clonard is still there; Greenan's shop is now a dwelling; and the west side of Clonard Gardens, where the Flax & Rayon mill used to be, is all new houses; Charleton's shop is bricked up; Tolan's the barber's is long since gone, I knew that; this side of the street is all derelict, breeze-blocked, holes knocked into holes; so on to the Falls. I go down the road a bit, almost as far as the library, then stop; I'd like to go down the Grosvenor Road, so I make a U-turn and stop at the lights at the Grosvenor Road junction, and I'm just wondering what's the point, it's Sunday and there's no traffic about, and certainly no policemen, when somebody mutters something in my ear, I turn, and I'm grabbed round the neck by this character, while someone else has me by the arm, twisted up my back, another has the other arm and I'm hauled off the bike, *Right — where're you going? Here, get him up against the railings — what do you think you're at?* — Legs kicked apart, arms slapped up, *Right, here, get him here — come on, MOVE* — and I'm dragged across the road into what used to be McQuillan Street, only it isn't there any more, into one of these hole-in-the-wall taxi places, arms up against the breeze-block wall, legs apart, frisked, and all the time,

You were seen coming from the Shankill.
Why did you make a U-turn?
Who are you?
Where are you coming from?
Why did you stop when you seen the car?
You know the car.
The car. Outside Sinn Féin headquarters.
You looked at it.
You looked at it.
You were seen. You were seen.
Coming from the Shankill.
Where are you from?
Where is he from?
The Falls? When? What street?
What was the number of the house?
How far down the street was that?
When was that?
What streets could you see from the house?
Cape Street? Yeah.
Frere Street? Yeah. Where was Cape Street?
Again. Who lived next door?
Next door again.
Why did you stop when you seen the car?
Why did you turn?
So you moved up the road? When?
How old were you then?
Where was that? Mooreland?
Where is that?
Stockman's? Where is that?
What's next?
Casement? Right. What's next?
You were seen.
Where do you live now?
Where's that?
So where did you live again?
Yeah, I know it's not there any more.
You just tell me what was there.
Again. No. 100. Where was that?
You were seen.

What's the next street down from Raglan Street?
Coming from the Shankill . . .

The questions are snapped at me like photographs.

The map is pieced together bit by bit. I am this map which they examine, checking it for error, hesitation, accuracy; a map which no longer refers to the present world, but to a history, these vanished streets; a map which is this moment, this interrogation, my replies. Eventually I pass the test. I am frisked again, this time in a regretful habitual gesture. *A dreadful mistake*, I hear one of them saying, *has been made*, and I get the feeling he is speaking in quotation marks, as if this is a bad police B-movie and he is mocking it, and me, and him.

I am released. I stumble across the road and look back; they have disappeared. I get on my bike, and turn, and go down the Falls, past vanished public houses — The Clock Bar, The Celtic, Daly's, The Gladstone, The Arkle, The Old House — past drapers, bakers, fishmongers, boot shops, chemists, pawnshops, picture houses, confectioners and churches, all swallowed in the maw of time and trouble, clearances; feeling shaky, nervous, remembering how a few moments ago I was *there*, in my mind's eye, one foot in the grave of that Falls Road of thirty years ago, inhaling its gritty, smoggy air as I lolled outside the door of 100 Raglan Street, staring down through the comforting gloom to the soot-encrusted spires of St Peter's, or gazing at the blank brick gable walls of Balaklava Street, Cape Street, Frere Street, Milton Street, saying their names over to myself.

Punctuation

This frosty night is jittering with lines and angles, invisible
    trajectories:
Crackly, chalky diagrams in geometry, rubbed out the instant
    they're sketched,
But lingering in the head. The shots, the echoes, are like
    whips, and when you flinch,
You don't know where it's coming from. This bullet, is your
    name on it?
For the moment, everything is X, a blank not yet filled in.

Walking in the black space between the stars, I'm avoiding
    the cracks in the pavement.
And in the gap between the street lights my shadow seems
    to cross itself. I can
See my hand, a mile away in the future, just about to turn
    the latch-key in the lock,
When another shadow steps out from behind the hedge, going
    dot, dot, dot, dot, dot . . .

Yes

I'm drinking in the 7-Up bottle-green eyes of the barmaid
On the *Enterprise* express — bottles and glasses clinking each
    other —
When the train slows with a noise like *Schweppes* and halts just
    outside Dundalk.
Not that unwontedly, since we're no strangers to the border
    bomb.
As the Belfast accent of the tannoy tells us what is happening

I'm about to quote from Bashō's *The Narrow Road to the Deep
    North* —
*Blossoming mushroom: from some unknown tree a leaf has stuck
    to it* —
When it goes off and we're thrown out of kilter. My mouth
    is full
Of broken glass and quinine as everything reverses South.

Revised Version

Trying to focus on the imagined grey area between Smithfield and North Street — jumbled bookstalls, fruitstalls, fleshers, the whingeing calls of glaziers and coal-brick men — I catch glimpses of what might have been, but it already blurs and fades; I wake or fall into another dream. I have before me Nesbitt's *The Changing Face of Belfast*, the first edition of 1968, and the second (revised) 1982 edition, which has somehow skimped on the ink, so that the dark threatening historicity of *High Street, looking east, 1851* — the stage-coach waiting, a one-legged man with a doomy placard tied to his back, two dogs fighting in the tramlines under the scratchy black clouds — has been replaced by a noon-day shimmer (we note the long morning shadows still) in which the dogs are merely playing, and the one-legged man proclaims salvation. We become aware of other shifts of emphasis, elisions and contractions, croppings: the observer taking a step backwards from *Victoria Square in the 1880s*, as if passing time has necessarily distanced the fixed past even more, and the new edition is a worn-out copy of the old; a photograph of The Ulster Institute for the Deaf and Dumb and Blind (1845-1963) becomes an old engraving of the same building; the entrance to Belfast Castle has vanished.

In waking life I expect streets which are not there. So, both versions of the *Demolition of Hercules Place, looking north, 1879* — one light, the other dark — suggest the ambivalence of this dilapidated present, the currency of time passing. For this could be now, 1987, as the Royal Avenue which the butchers' shambles of Hercules Place was to become is, in its turn, torn apart and a huge vista yawns through the vanished Grand Central Hotel (built to service a Central Railway Station that never was to be) to the Belfast Mountains, last refuge of the wolf and rebel. Transpose the dates: in 1879, two men in the right bottom corner have moved too quickly for the shutter; they are ghosts, wavering between memory and oblivion. Then a haze begins in the middle distance, the grainy dust of blitz sites and bad printing.

For everything is contingent and provisional; and the subjunctive mood of these images is tensed to the ifs and buts, the yeas and nays of Belfast's history. Going back another lifetime, to 1808, we find that *Mr Williamson proposes to make a new map of the town, but from the streets lately made, and the uncertain direction of others, it will be spring before any further progress will be made.* Spring became summer, autumn, winter; 'the map does not seem to have been produced'. It lives on in our imagination, this plan of might-have-beens, legislating for all the possibilities, guaranteed from censure by its non-existence. For maps cannot describe everything, or they describe states of mind, like Dubourdieu's 'very incorrect' *Plan of Belfast in 1811,* which shows *streets and blocks of buildings which have never existed; and also a bridge across the Lagan which was proposed but not carried out.* John Mulholland's Plan of 1788, dedicated to the Earl of Donegall, who owned half the town, shows a grand never-to-be canal flowing down the line of what was to be Chichester Street from the front of the White Linen Hall, now the City Hall, echoing the second Venice dreamed by George Macartney, Sovereign of Belfast in the late 1600s. Here too are 'intended streets', miasmas, projections on the reclaimed sleech which lies between the *ancient folded purple grits and shales of North Down and the tilted black basalts of Antrim, where on both sides of the river's mouth the valley sides fall back as if to form a great cup destined to hold the brimming city* — teetering and spilling, distilled from thin air, this intoxicating draught of futures swallowed at one gulp, as someone sets another up. We have seen Phillips' *New Cutt River* (on his Plan of 1685) before: not only does it almost follow the line of Mulholland's dream-canal, but it suggests the 1987 Concept Plan for Laganside, where a 'new cut' will make an island out of Maysfield, and the Blackstaff river is deculverted to form a marina; our architect has drawn little boats and happy figures here, absolving the stench and excrement and rubbish of the present. Here is the Eden of the future — gardens, fields, streams, clear water — looking like the banished past, before linen, ships, tobacco, ropes. We are going back to the source, as it is proposed that the Farset, which gave the town its name, be opened up again, this clear blue line leading up to the Albert Clock. Going back to Phillips, what are we to make of this *earthen rampart built in 1642, already partly obliterated at its north end?* Obliterated? Never finished? Proposed? And do we trust this *improvement made out on the strand?*

Improve, wipe out, begin again, imagine, change: the map appended to the Parliamentary Report of 1859 *shows very clearly the improvements effected by the making of Victoria Street and Corporation Street, which are laid down on the map over the old lanes and small streets, as follows*; so we follow the ghosts of Forest Lane, Weigh-House Lane, Back Lane, Elbow Lane, Blue Bell Entry, Stone Cutter's Entry, Quay Lane, Ireland's Entry, names that seem to spring up from an invented past. Or here, in 1853, we are shown *the Municipal Boundary of the Borough before its extension in 1853; after its extension; the Boundary of the Lighted and Watched Districts,* recalling the ordinance of 1680, that *Lights in Lanthorns be hunge at every other house doore or window time aboute in ye dark Nights from ye houres of six to tenn . . . to prevent disorders and mischeife,* later amended to *at their respective doores or shops one Lanthorne and candle lighted from ye houre of seaven oClock till ten at night when it is not moon-shine in ye saide houres . . .*

As we shift sideways into the future of 30 August 1823, ignoring the *rival schemes to produce gas from the oil of Irish basking sharks,* we can clearly read a letter 60 yards distant from High Street's *extra large light in the form of a dolphin's head*; before we understand what it is telling us, or appreciate *the clear effulgence of a cloudless atmosphere illumined by the moon,* there is a whiff of ozone, a blue flicker, and we find ourselves stumbling through a ruinous Gasworks — midnight echo-chambers, clangorous retorts — as the 1300 miles of piping give up the ghost — a tiny whisper and a hiccup.

The maps are revised again, as a layer of toxic spoil would have to be removed from the whole site and the view across the Lagan from the Ormeau embankment completely transformed by the obliteration of the gas-holders. The jargon sings of leisure purposes, velodromes and pleasure parks, the unfurling petals of the World Rose Convention. As the city consumes itself — scrap iron mouldering on the quays, black holes eating through the time-warp — the Parliamentary Under-Secretary of State for the Environment announces that *to people who have never been to Belfast their image of the place is often far-removed from the reality.* No more Belfast champagne, gas bubbled through milk; no more heads in ovens. Intoxication, death, will find their new connections. Cul-de-sacs and ring-roads. *The city is a map of the city.*

The Mouth

There was this head had this mouth he kept shooting off.
    Unfortunately.
It could have been worse for us than it was for him.
    Provisionally.
But since nothing in this world is certain and you don't know
    who hears what
We thought it was time he bit off more than he could chew.
    Literally.

By the time he is found there'll be nothing much left to tell
    who he was.
But of course some clever dick from the 'Forscenic Lab'
    reconstructs
Him, what he used to be — not from his actual teeth, not his
    fingerprints,
But from the core — the toothmarks of the first and last bite
    he'd taken of
This sour apple. But then we would have told them anyway.
    Publicity.

The Knee

His first bullet is a present, a mark of intelligence that will
End in the gutter behind The Clock Bar, since he keeps
    on doing what
He's not supposed to. The next one is for real, what we've
    just talked about.
It seems he was a hood, whatever, or the lads were just being
    careful.
Two and two were put together; what they added up to
    wasn't five.

Visiting time: he takes his thirteen-month-old son on his
    other knee.
Learning to walk, he suddenly throws himself into
    the staggering
Distance between his father and his father's father, hands
    held up high,
His legs like the hands of a clock, one trying to catch
    up on the other.

Brick

Belfast is built on *sleech* — alluvial or tidal muck — and is built *of* sleech, metamorphosed into brick, the city consuming its source as the brickfields themselves were built upon; sleech, this indeterminate slabbery semi-fluid — *all the public buildings*, notes Dr Pococke, visiting the town in 1752, *are founded on a morass* — this gunge, allied to *slick* and *sludge, slag, sleek* and *slush*, to the Belfast or Scots *sleekit* that means sneaky, underhand, not-to-be-relied-on, becoming, in the earnest *brick*, something definite, of proverbial solidity — *built like a brick shit-house*, we say; or, in dated slang, *you're a brick*. Yet even this paradigm of honesty has its verbal swamp. Its root is in *break*, related to the flaw in cloth known as a *brack*; worse, it is a cousin of *brock* — not the hardy badger, but rubbish, refuse, broken-down stuff, pig-swill, which is maybe why a German lager of that name never caught on in Northern Ireland. In anger, you might *come down like a ton of bricks* on someone; the victim might *shit a brick*. The subversive half-brick, conveniently hand-sized, is an essential ingredient of the ammunition known as 'Belfast confetti', and has been tried and trusted by generations of rioters; it is also known here as a *hicker* or a *heeker*, a word which seems to deal in the same currency as *hick, hack* and *howk*, pronounced *hoke* in these parts, meaning to dig or burrow; perhaps the defiant badger is in there somewhere after all, related to the superlative *wheeker*, which is another way of saying a *cracker*, something which is outstanding or *sticking out*.

   Coal-brick — moulded from the brock of *slack* and coal-dust — is here pronounced *breek*, reminding us of breeks, britches, bifurcations and alternatives, the breech of a gun. One of my abiding memories is the street-cry of the coal-brick man hawking his handcart through the smoggy backstreets, the bricks still steaming from the kiln — a long drawn-out *co-o-o-a-l br-e-e-e-k* ending in a glottal exclamation mark and mingling with the gulder of the brock-man or refuse-man, who bore with dignity and patience his occupational aroma of rotting tea leaves and potato skins.

Both were important links in the great chain of being which discarded nothing, the very building-blocks of matter recycled — milk-bottle tops, string, brown paper, rags; here I recall the rag-man's shed with its brick floor, mounds of old clothing, the musk of stale sweat. A world of cast-offs, hand-me-downs, of new lamps for old, realized in the incessant unravelling of my mother as woollen jumpers became scarves and socks and I held my arms at arm's length while she wound and wound. As the tall chimneys and the catacomb-like kilns of the brickworks crumbled back into the earth, the very city recycled itself and disassembled buildings — churches, air-raid shelters, haberdashers, pawnshops — were poured into the sleech of the lough shore to make new land; vast armies of binmen or waste-disposal experts laboured through the years transforming countless tons of brock into *terra firma*; the dredged-up sludge of the Lagan became Queen's Island, that emblem of solid work and Titanic endeavour.

᠆

Our new semi-detached house in Andersonstown — we moved there in 1955 — was built of *rustic* brick, an epithet I confused with *rusty*, for the material, rough-cast to mimic the weathered brick of rural cottages, seemed corroded, pitted, burnt. It seemed a paradox that the house itself was new, smelling of bare plaster and wood-shavings. Behind us was about half an acre of not-yet-built-on land; not sleech, for we had forsaken the lowlands of the Lower Falls, but a truer clay, red, thick, heavy, satisfying, that could be moulded by hand. Through the clay there flowed a tiny stream surrounded by hawthorn hedges that were once a field division, where we built tree-houses and furtive shacks we believed invisible to adult eyes.

The stream itself had a magical secret quality, and I and my best friend Noel explored its banks in microscopic detail, performing evermore complex feats of miniature engineering in a series of dams, canals, harbours, breakwaters, run-offs, cul-de-sacs and overspills. We built and sank navies. We dug out fist-sized catacombs in its banks, under the clear water, and in them placed the corpses of birds, mice and frogs; months later we returned to them, probing, finding delicate clean skeletons. And from the clay itself we made towns and cities. These were guarded by bulwarks, ditches, palisades and outworks, for a necessary condition of the city was its eventual destruction; this was achieved by a catalogue of wars whose weapons were marbles, pebbles, or pellets moulded from clay — flicked by hand, since we considered catapults too brutal, the ultimate deterrent. These were elaborate sagas of advances, forays, skirmishes and truces, agreed-on interludes for repair or consolidation. My defences were always the first to go, the laying waste of my city a *fait accompli*. Noel's engineering was of a higher order. Where I would roll out sheets of clay and make slab walls, he would patiently make individual tiny bricks, building them up in such a way that if one brick was taken out the structure would remain intact. His cities were fascist states; mine, a house of cards. My forts and palaces in ruins, we would join forces to destroy his stubborn battlements. I loved and admired him deeply, for his natural superiority extended to other domains: he was the fastest runner in the new estate; he had a peerless stamp collection; and he could fart at will. One day he asked me if I would like to be him. Perhaps he was asking if I loved him, or saying that he loved himself. At any rate, I said yes. Some time later his family moved. I was devastated. I sulked around the house for weeks. The magical half-acre was now a patch of arid waste-land. The stream was a gutter. Bit by bit, I made other friends; the intense detail came back, if only for a while. For the land we inhabited has long since been built over; the stream, the hawthorn hedges and the underwater cemetery are gone. Belfast has again swallowed up the miniature versions of itself in its intestine war.

The inevitable declension: *Brick.*

Brack.

Brock.

Apparition

The angelic old woman at the Friday morning second-hand
    market
Licks her finger and thumb and plucks little balls of fluff
    from off a jumper.
She smoothes out the wrinkles in a linen blouse and holds
    it to the light
And light shines through to meet the nearly-perfect sky-blue
    of her eye. Then
She dangles a 1940s pinstripe suit at arm's length, as if
    measuring a corpse.

It reminds me of the character I met one night in The Hole-
    in-the-Wall Bar
Who was wearing a beat-up World War II flying-jacket frayed
    and split at the seams.
One arm was nearly hanging off. 'Just back from Dresden?',
    cracked the barman.
'Don't laugh,' spat the character, 'my father was killed in this
    here fucking jacket.'

Night Out

Every Thursday night when we press the brass button
    on the galvanized wire mesh gate
A figure appears momentarily at the end of the strip-lit
    concrete passageway,
Then disappears. The gate squeaks open, slams shut almost
    instantly behind us.
Then through the semi-opaque heavy-duty polythene swing
    doors they might have taken
From a hospital. At the bar, we get the once-over once again.

Seven whiskeys later, the band is launching into 'Four Green
    Fields'.
From somewhere out beyond the breeze-block walls we get
    a broken rhythm
Of machine-gun fire. A ragged chorus. So the sentence
    of the night
Is punctuated through and through by rounds of drink,
    of bullets, of applause.

Intelligence

We are all being watched through peep-holes, one-way mirrors, security cameras, talked about on walkie-talkies, car phones, Pye Pocketfones; and as this helicopter chainsaws overhead I pull back the curtains down here in the terraces to watch its pencil-beam of light flick through the card-index — *I see the moon and the moon sees me*, this 30,000,000 candle power gimbal-mounted Nitesun by which the operator can observe undetected, with his infra-red goggles and an IR filter on the light-source. Everyone is watching someone, everyone wants to know what's coming next, so the lightweight, transparent shield was a vast improvement over the earlier metal one because visibility was greatly increased and — an extra bonus — gave better protection against petrol and acid bombs which could flow through the grill mesh of the metal type . . .

Or we note in passing that some walls in the city have been whitewashed to the level of a man's head so that patrolling soldiers at night are silhouetted clearly for snipers; or that one of these patrolling soldiers carries a Self-loading Rifle with an image intensification night-sight; that paint bombs are usually reserved for throwing at the vision blocks of APCs and armoured cars; and that passive observation is possible even on the darkest of nights, since the ambient light is amplified by this Telescope Starlight II LIEI 'Twiggy' Night Observation Device. Failing that, the 2B298 surveillance radar can identify a moving man at 5,000 metres by the blips on its console. We track shadows, echoes, scents, prints; and in the interface the information is decoded, coded back again and stored in bits and bytes and indirect addressing; but the glitches and gremlins and bugs keep fouling-up, seething out from the hardware, the dense entangled circuitry of backstreets, backplanes, while the tape is spooling and drooling over alphanumeric strings and random-riot situations; it seems the real-time clock is ticking away in the memory-dump, so look, let's get the relocating loader, since contrary to expectations water-cannon proved only marginally successful; few rioters seemed unduly convinced by a heavy soaking, especially in summer; better to use a random-access Monte Carlo method so that this clicking ticking Russian roulette will pay the house percentage, and we can then facilitate the provision of all manner of lighting devices, primarily to illuminate the removal of barriers which proliferated through the cities:

bread-vans, milk-carts, telegraph poles, paving-stones, lime trees, chestnuts, hawthorns, buses, tyres, fishing-lines, prams, JCBs, coal, shopping-trolleys, cement-mixers, lamp-posts, hoardings, people, sand, glass, breeze-blocks, corrugated iron, buckets, dustbins, municipal waste-bins, scaffolding, traffic signals, garden sheds, hedges, milk-churns, gas cylinders, chimney-pots, snow, oil-drums, gates, crazy paving, orange crates, fences, weighing-machines, earth, automatic chewing-gum dispensers, news-stands, camera tripods, ladders, taxis, dismantled football stadia, bicycles.

Keeping people out and keeping people in, we are prisoners or officers in Bentham's Panopticon, except sorting out who's who is a problem for the naive user, and some compilers are inclined to choke on the mixed mode — panopticons within panopticons —

The Building circular — an iron cage, glazed — a glass lantern about the size of Ranelagh — The Prisoners in their Cells, occupying the Circumference — The Officers (Governor, Chaplain, Surgeon, &c.), the Centre.

By Blinds, and other contrivances, the Inspectors concealed (except in so far as they think fit to show themselves) from the observation of the Prisoners: hence the sentiment of a sort of invisible omnipresence. — The whole circuit reviewable with little, or, if necessary, without any, change of place.

One station in the Inspection-Part affording the most perfect view of every Cell, and every part of every Cell, unless where a screen is thought fit occasionally and purposely to be interposed.

Against Fire (if, under a system of constant and universal inspection, any such accident could be apprehended), a pipe, terminating in a flexible hose, for bringing the water down into the central Inspection-Room, from a cistern, of a height sufficient to force it up again under its own pressure, on the mere turning of a cock, and spread it thus over any part within the Building.

For Visitors, at the time of Divine Service, an Annular Gallery, rising from a floor laid immediately on the ceiling of the Central Dome, the superior surface of which serves, after descent, for the reception of Ministers, Clerk, and a select part of the Auditory: the Prisoners all round, brought forward, within perfect view and hearing of the Ministers, to the front of their respective Cells.

Solitude, or limited Seclusion, ad libitum. *But, unless for punishment, limited seclusion in assorted companies is preferable: an arrangement, upon this plan alone, exempt from danger. The degree of Seclusion fixed upon this may be preserved, in all places, and at all times, inviolate. Hitherto, where solitude has been aimed at, some of its chief purposes have been frustrated by occasional associations.*

The Approach, one only — Gates opening into a walled avenue cut through the area. Hence, no strangers near the building without leave, nor without being surveyed from it as they pass, nor without being known to come on purpose. The gates, of open work, to expose hostile mobs: On the other side of the road, a wall within a branch of the road behind, to shelter peaceable passengers from the fire of the building.

Hence the open chain-link fencing on the open routes between areas of demarcation, the lazy swivelling eye of the security camera; the invisibility of jails on maps, these blank zones — on this 1986 reprint of the 1920 Ordnance plan of North Belfast, for instance, where *the interesting panopticon shape of the gaol is not shown here for securiry reasons,* though it is *a sad reflection that apart from the one surviving farm* (which, in any case, is now a barracks) *the only spaces on this map are the prison exercise yard and the paradeground of the military barracks* (which is half a barracks now, and half a high-rise urban complex, only the prison remains inviolate) — a sad reflection on what, on this ubiquitous dense graffiti of public houses, churches, urinals, bonding stores, graving docks, monuments, Sunday schools and Orange halls — terraces and terraces of kitchen houses, one-up-one-down

186

houses, parlour houses, town houses, back-to-back and front-to-back and back-to-front houses — flour mills, swivel bridges, goods sheds, drinking fountains, laundries, spinning mills, foundries, coffee stalls, Gallaher's tobacco factory spewing smoke and snuff and gouts of steam over railways, tramways, coal-quays, and I see now through the time-warp something like the Belfast of *Odd Man Out* as the camera pans down from some aerial vision (the VTO craft pioneered by Shorts?) into a mass of chimney stacks and mill-stacks churning out this Titanic smoke over the spires and cupolas; suddenly, I have just climbed the Whiterock Loney to Black Mountain, and my father and I are sitting in the Hatchet Field as he smokes a Gallaher's Park Drive and points out, down in the inferno, Clonard Monastery, the Falls Road, Leeson Street, the Clonard Picture-House, and the tiny blip of our house that we both pretend to see — down there, in the Beechmount brickfields, I can nearly see James Mason squatting in the catacomb of a brick kiln where I played Soldiers and Rebels, these derelict cloisters half-choked with broken brick and brick-dust, that are now gone, erased, levelled back into the clay, like all this brick-built demolition city, like this house we strain our eyes to see through the smog, homing in through the terraces and corner shops and spires and urinals to squat by the fire — coal-brick smouldering and hissing — while my father tells me a story . . .

PART THREE

. . . people . . . in their daily walks continued
to follow streets that no longer existed,
but were only imaginary tracks through
a razed and empty section of Florence.

— Kevin Lynch,
The Image of the City

I've just put on this
borrowed armour: second-hand
cold freezes my bones.

— Buson

Bed-time Story

The sound effects were really very simple: a creaky leather wallet
       — here,
The speaker reached into his pocket and produced the very
       article —
Might stand for the marching boots of the Seven Dwarfs.
       Almost instantly,
I stepped into my father's creased, enormous shoes, their
       puckered insole ridges:
Cold, cold, so many hours until he comes back trudging through
       the snow,
The empty canvas sack around his neck; but never empty-
       handed — always promises
Of stories, or postcards left in limbo, *Not Known At This
       Address.* On the back,
*You'll never guess who I met here — I'll tell you all about it
       when I see you.*
Or bits of hairy twine come snaking out, the same gruff texture
As his navy-blue, tobacco-scented serge. The braid. The black
       mirror of his cap-peak.

And in the ink-dark celluloid, confused images of the narrative
       appear:
Disney's artists gather round like dwarfs, or ravens, as Disney
Flaps his arms to illustrate the story. He imitates a talking bird.
His hand opens and shuts like a beak. He gets them to do the
       same, to feel
The movement, the whole body swept along in mimicry, as they
       get it down
On paper. *He seemed to make it up as he went along.* Or maybe
       these were dreams,
Rehearsed for nights until they dawned into a blue configuration
Set off by floating, regal clouds; as if, already spoken-for and
       animated,
The day proclaimed its destination, knowing what was coming
       next. The way
A flock of birds will make a fist. Which flits open, shuts again,
       then vanishes.

190

For the blue is the sky of an airmail letter, the clouds are puffs
    of smoke
Which punctuate my father's story. I see his fingernail is stained
    with nicotine,
Or maybe that's a trick of the light, the yellowish burnt umber
    which precedes
A thunderstorm. He is sprawled out on the sofa, I am in
    the rowing-boat
Between his knees. A squall will figure shortly, summoned-up
    from nowhere;
As this episode draws to a close, the castaway will cling
    to broken spars,
The tatters of his once-proud enterprise. By the island of
    tomorrow he will know
If he is drowned or saved; as yet, he's in the dark, treading
    amber water.
And now the time-lapsed, wind-torn envelope is swallowed
    in the cobalt night,
My father lies asleep; he's been abroad since early morning.

His hands are folded on his chest, as if fastened on a rosary.
He has gathered silence over him, like his overcoat I drape
    around me.
I feel its snowbound, dangling weight, the broad cuffs where
    my hands are lost,
The trailing hem. The regal crown of his cap. The cool damp
    head-band.
I touch the shining peak. Then the coarse weave of the sack.
    The glinting buckles.
I put on the leather harness. I step into the shoes again, and
    walk. I will deliver
Letters, cards, important gifts. I roll up a sleeve, and put
    my hand into his pocket.
His wallet. I open up its creaking leather palms, and I am rich:
I see myself in this, his photograph of me. He coughs, and stirs;
    his hands
Begin to sleepwalk, as if managing Pinocchio's wooden limbs.

In Kyoto, still
longing for Kyoto: cuck-
oo's two time-worn notes.

— Bashō

Jawbox

What looks to us like a crackly newsreel, the picture jumping
 with flak,
Was clear as day, once. But that's taken as read, since this
 is a 'quotation'
In the main text of the film, which begins with someone
 flicking open
The glossy pages of a *Homes and Gardens* kitchen supplement:
 Sink or Swim, the caption
Says, *The Belfast sink combines old-fashioned charm with tried
 and tested*
Practicality ... 'Why Belfast?', the character begins to ponder —
 he puts the accent
On the *fast*, as if the name was Irish, which it was (or is); this
 is how
His father says it, just as, being from Belfast, he calls the sink
 a 'jawbox'.

At first you think the screen's gone blank, till you realize
 the camera
Has focussed on the sink itself: it has eaten up the whole
Picture. Then it backtracks, to reveal a Forties kitchen with
 a kind of wartime
Atmosphere: an old bakelite Clydesdale radio glows in the
 corner, humming
Over names like Moscow, Hilversum, Berlin. There's those jugs
 with blue and white
Striped bars, which give a premonition of the future (still our
 past) — filled
With flowers, they're déjà vu before their time, just as the sink,
 retired now
To the garden, overflows with hyacinths, geraniums.

There's something threatening about the kitchen — knives, glass,
 the epileptic
Buzzing of the overhead fluorescent strip, the white glaze
 blotched with calligraphic

Tea leaves. Something in the pattern brings to mind
an ornamental
Slightly murderous detail, and the picture changes with a click
to show
The handcuffed metal *X*s of an old-style elevator gate.
Someone's going down —
Chinese shadows flicking off and on across the various floors —
to the Forensic Lab.
It's like suspicion, this weightless feeling in his stomach; and
the clickety-clack
Reminds him of a railway journey, interrupted, for the seventh
time that week,
By a bomb on the line between Dundalk and Newry. Or
Newry and Dundalk, depending
Where you're coming from: like the difference between
Cambodia and Kampuchea.

Shepherded on board an Ulsterbus, knowing now that the
appointment won't be kept,
His attention wanders out across the rushy unkempt landscape,
where a white dot
Concentrates his gaze. He lurches nearer. A hedge, a stone wall,
gets in the way,
And then, brimming with water, wind-skimmed, rippled —
he remembers how
He used to scoop an icy draught from it — the Belfast sink
reveals itself.
It's now a cattle-trough, ripped out from a deconstructed
farmhouse renovated
In the 'hacienda' style — not inappropriately, since 'South
of the Border
Down Mexico Way' is a big hit in these parts. Just then the border
passes through him
Like a knife, invisibly, as the blip of the bus is captured on
surveillance radar.

What's been stirring in his memory, like tea leaves stirred in
    water —
He's elbow-deep in it, fingers trying to unblock the plug-hole
    — is the half-gnawed
Apple found at the *mise en scène*. The body, face-down
    on the steaming
Freshly-tarmacked road. He bites into the core, imagining his
    mouth's interior.
That twinge, an old occlusion. The tooth he broke on the rim
    of the jawbox
When he was eight. Blood-spattered white glaze; dilating, red
    confetti.
He spits out the pips and stares at the imaginary pith, seeing
    himself engraved there:
Furrows, indentations, grooves, as crisp as fingerprints. A little
    hinge of skin.

The mouth suggests the body —
Biting, grinding, breathing, chewing, spitting, tasting; clenched
In a grimace or a smile — his child's body, hunched in the dark
    alcove underneath
The sink, sulking, tearful, wishing he was dead. Imprisoned
    by so many
Small transgressions, he wants to break out of the trap. He's
    caught between
Bel*fast* and *Bel*fast, in the accordion pleats between two
    lurching carriages
Banging, rattling, threatening to break loose, as he gets
    a terrifying glimpse
Of railway sleepers, blotchy gravel flicking past a smell
    of creosote and oil and urine.

The coupling snaps; another mouth floats into view, its rust-
    tinged canine edges
Sealed in labelled see-through polythene; there's an O of
    condensation. From the cloud

A face begins to dawn: something like his own, but thicker,
 coarser, Jekyll
Turning into Hyde — an Englishman into an Irishman —
 emerging from the bloom
Behind the mirror. Breathed-on, becoming whole,
 the murderer is hunched
Behind the hedge. One bite from the apple, as the victim's
 Ford Fiesta trickles
Up the driveway. The car door opens. The apple's thrown away.

There's a breath of fresh tar. The scent will always summon
 up that afternoon,
As it blossoms into apple, into mouth. It's hanging in the air
 as Dr Jekyll finally
Makes it into Belfast. Beyond the steamed-up window, the half-
 dismantled gasworks
Loom up, like a rusty *film noir* laboratory — carboys, vats,
 alembics, coils, retorts.
It's that effect where one image warps into the other, like
 the double helix
Of the DNA code, his footsteps dogged throughout the action
 by another. Or
A split screen might suggest the parallels of past and present,
 Jekyll ticking
Downwards in the lift, as Hyde runs down the spiral stairwell.
 Till they meet.

What looks to us like a crackly newsreel, the picture jumping
 with flak,
Is the spotted, rust-tinged mirror screwed above the Belfast
 sink. Jekyll's head
Is jerking back and forward on the rim. Red confetti spatters
 the white glaze.
The camera backtracks to take in a tattered *Homes and Gardens*
 kitchen supplement.

A pair of hands — *lean, corded, knuckly, of a dusky pallor,*
   and thickly shadowed
With swart hair — come into view, and flick the pages
   of the magazine.
Bel*fast*, the voice says, not *Bel*fast. Then the credits roll.

Darkness never flows
except down by the river:
shimmering fireflies.

— Chiyo

John Ruskin in Belfast

As I approached the city the storm-cloud of the Nineteenth
 Century
Began to wheel and mass its pendulous decades; the years grew
 weighty, slate-grey,
Palpable, muttering with dark caesurae, rolling in a clattering
 mockery
Of railway-luggage trains. All this while, the minutes seethed
 forth as artillery-smoke
Threatening to collapse into a dank fog. A single gauzy patch
 of iris blue —
All that remained of the free azure — contracted, shrank into
 oblivion
Till it became all pupil, olive-black, impenetrable; jagged
 migraine lightning
Flashed in the dark crock of my brain.

Like Turner, lashed to the mast of the *Ariel*, the better to see
 what he later painted —
The unwearied rage of memory, no distinction left between
 the sea and air —
I am riding out the hurricane, the writhing cloudscape
 of the sea collapsing
Into masses of accumulated yeast, which hang in ropes and
 wreaths from wave to wave;
Gouts and cataracts of foam pour from the smoky masts
 of the industrial Armada
As the wrack resolves itself in skeins and hanks, in terraces
 and sinks and troughs;
The air is sick with vitriol, the hospital-sweet scent of snuff,
 tobacco, linen.
And the labyrinthine alleyways are bloody with discarded
 bandages, every kind of ordure:
The dung of horses, dogs and rats and men; the knitted,
 knotted streets
Are crammed with old shoes, ashes, rags, smashed crockery,
 bullet casings, shreds

Of nameless clothes, rotten timber jaggy with bent nails,
    cinders, bones and half-bricks,
Broken bottles; and kneaded into, trampled, or heaving,
    fluttering, dancing
Over all of these, the tattered remnants of the news, every kind
    of foul advertisement,
The banner headlines that proclaim an oceanic riot, mutilated
    politics,
The seething yeast of anarchy: the very image of a pit, where
    a chained dwarf
Savages a chained bulldog.

As I strove against this lethargy and trance within myself,
    dismembered
Fragments of my speech, *The Mystery of Life and Its Arts*,
    swam up through the cumulus:
This strange agony of desire for justice is often, I think, seen
    in Ireland —
For being generous-hearted, and intending always to do right,
    you still neglect
External laws of right, and therefore you do wrong, without
    conceiving of it;
And so fly into wrath when thwarted, and will not admit
    the possibility of error . . .
See how in the static mode of ancient Irish art, the missal-painter
    draws his angel
With no sense of failure, as a child might draw an angel, putting
    red dots
In the palm of each hand, while the eyes — the eyes are perfect
    circles, and,
I regret to say, the mouth is left out altogether.

That blank mouth, like the memory of a disappointed smile,
    comes back to haunt me.
That calm terror, closed against the smog and murk of Belfast:
    Let it not open
That it might condemn me. Let it remain inviolate.

Or let that missing mouth be mine, as, one evening in Siena
I walked the hills above, where fireflies moved like finely-
        broken starlight
Through the purple leaves, rising, falling, as the cobalt
        clouds — white-edged, mountainous —
Surged into thunderous night; and fireflies gusted everywhere,
        mixed with the lightning,
Till I thought I'd open up my mouth and swallow them,
        as I might gulp the Milky Way.

When the last star fades into the absolute azure I will return
To where 'The Dawn of Christianity', by Turner, hangs in
        Belfast in its gilt frame:
Airy, half-discovered shades of aqua, the night becoming hazy
        milk and pearl,
The canvas is a perfect circle; and as I gaze into its opalescent
        mirror
I try to find its subject, 'The Flight into Egypt'. A palm tree
        beckons
Like an angel's hand: words issue from the sealed tomb of his
        mouth — *Be thou there*
Until I bring thee word — and the Holy Family vanishes into
        the breathed-on mirror
Where the Nile-blue sky becomes the Nile, abandoning
        the Empire
To its Massacre of Innocents, the mutilated hands and knees
        of children.

Eleven horsemen —
not one of them turns his head —
through the wind-blown snow.

— Shiki

Narrative in Black and White

Now take these golf balls, scattered all around the place,
    which since
The reproduction's blurred, you'd easily misconstrue
    as ping-pong —
You can't make out the dimples. But they're different
    as chalk and cheese:
Ever get hit by a golf ball? You'd know all about it. And
    perhaps
The golf club in the bottom corner is no give-away. People
    have been known
To mistake it for a gun. And the disembodied plus-fours
Might be army surplus. No, all these things are dangerous
    enough,
According to whose rules you play. Which is maybe why
    they're put there,
Where you'd least expect them, floating against the façade
    of the Europa.

Hotel, that is. You know it? Looks as if it's taken from
    a photograph,
Down to the missing *E* of the logo, the broken windows,
    which they only got
Around to fixing last week. Things drift off like that,
    or people drift in.
Like Treacy, who it's all about, according to the guy who
    painted it.
This splash of red here: not blood, but a port-wine stain
    or strawberry mark
That Treacy carried all his life, just here, above the wrist-
    watch. Any time
You saw him sitting he would have his right hand over it.
    Like this.
Too easily recognized, he didn't like. This is where the black
    gloves
Come in, gripping the revolving foyer doors. Or maybe one
    of them
Is raised, like saying *Power* — to the people, to himself, whatever.

Billiard balls? Well, maybe. Certainly these random scratches
  on the canvas
Suggest the chalk marks on a green baize, a faded diagram
  from which
You'd try to piece together what the action was. Like trying
  to account
For Treacy's movements. Though on the night in question,
  according to the barman
In The Beaten Docket, he'd staggered in from some win
  on the horses,
Slaps a tenner on the counter, and orders a 'Blue Angel'. Blue
  what?
Says the barman. Angel, Treacy says, Blue Bols, vodka, ice,
  a drop of sugar.
Oh, and top it up with whipped cream. I say this just to show
  the sort
Of him, like someone who a year or two ago would not have
  known cocktail
From a hen's arse. You're sure, the barman says, you
  wouldn't like a straw?

The staircase is important. The zig-zag is like taking one step
  forward,
Two steps back. For who would take the stairs up thirteen
  floors when
He could take the lift? The reason why, the power had gone
  that night.
So only one way in, and one way out. As sure as meeting your
  own shadow.
This, I think, is what the mirror represents. Like, everybody
  knew about the split,
And what side Treacy ended up on. Of course, the detail's lost;
You have to see it like it is, original. The colours, the dimensions.
Even the frame, like someone spying through binoculars, is
  saying something:
I'm watching you; but you, you can't see me. Ping-pong.
  Yin-yang.

So here is Treacy, at the wrong end of the telescope,
    diminishing.
He was seen in this bar, that bar. Like, what I'm saying is
    that anybody
Might have fingered him. So the man on the thirteenth floor
    sits pat.
He draws back the curtain. He stares through the kaleidoscope
    of snow
And sees what's coming next. Treacy's footsteps. Game, set
    and match.
They found him in the empty room. The face was blown off.
    They rolled down
One black glove. A Rorschach blot. The Red Hand, as he
    called himself.

Me? I knew him like a brother. Once. But then our lives grew
    parallel, if
Parallel is never meeting. He started dressing up and talking
    down. What
He would and wouldn't do. And people don't go shooting off
    their mouths like that.

Wild rough seas tonight:
yawning over Sado Isle,
snowy galaxies.

— Bashō

Hamlet

As usual, the clock in The Clock Bar was a good few minutes
    fast:
A fiction no one really bothered to maintain, unlike the story
The comrade on my left was telling, which no one knew for
    certain truth:
Back in 1922, a sergeant, I forget his name, was shot outside
the National Bank . . .
Ah yes, what year was it that they knocked it down? Yet, its
    memory's as fresh
As the inky smell of new pound notes — which interferes with
    the beer-and-whiskey
Tang of now, like two dogs meeting in the revolutionary 69
    of a long sniff,
Or cattle jostling shit-stained flanks in the Pound. For *pound*,
    as some wag
Interrupted, was an offshoot of the Falls, from the Irish, *fál*,
    a hedge;
Hence, *any kind of enclosed thing*, its twigs and branches
    commemorated
By the soldiers' drab and olive camouflage, as they try to melt
Into a brick wall; red coats might be better, after all. *At any rate,*
This sergeant's number came up; not a winning one. The bullet
had his name on it.
Though Sergeant X, as we'll call him, doesn't really feature
    in the story:
The nub of it is, *This tin can which was heard that night,*
trundling down
From the bank, down Balaklava Street. Which thousands heard,
and no one ever
Saw. Which was heard for years, any night that trouble might be
Round the corner . . . and when it skittered to a halt, you knew
That someone else had snuffed it: a name drifting like
    an afterthought,
A scribbled wisp of smoke you try and grasp, as it becomes
    diminuendo, then
Vanishes. For *fál* is also *frontier, boundary*, as in *the*
undiscovered country

From whose bourne no traveller returns, the illegible, thorny
    hedge of time itself —
Heartstopping moments, measured not by the pulse of a wrist-
    watch, nor
The archaic anarchists' alarm clock, but a mercury tilt device
Which 'only connects' on any given bump on the road. So,
    by this wingèd messenger
The promise 'to pay the bearer' is fulfilled:

As someone buys another round, an Allied Irish Banks £10
    note drowns in
The slops of the counter; a Guinness stain blooms on the
    artist's impression
Of the sinking of *The Girona*; a tiny foam hisses round
    the salamander brooch
Dredged up to show how love and money endure, beyond
    death and the Armada,
Like the bomb-disposal expert in his suit of salamander-cloth.
Shielded against the blast of time by a strangely-mediaeval
    visor,
He's been outmoded by this jerky robot whose various
    attachments include
A large hook for turning over corpses that may be booby-trapped;
But I still have this picture of his hands held up to avert
    the future
In a final act of *No surrender*, as, twisting through the murky
    fathoms
Of what might have been, he is washed ashore as pearl and
    coral.

This *strange eruption to our state* is seen in other versions
    of the Falls:
A no-go area, a ghetto, a demolition zone. For the ghost,
    as it turns out —
All this according to your man, and I can well believe it —
    this tin ghost,

Since the streets it haunted were abolished, was never heard
again.
The sleeve of Raglan Street has been unravelled; the helmet
of Balaklava
Is torn away from the mouth. The dim glow of Garnet has gone
out,
And with it, all but the memory of where I lived. I, too, heard
the ghost:
A roulette trickle, or the hesitant annunciation of a downpour,
ricocheting
Off the window; a goods train shunting distantly into a siding,
Then groaning to a halt; the rainy cries of children after dusk.
For the voice from the grave reverberates in others' mouths,
as the sails
Of the whitethorn hedge swell up in a little breeze, and tremble
Like the spiral blossom of Andromeda: so suddenly are shrouds
and branches
Hung with street lights, celebrating all that's lost, as fields are
reclaimed
By the Starry Plough. So we name the constellations, to put
a shape
On what was there; so, the storyteller picks his way between
the isolated stars.

But, *Was it really like that?* And, *Is the story true?*
You might as well tear off the iron mask, and find that no one,
after all,
Is there: nothing but a cry, a summons, clanking out from
the smoke
Of demolition. Like some son looking for his father, or
the father for his son,
We try to piece together the exploded fragments. Let these
broken spars
Stand for the Armada and its proud full sails, for even if
The clock is put to rights, everyone will still believe it's fast:
The barman's shouts of *Time* will be ignored in any case, since
time

Is conversation; it is the hedge that flits incessantly into
    the present,
As words blossom from the speakers' mouths, and the flotilla
    returns to harbour,
Long after hours.

FIRST LANGUAGE

(1994)

for Deirdre

La Je-Ne-Sais-Quoi

I bhfaiteadh na súl
I ndorchadas an lae
Bhrúigh do bhéal go tobann
Ar mo bhéalsa
Agus slogadh mé go glan
I gclapsholas domhain do phóige.

I bhfaiteadh na mbéal
I bhfriotal na súl
Fáscadh agus teannadh
Go dtí nach raibh ann
Ach scáth an scátháin eadrainn,
Tocht i do chluais istigh.

Mé i mo thost anois,
Dlaoithe chasta do chainte
Ina luí go dlúth ar urlár snasta,
Mé á scuabadh, mé á scaipeadh
Go béal an dorais,
Séideán beag amuigh.

Second Language

English not being yet a language, I wrapped my lubber-lips
    around my thumb;
Brain-deaf as an embryo, I was snuggled in my comfort-
    blanket dumb.

Growling figures campaniled above me, and twanged their
    carillons of bronze
Sienna consonants embedded with the vowels *alexandrite,*
    emerald and *topaz.*

The topos of their discourse seemed to do with me and
    convoluted genealogy;
Wordy whorls and braids and skeins and spiral helices,
    unskeletoned from laminate geology —

How this one's slate-blue gaze is correspondent to
    another's new-born eyes;
Gentians, forget-me-nots, and cornflowers, diurnal
    in a heliotrope surmise.

Alexandrine tropes came gowling out like beagles, loped and
    unroped
On a snuffly Autumn. Nimrod followed after with his bold
    Arapahoes,

Who whooped and hollered in their unforked tongue. The trail
    was starred with
Myrrh and frankincense of Anno Domini; the Wise Men
    wisely paid their tariff.

A single star blazed at my window. Crepuscular, its acoustic
    perfume dims
And swells like flowers on the stanzaic-papered wall.
    Shipyard hymns

Then echoed from the East: gantry-clank and rivet-ranks, Six-
    County hexametric

Brackets, bulkheads, girders, beams, and stanchions;
    convocated and Titanic.

Leviathans of rope snarled out from ropeworks: disgorged
    hawsers, unkinkable lay,
Ratlines, S-twists, plaited halyards, Z-twists, catlines; all had
    their say.

Tobacco-scent and snuff breathed out in gouts of factory
    smoke like aromatic camomile;
Sheaves of brick-built mill-stacks glowered in the sulphur-
    mustard fog like campaniles.

The dim bronze noise of midnight-noon and Angelus then
    boomed and clinked in Latin
Conjugations; statues wore their shrouds of amaranth;
    the thurible chinked out its smoky patina.

I inhaled *amo, amas, amat* in quids of *pros* and *versus* and
    Introibos
Ad altare Dei; incomprehensibly to others, spoke in Irish.
    I slept through the Introit.

The enormous Monastery surrounded me with nave and
    architrave. Its ornate pulpit
Spoke to me in fleurs-de-lys of Purgatory. Its sacerdotal gaze
    became my pupil.

My pupil's nose was bathed in Pharaonic unguents of dope
    and glue.
Flimsy tissue-paper plans of aeroplanes unfolded whimsical
    ideas of the blue,

Where, unwound, the prop's elastic is unpropped and balsa-
    wood extends its wings
Into the hazardous azure of April. It whirrs into the realm
    of things.

Things are kinks that came in tubes; like glue or paint
   extruded, that became
A hieroglyphic alphabet. Incestuous in pyramids, Egyptians
   were becalmed.

I climbed into it, delved its passageways, its sepulchral
   interior, its things of kings
Embalmed; sarcophagi, whose perfume I exhumed in chancy
   versions of the *I-Ching*.

A chink of dawn was revelated by the window. Far-off cocks
   crowed crowingly
And I woke up, verbed and tensed with speaking English;
   Ilisped the words so knowingly.

I love the as-yet morning, when no one's abroad, and I am like
   a postman on his walk,
Distributing strange messages and bills, and arbitrations with
   the world of talk:

I foot the snow and almost-dark. My shoes are crisp, and bite
   into the blue-
White firmament of pavement. My father holds my hand and
   goes blah-

Blah with me into the ceremonial dawn. I'm wearing tweed.
   The universe is Lent
And Easter is an unspun cerement, the gritty, knitty, tickly
   cloth of unspent

Time. I feel its warp and weft. Bobbins pirn and shuttle in
   Imperial
Typewriterspeak. I hit the keys. The ribbon-black clunks out
   the words in serial.

What comes next is next, and no one knows the *che sera* of it,
   but must allow

The Tipp-Ex present at the fingertips. Listen now: an angel
   whispers of the here-and-now.

The future looms into the mouth incessantly, gulped-at and
   unspoken;
Its guardian is intangible, but gives you hints and winks and
   nudges as its broken token.

I woke up blabbering and dumb with too much sleep. I rubbed
   my eyes and ears.
I closed my eyes again and flittingly, forgetfully, I glimpsed
   the noise of years.

A Date Called Eat Me

The American Fruit Company had genetically engineered
    a new variety of designer apple,
Nameless as yet, which explored the various Platonic ideals
    of the 'apple' synapse.

Outside the greengrocer's lighted awning it is dusky
    Hallowe'en. It is
Snowing on a box of green apples, crinkly falling on the tissue
    paper. It is

Melting on the green, unbitten, glistening apples, attracted
    by their gravity.
I yawned my teeth and bit into the dark, mnemonic cavity.

That apple-box was my first book-case. I covered it in wood-
    grain Fablon —
You know that Sixties stick-on plastic stuff? I thought
    it looked dead-on:

Blue Pelicans and orange Penguins, *The Pocket Oxford*
    English Dictionary;
Holmes and Poe, *The Universe*, the fading aura of an apple
    named Discovery —

I tried to extricate its itsy-bitsy tick of rind between one tooth
    and another tooth,
The way you try to winkle out the 'facts' between one truth
    and another truth.

Try to imagine the apple talking to you, tempting you like
    something out of Aesop,
Clenched about its navel like a fist or face, all pith and pips
    and sap

Or millions of them, hailing from the heavens, going *pom,*
    pom, pom, pom, pom

On the roof of the American Fruit Company, whose computer
banks are going *ohm* and *om*.

They were trying to get down to the nitty-gritty, sixty-four-
thousand dollar question of whether the stalk
Is apple or branch or what. The programme was stuck.

The juice of it explodes against the roof and tongue, the cheek
of it.
I lied about the Fablon, by the way. It was really midnight
black with stars on it.

Grass

We'd done a deal of blow, and dealt a hand or two of Brag,
Which bit by bit became a bloody Patience, except no one
Seemed to twig which hand was which, or who was who
    or whom
Or what was ace or deuce.

Hardly any shock, when in the general boggledybotch,
    the budgie
Unlatched himself from out the room, and what he cheeped
    and Canterburied
Wasn't Gospel — which hardly gave a fiddler's, since the flats
    were on the bias
Or on the juice.

It was the circumbendibus of everything that got us locked
And scuttered, the Anno Domini of what had happened
    yonks before
Our time, and that is why we languish now in Anguagela Jail,
    while he
Is on the loose.

For what the blatherskite had shit was mouth a bow-wow
Word or two and let the echolalia hang out — which the
    Powers-that-Be
Lapped up, since they never liked to Brian O'Lynn the sup
    without
Its inkling of Vermouth.

What we had on us would do and, if not, they'd make it more,
The way an ounce of dope becomes a key. They took it down
    in notes
Contemporaneously, and the brief told us to sing our prayers,
    but not the sort the boys
Learn in Maynooth.

My curse upon this few-cards-missing-from-the-deck who
    lately soldiered o'er

From Cant; Archbishoply he took us in. But his crinkum-
　　crankum ways
Will lead him to Brazil, if that is what he thinks he is as hard as;
He'll do his bird in Braggadocia and learn the truth.

Two to Tango

Whether you want to change your face or not's up to yourself.
    But the bunk of history
They'll make up for you. Someone else's shoes. They can put
    you anywhere. Where's a mystery.

Aromas, sounds, the texture of the roads, the heaviness
    or lightness of the air —
All these contribute to the sense of place. These things are
    what we are,

Though mitigated by ourselves. The details might be
    anywhere, so long as a romantic atmosphere
Is evoked. But to mention Africa, the Middle East or Russia
    is anathema.

It's not the money. Money enters into it, but doesn't talk.
    I do that.
I fill the blanks they know already. I'm the jammy centre
    in the doughnut.

Introspection must serve a purpose beyond the simple passing
    of time:
That bit of dialogue, recalled, might prove to be the clue that
    solves the crime.

And Belfast isn't like Beirut, although I've never been there.
    It's what it is:
Agendas, bricks and mortar, interfaces. Others in the structure
    like me. *Veritas.*

Dialogue can act as a transition bridge: for example, *I've been*
    meaning to talk to you,
He said, *I hear you've got the job . . . that you'll have to move*
    to Tokyo . . .

They can't let on I'm there. There's nothing down on paper.
    What there is is code.

Alone? I'm sometimes. Very. Very. Sometimes very hot and
sometimes very cold.

She watched the way the hair on his wrist curled round
the band of his wrist-watch:
This is an example of 'initial entanglement', from which
it's difficult to wrench

Herself. Others might be fragrances, like melted candle-wax;
sometimes, even, sweat.
And the timepiece might be Philippe Patek, but never, under
any circumstances, Swatch.

You find ways around it, yawning, getting up to 'go out for
a couple of hours'.
They make the place secure for you. It's like a Twilight Zone
where they exert their Special Powers.

And you make sure you don't repeat yourself. Change the
routine ever
So slightly. Tell no one, I mean no one, what you're up to.
Never. Never. Never.

Use slang and buzz-words sparingly. Use body language tags,
especially for men:
He punctuated his words with repeated clicks of his Mont Blanc
ballpoint pen.

For when you stop saying *never*, that's when you'll get dead.
You'll put your sweet lips
A little too close to the phone and talk of *always* in a fatal
momentary lapse.

And then you think, not to repeat yourself is not real life. And
so you do.
You develop mannerisms. Tics and tags, without them looking
like they're pseudo.

And contrast is important, between male and female dialogue.
    Then there's changes of identity;
But be careful of the cliché where the protagonist is torn
    between identical

Twins. A hero, me? I'm not. It's just a game. I'm saving lives?
    Perhaps.
It's like a sentence crammed with grammar, phrases, ages,
    hyphens, stops.

Is this a faction or a *roman fleuve* (more commonly called
    generational
Or *saga*)? Decide before you start, work out your plot, then
    go for it. *Be inspirational.*

One side says this, the other that. You work it out yourself
    and walk between the story lines.
What's true is what you do. Keep your head down. Know
    yourself. Ignore the starry skies.

Ovid: *Metamorphoses*, V, 529–550

Persephone ate seven pomegranate seeds. So what? I'll tell you
  what —
It doesn't do to touch strange fruit, when it's forbidden
  by the Powers-
That-Be. Who put you on a hunger strike which, if you break,
  you'll stay put
In the Underworld. It doesn't do to get caught out. Watch
  out for prowlers.

She'd wandered into Pluto's murky realm; plucked the dull-
  orange bubble.
Split the cortex. Sucked. And who was salivating in the bushes'
  dark interior
But Ascalaphus. Stoolie. Pipsqueak. Mouth. He spilled
  the beans on her, he blabbed —
Straight off he shot, and knocked, knocked, knocked
  on Heaven's iron door.

But she spat back as good as she had got: unholy water from
  the Phlegethon
She slabbered on him. His eyes yellowed, drooled, and grew.
  His neb became a beak.
He sprouted spermy wings. Hooked talons shot from his
  fingers. His body dwindled
Into mostly head. All ears, all eyes: touts everywhere,
  potential freaks,

Beware. For now he is the scrake-owl, Troubles' augury
  for Auld Lang Syne,
Who to this day is harbinger of doom, the gloom of Pluto's
  no-go zone.

Four Sonnets

1

The crushed carapaces of watches ticked on the pavement.
Passersby ignored them.

Put your ear to the street, you will hear the underground
streams of Belfast.

'The bodies that clothe them are enfeebled,' said the Dalai
Lama momentarily.

The seagulls' white *ms* skittered and mewed behind the noisy
Doppler-red fire engines.

But it is business as usual and there is already new glass to be
stared through.

All over the city the stopped clocks told each other the different
wrong times.

The black electric flex snaked through the air-vent to remind
you of a bug.

'Planting through the new man-made membrane can be a bit
fiddly.'

With his fingernail and quick he unlatched the little crucifix's
coffin-lid.

'This morning's lesson is "psychotherapeutic evaluation".
Multiple choices are allowed.'

Don't ever sit around in your costume. Don't *ever* put your
puppet face-down.

'*Not* business solutions.' 'But there are so many lookalikes.'
'Wrong again.'

I lost the key to the refreshment centre. Babies. Splits. Cidona. Squash. Dash.

He breathed Gethsemane. They began to search the labyrinth of the thumb-print.

2

He splashed Polish spirit on his wrist, set fire to it, and didn't burn.

Tomorrow? That's the Twelfth of Nevuary, man — like, O, Zero, Nought, Nix.

One of the puppets is 'The Disjointed Policeman'. Then there's Punch. They share the truncheon.

There *are* so many lookalikes. The way you know the black boxer by his white shorts.

It was printed on Weetabix paper with some dense black ink by a former Soviet.

He did his chicken-with-the-head-cut-off walk, then staggered out. No strings attached.

I examined the calamine-lotion-pink of the tax form till I was tired.

'The South Georgian onions had a bad spring, so Anton decided to use the Spanish instead.'

The cidermen were in direct contravention of an alcohol-free zone.

'Everybody cries. Some like you did. Some inside. What you did's better.'

In the Conrad Hotel the delegates walked round pretending not to read their name-tags.

There's a space the thickness of rice-paper between your feet and the stage.

'It's a non-consumptive, non-polluting industry,' said the injection apparatus operator.

The legs hang from the shoulder. The heads are kept separate from the bodies.

3

The white security tape has been taken away, but I wouldn't go out, if I were you.

After I changed the ribbon I realized everything was finger-printed.

The deaf-mute held a lemon in his hand for want of a better word.

'Well, one day the statue was there, and the next it wasn't.'

When the innocent was released he was speedily embraced by Special Powers.

Why the shattered window, when the door's unlatched and creaking?

It's the aerosol 'pine' aroma that goes with the log-effect electric fire.

The holes were drilled in the scales of Justice to let out
the rainwater.

Like the man says, 'You don't have to know how a thing
works to know it *isnae* working.'

Summer lightning: the blackthorn hedge wavered like a foot
patrol.

He had his two arms full of analogue and digital, Arabic and
Roman watchstraps.

I opened the fridge; a blast of cold air slapped me in the face
like light.

'He's trying to play the crocodile — and what is he? He's
the lizard under the rock.'

I was trying to tell the time when I swallowed a lemon pip
from my sixth or seventh gin-and-tonic.

4

Who is the leader? What is the gang? Give me the initials
of the gang!

'Magenta' summoned up the battle of Magenta.

'Prisoners on the roof are dismantling the roof in a desperate
bid for freedom.'

I spilled the milk. A little, dog-eared map of Ireland sprawled
on the Axminster.

He was full as a goog or a sheugh. Legless. Half-cut. Half-lit.
Getting there.

In February the ice-cream chimes played 'The Teddy-Bears' Picnic'.

The sniffer dog wriggled its way into focus the way it waggled its tail.

They were attached to each other in the loops of Messerschmidt and Hurricane.

First the bare notes. Then staccato. Then the off-beat. Counterpoint. *Stop*. You forgot the soul.

The tickly corrugations of the Tintawn that he barefoot crept downstairs upon.

You mistook the Californian oranges for Seville. One is bumpier.

It was the way he noticed the man who was playing the saw had only a leg.

Be Born Again! Be Saved! Wash yourself in the Blood of the Lamb!

On Not Remembering Some Lines of a Song

It's the pawl-and-ratchet mechanism
Of one of those antique, whirligig-type, wooden rattles, only
Some of the teeth are missing. Or there's fluff
On the needle of the pick-up, and bursts of steam —
Ampersands, asterisks, and glottal stops — puff round
The words, like those signals in the distance
That announce the almost-imminent arrival
Of the train which everyone had given up for lost.

*If I'd been you, I wouldn't have started
Off from here*, the anxious tourist was informed. He'd come
Prepared for rain, but dusk was streaming
Down on the little station, on
His orange oilskins. Over and above the musk
Of creosote and hawthorn he could just make out
The pipe bands struggling homewards, the skirts
Of clouds obscured by twilit music.

That windblown, martial girn and drone reminded me
I came from the wrong side of the tracks.
The criss-cross meaning of their Black Watch tartan
Was a mystery to me, and I could never fathom
How they synchronized
The swing of their hips, kilts waving like a regiment
Of windscreen-wipers, so the drizzle doesn't fog
Their automatic pilot.

It's coming back in dribs and drabs, for nothing ever
Is forgotten: it's in there somewhere in the memory-bank,
Glimmering in binary notation. I think you have to find
That switch between the *off* and *on*, the split chink
Through which you peer with half an eye
And glimpse the other, time-drenched world.
A jitter of fragmented birdsong, in which the microtones
Are birds, twittering between the staves.

And the demarcation lines of white tape
Drifted into side streets, tangled up with children's skipping-
Ropes, the hide-and-seek of counting-rhymes.
Evening draws in like a hyphen: the parade
Had ended hours ago
And the Sabbath quiet of that Monday
Had been long implicit in the festival agenda
As the marchers learned to walk again by rote.

The regalia were consigned to the future blue
Where a fancy skywriter lets the message bloom and fluff
And then dissolve before our eyes
Until everything is indecipherable, the blown wisps
Of letters becoming an 'acoustic perfume'. And
The slogan was so perfect, so much
In tune with television jingles, that it seemed to breathe
From everybody's mouths

As if freshly minted there, this squeezed-out root of toothpaste
That bears the tang of aromatic speech. It oozes
From the floodlit shrubbery
Where gypsy moths are whirling in commemorative World War I
Camouflage, describing Celtic dogfights, loop-
The-loops and tangents. For everything blooms out of season:
Surely the children had anticipated all of this, these frosty nights;
They counted out the gabbled alphabet of stars.

Apparat

Unparalysed, the robot bomb-disposal expert inched and
tacked across the mezzanine
As casually as someone to be barbered sits relaxing with
a magazine.

It was using 'deep creep' and 'infinite hair', conversing in its
base-of-two conundrum.
Its chips were bugged like all the toasters in the apparatchniks'
condominium.

Turnbull twiddled with the radio controls. He twitched his
robot's claws.
He felt the Mobile Ordinance Disposal Unit index through
its dictionary of clues.

Umbilical, he was in the waiting room. Barberlike, he opened
up his case of instruments.
He was beckoned by the realms of Nod. He entered in with
incense and Byzantine vestments.

The smart bomb got the message and intoned the right
liturgical analysis.
Latinate, they swapped explosive bits and pieces; they re-
emerged in Nemesis.

The Brain of Edward Carson

They cracked the skull and watched its two halves creak
     apart, like the decks
Of some Byzantine trireme. The herringboned, zipped oars,
     the chains and shackles.
The bronze circuitry. The locks. The titanic, legal depositions
     of the cells.
The hammered rivets. The rivetted, internal gaze. The screws.
     The nails.
The caulked bulwarks. The slaves, embalmed in honeycomb
     prismatic.

Barbaric instruments inserted there, like hook and razor, iron
     picks
By which they will extrapolate its history: the bronze, eternal
     static
Of his right, uplifted hand. The left hand like a shield. The
     bolted-on, external
Eyes. The seraphic frown. The borders and the chains
     contained therein. The fraternal
Gaze of the Exclusive Brethren: orange and bruised purple,
     cataleptic.

The map of Ulster opened up, hexagonal and intricate,
     tectonic:
Its shifting plates were clunked and welded into place by laws
     Masonic.
The ladder and the rope. The codicils. The compasses by
     which they sail
Uncharted futures. The outstretched hand. The crown. The
     sash. The secret nail.
And then disintegration intervened, the brain eluded them:
     Sphinxlike, catatonic.

Opus 14

Hole Blown in Baroque Splendour of Opera House (designed
  by Frank Matcham):
The Security Forces were specifically looking for terrorists but
  spectacularly failed to catch them.

∽

Newly-appointed innumerate Chancellor of the Exchequer
  What-Do-You-Call-Him Clarke
Was counting his stars in twos like the innumerable animals
  in Noah's Ark.

∽

Did you know that 'the set of all objects describable in exactly
  eleven English words'
Is called an 'R-Set'? I didn't. It was dreamed up by the people
  who put the 'surd' in 'absurd'.

∽

Spokesman for censored political party spoke in someone
  else's lip-synch
So perfectly, you'd think it was the man himself, though much
  of this is double-think.

∽

So I woke up this morning with yet another wrong solution
  to Fermat's Last
Theorem, which bore about the same relationship to global x
  as does the world to Atlas.

∽

He had a pocketful of pocket calculators, palindromes, and
  anagrams. The Name

Of Names eluded him as yet, but he was working on it and
  had found the Name of the Game.

⌒

The idea was that one and one made three, like in the Holy
  Family
Or Trinity, where 'three' is pronounced 'tree', as in the Irish
  Christian Brother's homily.

⌒

I think this goes to show that Cajori's study of mathematical
  symbols
Is in part, like not to see the wood for trees, a graveyard for
  dead symbols.

⌒

For you can deconstruct all sorts of words from 'England':
  angel, gland and *dangle*;
It's the way the Germans have captured the Gaolainn-speaking
  industry in Dingle.

⌒

Sums are funny. *Wars 2. Legs 1. Wives 2. Children 4. Wounds
  2. Total 11.* You know?
Which reminds me to go and check out Nik Cohn's book *Yes,
  We Have No.*

⌒

Bananas is understood. It's not known by many, or maybe
  it is, that Cohn's from Londonderry or Derry,
Which might account for the ambivalence of the fact of the
  Foyle's not having a ferry.

Of course, it has this double-decker bridge, at which you're
    doubly checked.
The soldier looks at you and then he looks at your picture.
    It's pronounced *echt*.

At the previous Chancellor's Last Supper he was seized
    by a sudden triskaidecaphobia
Which took him to the fourteenth floor, where he became
    immersed in a conference of bankers from the Bank
    of Wachovia.

It likes to do that. *Wachovia*. Which brings me back to
    baroque Opera House designed by Frank.
The googolplex security net had been full of innumerable holes
    held together by string, to be frank.

Drunk Boat

after Rimbaud, 'Le Bateau Ivre'

As I glided down the lazy Meuse, I felt my punters had gone
    AWOL —
In fact, Arapahoes had captured them for target practice,
    nailing them to stakes. Oh hell,

I didn't give a damn. I didn't want a crew, nor loads of Belgian
    wheat, nor English cotton.
When the whoops and hollers died away their jobs were well
    forgotten.

Through the tug and zip of tides, more brain-deaf than
    an embryo, I bobbled;
Peninsulas, unmoored and islanded, were envious of my
    Babel-babble.

Storms presided at my maritime awakening. Like a cork
    I waltzed across the waves,
Which some call sailors' graveyards; but I despised their
    far-off, lighted enclaves.

As children think sour apples to be sweet, so the green sap
    swamped the planks
And washed away the rotgut and the puke, the rudder and
    the anchor-hanks.

I've been immersed, since then, in Sea Poetry, anthologized
    by stars,
As through the greenish Milky Way a corpse drifts down-
    wards, clutching a corrupted spar;

When suddenly, those sapphire blues are purpled by Love's
    rusty red. No lyric
Alcohol, no Harp, can combat it, this slowly-pulsing, twilit
    panegyric.

I've known lightning, spouts, and undertows, maelstrom
        evenings that merge into Aurora's
Blossoming of doves. I've seen the Real Thing; others only get
        its aura.

I've seen the sun's demise, where seas unroll like violet,
        antique
Venetian blinds; dim spotlight, slatted by the backstage work
        of Ancient Greeks.

I dreamed the green, snow-dazzled night had risen up to kiss
        the seas'
Blue-yellow gaze, the million plankton eyes of phosphor-
        escent argosies.

I followed then, for many months, the mad-cow waves of the
        Antipodes,
Oblivious to the Gospel of how Jesus calmed the waters,
        walking on his tippy-toes.

I bumped, you know, into the Floridas, incredible with
        pupil-flowers
And manatees, which panther-men had reined with rainbows
        and with Special Powers.

I saw a whole Leviathan rot slowly in the seething marsh, till
        it became
All grot and whalebone. Blind cataracts lurched into
        oubliettes, and were becalmed.

Glaciers and argent seas, pearly waves and firecoal skies!
        A tangled serpent-cordage
Hauled up from the Gulf, all black-perfumed and slabbered
        with a monster's verbiage!

I would have liked the children to have seen them: goldfish,
        singing-fish, John Dorys —

My unanchored ones, I'm cradled by the tidal flowers and
lifted near to Paradise.

Sometimes, fed-up with the Poles and Zones, the sea would
give a briny sob and ease
Off me; show me, then, her vented shadow-flowers, and
I'd be like a woman on her knees . . .

Peninsular, I juggled on my decks with mocking-birds and
ostriches
And rambled on, until my frail lines caught another upside-
down, a drowned Australian.

Now see me, snarled-up in the reefs of bladderwrack,
or thrown by the waterspout like craps
Into the birdless Æther, where Royal Navy men would slag
my sea-drunk corpse —

Smoking, languorous in foggy violet, I breathed a fireglow
patch into
The sky, whose azure trails of snot are snaffled by some Poets
as an entrée —

Electromagnets, hoof-shaped and dynamic, drove the
Nautilus. Black hippocampuses
Escorted it, while heat-waves drummed and blattered on
the July campuses.

Me, I shivered: fifty leagues away, I heard the bumbling
Behemoths and Scarabs;
Spider spinning in the emerald, I've drifted off the ancient
parapets of Europe!

Sidereal archipelagoes I saw! Island skies, who madly
welcomed the explorer;
O million starry birds, are these the endless nights you dream
of for the Future?

I've whinged enough. Every dawn is desperate, every bitter
   sun. The moon's atrocious.
Let the keel split now, let me go down! For I am bloated, and
   the boat is stotious.

Had I some European water, it would be that cold, black
   puddle
Where a child once launched a paper boat — frail butterfly —
   into the dusk; and huddled

There, I am no more. O waves, you've bathed and cradled
   me and shaped
Me. I'll gaze no more at Blue Ensigns, nor merchantmen, nor
   the drawn blinds of prison-ships.

Second Nature

after Seán Ó Ríordáin, 'Malairt'

'Come over here,' says Turnbull, 'till you see the sorrow
    in the horse's eyes;
If you had hooves as cumbersome, there would be gloom
    in your eyes too.'

And it was clear to me, that he had understood the sorrow
    in the horse's eyes
So well, had dwelt so long on it, that he was plunged in
    the horse's mind.

I looked over at the horse, that I might see the sorrow
    pouring from its eyes;
I saw the eyes of Turnbull, looming towards me from
    the horse's head.

I looked at Turnbull; I looked at him again, and saw
    beneath his brows
The too-big eyes that were dumb with sorrow, the horse's
    eyes.

Correspondances

after Baudelaire, 'Correspondances'

Nature is a Temple: its colonnaded trunks blurt out, from time
    to time, a verdurous babble;
The dark symbolic forest eyes you with familiarity, from
    the verge of Parable.

Self-confounding echoes buzz and mingle through the gloomy
    arbours;
Vowels, perfumes, stars swarm in like fireflies from
    the midnight blue of harbours.

The quartet yawns and growls at you with amber, rosin,
    incense, musk;
Horsehair on the catgut is ecstatic with its soul and spirit
    music —

Prairie greens, the *oms* and *ahs* of oboes, soft as the bloom
    on infant
Baby-skin; and other great hits, smothered in the triumph
    of the infinite.

All Souls

The un*Walkman* headphones stick out awkwardly, because
   they are receiving
Not the packaged record of a song, but real-time input, a form
   of blah
Alive with intimations of mortality, the loud and unclear
   garbled static.

It's the peripatetic buzz of static, like it was a Hallowe'enlike
   weather
That you rarely get at Hallowe'en. The mushrooms
   mushroomed as per
Usual, that is to say, in subterfuge, slowly dawning through
   on Instamatic.

Like putting on spectacles, when what it was was blurred, then
   swims
Into your focus. You can see they come from the Planet *X*,
   with their walkie-
Talkies, the heavy warbling of their heavy Heaney tyres and
   automatic,

Gyroscope-type-tank-surveillance technique, their faces
   blacked like
Boots. Their antennae quivered on that Hallowe'en
   encountered just beyond Sans
Souci. It was, in fact, outside the Fire Station, and the firemen,
   with Platonic

Abandon, were going through their exercises, rehearsing for
   the Fire,
The Bomb, the Incident, some routine dot on the dial, where
   the wireless
Lights with intimations of Hilversum or Moscow, and
   the Radio Symphonic

244

Orchestra is playing someone's Dead March through
   the whistles and the static
Of the dark you listen to. To which you listen, like routine
   intimations
Of the precinct where the oblique Mandarins decreed antique

Examinations. Then the sound was turned up suddenly,
   anorectic candidates
Blew their fuses; they had failed to comprehend their
   hierophantic elders, who
Laid the rubric down so many yonks ago in ancient mnemonic.

Demonic intimations went on daily; routine, undercover
   orchestrations
Of the nominated discipline of alphabetic, proscribed areas
That ended, as they always do, in tragic, tired recriminations;
   rhetoric.

It then occurred the Firemen had a Ball, it was at Hallowe'en.
   Ecstatically, they
Didn't have false faces on. They were plastic, not explosively,
   but faces. Then
They tore their faces off. Un*Walkman*like. Laconic.
   Workmanlike.

From the Welsh

Mountain snow, my drift is deep and thick; the sheep are walking on the rooftops.

Mountain snow, the milk is icy; I skim it off to get down to the bottom of it.

Mountain snow, the fences under snow; without them, who will know his neighbour?

Mountain snow, I climbed it yesterday; eventually, my head came through the clouds.

Mountain snow, the eggs are fragile; numbed fingers cannot handle them.

Mountain snow, the ducks are out of water; they slither out of kilter on the ice.

Mountain snow, the preacher shuts his Bible; his words are swallowed in the dark.

Mountain snow, the moorcock crows; his loneliness betrays him to the hunter.

Mountain snow, the English are at odds with one another; some of them are learning Welsh.

Mountain snow, no light to read a book by; heads are buried under bedclothes.

Mountain snow, one eye squeezed against the cold, the hunter is a Cyclops.

Mountain snow, a sheep is sprawling in the ditch; one by one the flock falls in with her.

Mountain snow, if words related what the mind knew none would be neighbours.

Mountain snow, and there is brawling in the tavern; it is probably the Irish.

Sonnet

As usual the little container of artificial milk spurted driblets
on my wrist.

The baby's furled and unfurled fists described the way it
bawled with its mouth.

'Welcome to Belfast, home of the best knee surgeons
in the world.'

She fried the fish fingers in cod-liver oil.

'Extra Mild? They'd be no good to me. I'd have to break off
the cork.'

I so admired the lip-print on the calling-card of the diminutive
Japanese 'hostess'.

'Let me know the details, including Designer, Printer, and
the length of run including variables.'

I knew he was a smoker because of the wrinkled eyes. The
pursed mouth.

Muldoon clutched the wheel of a convertible Hillman Imp
with the canopy rolled back.

There was a wild rumour that the live band had been lip-
synched by a rival organization.

'I apologize if I did not sign the letter that accompanied
the interview. If I did, forget this note.'

I knew he couldn't be a gardener because of the hours he spent
with seed catalogues.

The bicycle shop exploded in a shower of cleats, straps, sprockets, spindles, cranks, ratchets, levers.

Not to mention the yellow fingers. I prefer the semi-skimmed myself.

Ovid: *Metamorphoses*, XIII, 439–575

They'd anchored off the coast of Thrace, Agamemnon and
    the comrades, waiting
For a calm; when suddenly, Achilles' ghost appears from
    nowhere, looking large
As life and twice as natural. Blood-shot glinting in his eye,
    he says,
'Forgetful of me, are you? Think my fame was buried with
    me? No, you'll have to pay
Your dues. Take you Polyxena, and put her through the usual
    rites of sacrifice. Her blood
Will be the mark of your respect.' The comrades looked at one
    another, and in that look
Became blood brothers. They dragged Polyxena from
    Hecuba, her mother.

They bring her to the altar. With sword unscabbarded,
    the priest is waiting.
Then, 'Take off your hands from me,' she says, and rips her
    bodice. Shows
Her throat. Her breast. 'I'll go as someone free. It's not
    my death that grieves me,
But my mother's life. And when she comes to claim my body,
    give it to her
Freely. Don't ask for gold as ransom for this corpse. Exchange
    it for her tears.'
And then she's stabbed and stabbed again, and still her last gasp
    shows no sign of fear.
The Trojan women keened her then, and all the other dead
    ones in the house of Hecuba and Priam.

Here's Hecuba: she stuck her lips to the flapping lips
    of the wound and sucked the blood.
Her hair was slabbered and bedraggled with it. Her salt tears
    watered it.
She clawed and scrabbed herself. Then, 'Daughter, last
    of all my pain, for what

Remains? — I stare into your wound and see my wound,
  my children slaughtered.
Achilles did your brothers in, and you, and emptied me. His
  very ghost
Abuses me. I who was queen. I was someone. Look at me.
  I'm nothing now. I spin my wool
As conversation-piece for that Penelope, who sniggers, "*That*
  was Hector's mother. *That* was Priam's wife."

'And can I be alive? How can I be? O Gods, have you reserved
  some more for me?
New funerals? New death? And who would think that Priam
  would be
Happy? Happy man is he in being dead. And will my daughter
  have a gorgeous funeral?
Pomp and ceremony? Not she. She's planted in this foreign
  heap of sand.
No, wait, no, stay — there's more. There's still my lovely imp,
My little Polydorus. He's alive. He'll keep me. Look after me.
  What *am* I at? I haven't washed
Her wound yet. Her bloodied face. Her wound. I'll get some
  water from the shore.'

Salt water: when she got there, what was there? She shut her
  eyes. She howled.
For what was there was Polydorus, dead. His wounds stared
  at her. The eyes of
The wounds. Their sockets. The emptiness of wounds. She
  petrified herself.
Her stony eyes grazed the ground. The sky. The ground again.
  The sky. And then
She opened sight itself and looked at him. His face. His eyes.
  His hands. His feet. All over.
And then it struck her. Polymestor. King of Thrace. He had
  to be behind it.
Polymester. I'll show him who was queen. Who is. I am.
  I'll be. I'll get him yet.

She's like a lioness, robbed of her cubs, who crouches, shivers,
  creeps in for the kill.
She howled again. Shook her bedraggled hair. Set out for him,
  and gained an interview.
Said she had some gold, she'd kept for Polydorus. That she'd
  give him,
Polymestor, for to keep in trust. Stashed away somewhere. He
  went with her. Yes. He'd give it
To her imp. Her latest son. He would. Then she got him
  in the secret place.
Oh yes. She got him rightly. Oh. Her claws tore out his eyes.
  And then her fingernails
Went in again. Not for his eyes. What eyes? He had no eyes.
  She plucked the dark from out the sockets.

And that was that. She got down on all fours and crawled.
  Shivered her haunches.
Growled. It's over. I have done my time. My time is done.
  What now? What
Will I be? Her jaw distended. Her arms and legs became all
  legs, and claws
Sprang from her toenails. Her bedraggled wiry coat was mired
  with blood.
There was this stone. She ran at it and gnarred at it and
  worried it.
She gawped her mouth to speak, and barked. She tossed
  the stone up
In the air. Her tongue lolled out. She barked and barked again,
  and gowls eternally around the Hellespont.

Contract

Demosthenes climbed the rungs of Larynx, diminuendo in its
    double helix.
He buzzed with words like *gremlin, glitch, Zeno's Paradox*,
    and *genetrix*.

Sparks and plumbers, carpenters and glaziers vocalized their
    trades' vernacular;
Priests hymned their rounds and hummed and hahhed
    the ropey new funicular.

So this was Brueghel's 'Babel', Lego-kit-like Pharaonic phasia-
Bricks, where everything is built in stages, ages, scaffolding,
    and phrases.

An eighth-month unstung tongue was clammed with gummed-
    up syllables
Of forceps: bumble, blunder, umbilicals, and garbled labials.

Then Principalities of angels glided in on wings of myth and
    moth,
Their pockets filled with pebbles; they put the thumby,
    stumbling bees in Plato's mouth.

Bagpipe Music

He came lilting down the brae with a blackthorn stick the thick
of a shotgun
In his fist, going *blah dithery dump a doodle scattery idle
fortunoodle* —
When I saw his will-o'-the-wisp go dander through a field
of blue flax randomly, abandonedly
Till all his dots and dashes zipped together, ripped right
through their perforations
Like a Zephyr through the Zodiac: the way a quadrille,
in its last configuration,
Takes on the branches of a swastika, all ribs and shanks and
male and female chromosomes;
Till I heard his voice diminish like the corncrake's in the last
abandoned acre —
Scrake tithery lass a laddle nation aries hiber Packie, he'd be

Oblivious to the black-and-tan, leaf-and-muck-bestrewn
squatting figure
Whose only obvious features are the almost-blue whites
of his two blue eyes, who crabs
From leaf to shadow, mesmerized by olive and burnt umber,
the khaki, lion patches
Of his Cockney accent, going *hang bang a bleeper doddle
doodlebug an asterix.*
The Pisces rod of his aerial twitched just now, as if he'd got
the message,
That the earth itself was camouflaged. Bluebells carpeted
the quivered glades, as,
Three fields away, the tick-tock of the grandmother reassures
us with the long extended
Skillet of its pendulum. The wife in all of this is sidelong,
poised Egyptian
In her fitted kitchen, though the pictograph is full of *Ireland's
Own*-type details, Virgin
Marys, blue and white plates ranged like punctuation
in the lull of memory.

254

The walls are sentences. We see the three walls and the fourth
    is glassy us.

Ocularity a moiety blah skiddery ah disparity: the shotgun
    made a kind of statement, two
Crows falling in a dead-black umlaut. 'The Lucky Shot',
    my man would say, and feed
Me yet another yarn: how you find a creeper in the
    undergrowth and yank,
And a rippled, ripped net shivers through its warp of black-
    damp earth aroma.
There's ink embedded in his two eyes blue, like children's
    dots. Listen close
Enough, you'll get the blooping of the retting dam, parturient,
    as bubbles
Pick and pock a morseway through the stench of rotting flax.
    For it seemed
The grandmother produced an alarm-clock from her
    psychobabble handbag.

That was at the checkpoint. Meanwhile, the trail was
    beginning to leak and waft
A way, but the sniffer dogs persevered in their rendition
    of 'The Fox Chase', lapping
And snuffling up the pepper-black stardust fibrillating
    on the paper, till
The interview was thwarted by Aquarius, a blue line
    on the map that was
Contemporaneous with its past. *Skirl girn a snaffle birdle
    girdle on the griddle howlin* —

Here a squad of black-and-white minstrels wheel in from
    Stage Right, or rather, they
Are wearing balaklavas, and it only looks like that, their
    grinning
Toothpaste lips, their rolling whites of eyes, their Tipp-Exed
    teeth, their Daz forensic

Gloves. They twirl their walking-sticks as thick as guns
    to marching tunes
That blatter in that fourth green field across the border,
    upstairs in a tent,
With Capricorn-skin drums and fifes, while Blavatsky hollers
    through a bullhorn,
Give ye thirty shillins for yer wan poun ten, yer wan poun ten,
    yer —
Fair exchange, they say, sure six of one and half-a-dozen
    of the brother —
I get the drift of the Bloo in the portable loo, John, like, it's one
    ping cancels out
The pong, going *January, February, March! April, May, June,*
    July!

He was blabbing with his Jew-or-jaw's harp finger on his
    lower lip, when the breech
Of the gun snapped out its breach of the peace. The linen
    handkerchief had got
A brack in it, somehow, the dots and dashes of some other's
    red. I tried to pin it down
Just then, or pen it down, but the Lambegs wouldn't let me,
    and anyway, my thumb
And finger's smeared up to the wrist with Lion ink. My hand
    is dis-
Located. The unmarked car came quietly, enquiringly, while
    in a no-go zone
Three streets away I heard two taxis crabbing, like Gemini
    in Gethsemane, which
Of them was black: *honk parp a bullet billet reverup and harp*
    a ballad
Scrake nithery lou a mackie nice wee neice ah libralassie . . .
Just before I put the thing to bed, I closed a pair of scorpion's
    inverted commas round it.
Tomorrow I would glance at the decapitated headlines, then
    flick forward to the Stars.

58

They'd rehearsed the usual Heinz variety of condoms, clocks,
   fertilizer, and electrical flex,
Plus a Joker's device which, someone claimed, had devolved
   from one of the Fifties *Batman* serial flicks —
Which proves there's nothing new *sub specie aeternitatis*,
   or it's part of the general, Heraclitean flux.

Like the orange-sized plastic tomato that glows on the Formica
   counter of the all-night caff,
Your actual's slantindicular as the letter zed, and a long shot
   from being all kiff,
As you'd guess from the blobs and squiggles they'd squidged
   on their chips and someone got on his cuff.

It was raining on the neon writing as they upped and offed and
   packed themselves into the pick-up truck;
The drizzly sound of the words seeped out and will-o'-the-
   wisped on the nearby railway track;
But when the deal came down and the *Enterprise* glimmered
   through, they'd be *n* cards short of a trick.

For they couldn't computate how many beans made five;
   a has-been Celticamerad had vizzed them to the Picts.
And, chauffed through the dark, they were well on the drag
   to becoming commemorative plaques —
Which is hickery-pickery, Indian smoke to the pipe of the
   aberkayheybo Hibernian Pax.

So it's mercury tilt and quicksilver flash as the Johnson
   slammed on the brakes
And it's indecipherababble bits and bods, skuddicked and
   scrabbled like alphabet bricks —
A red hand. A rubber glove. The skewed grin of the clock.
   A clip of ammunition. A breastpocketful of Bics.

Ark of the Covenant

1

They palmed it in and hid it in a bog, invisibly, between
    the Islands of Carnmoon
And Island Carragh South: a strange device, concocted from
    the inner workings
Of a fertilizer bag and someone's fertile brain — gyres and
    gimbals, wires and moans.

A vulgate apologia was on the cards already, the orchestra
    of palms upturned and weighed.
It would be interpreted, dismantled, in iodine ablutions
    of The News
Which comes before The Weather: thunderclouds that move
    in symphonies of woad.

Soldiers painted like the palm-and-finger paintings of a child,
    smears of black
Which underline their eyes like eyebrows, so's the light
    won't blind them: they are
Egyptian, mummified and profiled in the *ignis fatuus* of check
    and road-block.

Scrawled hieroglyphs elaborate the black slick of the road.
    Witnesses
Are called upon, but the ink has lightened into amethyst, and
    soon its blue will be
Invisible, as new ideas dawn across the moss. A great
    Panjandrum will construe their Whatnesses.

2

They trojan-horsed it in and stashed it in a bog, intentionally,
  between the Islands of Carnmoon
And Island Carragh South: a palpable device to suit
  the nomothetic military,
Their *sotto voce* blacks and tans; to second-guess the language
  of their brief campaign.

They read it in the Vulgate, words which spoke with high
  authority of semaphore
And palms. And psalms were evident in thunderclouds
  as pyramidal rays of light
Engraved in blue-ish tints, when God's eye glitters through
  the cloudy hemisphere.

He is painted like a waterfall or thundercloud of beard and
  icon, topaz
Frown that condescends to Bethlehem, where shepherds
  watch by night across
Carnmoon, hunched carmine in the lanternlight, as they
  rehearse the day's momentous topics.

They are the witnesses of snowflake-lazy galaxies, who
  prophesy the moon,
Blue moon that indicates a Second Coming is at hand.
  It is a trip that might be
Wired or not, a trap of wired-up jaws from which ensues
  the vulgate moan.

3

They hushed it in, in its impenetrable black: a bag, a coalsack
    isolated in Carnmoon.
It seethed with good intentions of its maker, trickling
    microseconds slow
As syllables which tick their clock as condensation drips
    in mushroom mines.

The dead black Vulgate of its text is barbed and gothic, and
    is inspired by Yahweh.
Its circuits have been dipped in the blackletter font. They have
    named it *Proclamation.*
And whosoever does not take the word on board will
    be forever called Yahoo

Who are doodled like the antlered stags and men in glyptic
    caves, ritual ochre
Hands imprinted there. The rubric of discarded bones has
    made it difficult to tell
Humerus from humus, as the sheep enact a huddled parliament
    on Carnmoon's snowy acre.

The animals were nodding witnesses, plumes of breath
    illuminated by the birth,
The icy straw. The frankincense and myrhh have taken
    on a cordite odour;
The movable star is relegated to the black bag, where it weeps
    amidst the weeping broth.

4

They'd bound it in a mock book buried in the bog between
    the Islands of Carnmoon
And Island Carragh South, and sniffed the glue and ichor
    of its perfect binding
And its veins. The dope-black seeds of its brain they wrapped
    in husk of cardamom.

Black Vulgate barbs and verbs were conjugated there with
    wired-up quips,
Hosannahs subjugated by the nomothetic tablature. It's
    writhing into future
Tense just now, elaborated by its wish to be, to match the pro
    quos to the quids.

Soldiers, camouflaged as hedges in the hedgeless bog, flit
    through the Islands of Carnmoon.
Their palms are blacked as if for fingerprinting, and the blue
    whites of their eyes
Illuminate the rubric of their Yellow Cards. They slant
    Egyptianly with dog and carbine.

One dog was witness, moaning through the scattered codices
    and hieroglyphs.
The alphabet of troops was learned by rote and entombed
    in the black aplomb
Of a police notebook: an abecedary sans eyes, sans teeth, sans
    everything, and sans serifs.

Ovid: *Metamorphoses*, XIII, 576–619

When Aurora heard about the fate of Hecuba, she didn't care.
She'd troubles of her own. Her own son Memnon, transfixed
    by Achilles'
Spear. He's set upon the pyre. They're going to burn him. She
    offers up a prayer
To Jove: commemorate him in some memorable way. The god
    nods, and says, well, yes.

Memnon's bonfire then collapsed in red and black, the charred
    beams hissed and flickered.
Greasy-thick smoke sputtered up and smutched Aurora's
Sky of rose and pearl. Soot and cinders flocked together
    in a bird-shaped aura
That becomes a bird. Like an opening fist, it creaks its wings.
    Squawks and flutters.

And then the squab engendered other birds innumerable. They
    wheeled
In pyrotechnics round the pyre. The Stukas, on the third
    approach, split
In two like Prods and Taigs. Scrabbed and pecked at one
    another. Sootflecks. Whirl-
Wind. Celtic loops and spirals chawed each other, fell down
    dead and splayed.

And every year from then to this, the Remember Memnon
    birds come back to re-enact
Their civil war. They revel in it, burning out each other. And
    that's a fact.

Opus Operandi

1

Fatima handed out twelve teaching modules of the 'empathy
  belly'
To the variously expectant fathers. Some were Paddy, and
  some were Billy.

Today's lesson was the concept 'Orange'. They parsed it into
  segments: some were kith,
And some were kin. They spat out the pips and learned to peel
  the pith.

Then the deep grammar of the handshake, the shibboleths
  of *aitch* and *haitch*:
It's a bit like tying knots, whether Gordian or sheepshank,
  clove or hitch.

In the half-dark of their lapidary parliament, you can just make
  out the shape
Of chimeras and minotaurs. Anthropomorphic goats are
  blethering to the demi-sheep.

It seems the gene-pool got contaminated. Everything was
  neither one thing nor the other;
So now they're trying to agree on a formula for a petition
  to the Author.

He's working overtime just now, dismembering a goose for
  goose-quills.
Tomorrow will be calfskin parchment, then the limitation
  clauses and the codicils.

2

Jerome imagined Babel with its laminates and overlapping
    tongues
And grooves, the secret theatre with its clamps and vices,
    pincers, tongs.

It's like an Ark or quinquereme he prised apart, to find
    the little oarsmen
At their benches. They looked somewhat surprised as he began
    the seminar

On hieroglyphs, using them as prime examples. They began
    to strain
Against the shackles of his language, his sentences, his full-
    stop and his chain.

He tapped the clinker-built antique and it disgorged
    its clichés.
He upturned it and it struggled like a turtle full of cogs
    and helices.

A school of clocks swarmed out from the Underwood's
    overturned undercarriage,
Full of alphabetical intentions, led astray by braggadocio
    and verbiage.

Typecast letters seethed on the carpet, trying to adopt
    its garbled Turkish
Convolutions. They were baffled by the script's *auctoritas*.

Bug-like, they attached themselves to the underside
    of the rug and hung there
Bat-like, colonized in non-pareils and minions, hugger-
    mugger.

3

Dr Moreau contemplated the Doormouse. It was wearing
    an elegant penguin
Suit. Moreau handed it his hat and went on in. He hoped
    the operetta would be sanguine.

Die Fledermaus was dressed up in his usual bat-suit.
    Crocodile-
Skin shoes. A cape for wings, and an absolutely Dracula-like

Dicky-bow. An as-yet-unbloodied bib. He bared his fangs
    as far back as the epiglottis
And began to aria an echolalia of aspirates and glottal stops.

Eventually he found a disguised Countess, and sunk an umlaut
    in her jugular.
He gargled in her tautonyms and phonemes, her Transyl-
    vanian corpuscular.

Her eyes drooled and grew as he imbibed her, as they glided
    through the mirror
And came out on the other side; then, clinging to each other,
    dimmed into tomorrow.

Moreau's yesterday was their tomorrow. His fossil study
    of the pterodactyl
Had led him to believe that man could fly, fuelled by iambics,
    alcohol, and dactyls.

Jerome drank the vision in. He put on his airman's snorkel
    and got into the bubble.
He gave the thumbs-up sign, and set the ultrasonic scan for
    Babel.

In his amphibian, the hero limped home in a grand Byronic Gesture; Fatima dismissed the Twelve; it was the end of therapy and embryonics.

Tak, Tak

for Piotr Sommer

It was on a crackly line from Sulejówek that I learned these first
    few words of Polish,
Meaning *Yes, Of course*, or *Is that so?* The static made me think
    perhaps a Police

Tap. It put me in mind of the Queen's own brand of blotting-
    paper, which is black,
So nobody can read the mirror image of Her private
    correspondence. *Tak?*

Black line, impenetrable-bakelite-black phone: viridian-
    beetle-black, the *tak, tak, tak*
As someone lifted or abandoned a receiver. He clicked
    the snooker cue into the rack;

Or *verbatim*, Vulgate-black like the inside of an unopened
    Bible —
*Cessaverunt aedificare civitatem. Et idcirco vocatum est ejus
    Babel.*

And in the bas-relief of Babel, serried regiments of Babylonian
    lions blink lazily
From lion-coloured tiles, imprinted on a ground of lapis lazuli.

The antique roar is deep-embedded, throttled in the Leo
    syrinx,
Eroded through with sand and microscopic bits of Sphinx.

Marduk brandished his articulated scorpion-tail.
   Nebuchadnezzar joined Him in the lapis monastery.
Blue glaze of tiles gazed round them, as they re-interpreted
   the Mystery.

They went from *A* to *B* by way of *Zed*, as far as they could
      figure it,
Which caused their ruination; they became a nation
   of abandoned ziggurats.

 ⁓

And it was on a crackly line from Sulejówek that I learned
      these lines of Polish,
Scrawled by Someone's moving finger in the urinously
   monumental palace —

Ceramic blue and white, glazed over by the whisperings
   of cisterns. It was underground,
Suddenly invaded by the *furioso*, off-course *tak, tak, tak*
   of trains relinquishing The Underground.

Latitude 38° S

1

Then they told the story of the satyr, who played the flute
    so brilliantly
In Phrygia, he tried to beat Apollo. Apollo won, of course; for
    extra measure, thought
He'd bring the satyr down another peg or two: stripped off
    his pelt, ungloving it from

Scalpwards down. And could he play then? With his fingertips
    all raw,
His everything all peeled and skinless? You saw the score
    of veins
Externalized, the palpitating circuits. The polythene-like
    arteries. The pulsing bag
Of guts you'd think might play a tune, if you could bring
    yourself to blow and squeeze it.

2

I flipped the tissue-paper and took in the Christian icon-
    ography.
Its daguerrotype-like, braille feel. The spiky instruments.
    The pincers.
The man who'd invented the saw had studied the anatomy
    of a
Fish's spine. From bronze he cut the teeth and tried them out
    on a boxwood tree.

That ancient boxwood flute of Greece will haunt him yet.
    Through olive groves
Its purple aura bleats through dark and sheep. The dozing
    shepherd
With his flute abandoned. Wrapped up in his mantle,
    independent, fast asleep.

3

I felt like the raw blob of a baby kangaroo that crawls the vertical
Fur of its mother, and falls eventually into the pouch, exhaustedly.
As Daedalus was herring-boning feathers into wings I was
The sticky, thumby wax with which he oozed the quills together.

I dropped my red blob on the letter-flap and sunk my
  suddenly-embodied
Thumb in it. The message inside was the obverse harp on an
  Irish ha'penny;
Bronze, unstrummable. It was there for someone else to flip.

4

Fletcher cut the nib of a quill with a Stanley knife and sliced
  the palp
Of his finger off. It quivered with its hinge of skin, then
  rivuletted
On the parchment. He didn't know where it was going. It
  obscured
The nice calligraphy that looked definitive: like a Proclamation
  or a Treaty.

In fact, he'd been trying to copy the *Inquit* page off the Book
Of Kells, as if it were a series of 'unquotes'. The way you'd
  disengage
The lashes of a feather, then try and put them back together.

5

The place was packed with expectant academics, but my
  marking slips
Had flittered away from the text. They'd been Rizla papers
  in another

Incarnation, when I'd rolled a smoke between my thumbs and
    fingers, teasing
Out the strands. I waffled on about the stet-detectors
    in the library

Basement, security requirements, conduits, wiring, laminates,
    and ducts.
Up above, the floors and stacks and filing systems, the elaborate
Machinery of books, where I materialized. I strummed their
    rigid spiny gamut.

6

There's a shelf of *Metamorphoses*. Commentaries. Lives. *The
    Mystery of Ovid's*
Exile. This is where the Phrygian mode returns, by way
    of an Australian stamp
That's slipped out from the covers, bearing the unlikely-
    looking lyre-shaped
Tail of the lyrebird. Printed in intaglio, it's playing a barcarole.

I think of it as clinker-built, Æolian, floating down the limpid
    river which —
Said Ovid's people — sprang from all the tears the country
    fauns and nymphs
And shepherds wept in Phrygia, as they mourned their friend
    the fettered satyr.

7

So they tell their stories, of the cruelty of gods and words
    and music.
The fledglings of the lyrebird's song. Its arrows. They stare into
The water — 'clearest in that Realme' — and see the fishes
    shingled,

Shivered, scalloped on the pebbles. The arrows of the wind
    upon the water,
Written on the water; rolled like smoke, the fluted breath that
    strolls
At midnight. They gaze into the stream's cold pastoral, seeing
Fossil ribs and saws embedded there, the fluteplayer's
    outstretched fingers.

The Albatross

after Baudelaire, 'L'Albatros'

Often, for a gag, the Jack Tars like to catch an albatross,
   Aviator
Of the high seas, who, following the navy, wants to be its
   Avatar.

But they slap him, Emperor of Blue, down on the salty planks.
   They taunt him.
Spat at, tripped up, his wings creak helplessly like oars, and
   haunt him.

This wingèd voyager, now bedraggled, ugly, awkward, how
   pathetic!
Someone pokes a pipe into his mouth, and someone else who
   mimics him is paralytic.

The Poet's like that Prince of Clouds, who soars above the
   archer and the hurricane: Great Auk
Brought down to earth, his gawky, gorgeous wings impede
   his walking.

The Ballad of HMS Belfast

On the first of April, *Belfast* disengaged her moorings, and
    sailed away
From old Belfast. Sealed orders held our destination,
    somewhere in the Briny Say.

Our crew of Jacks was aromatic with tobacco-twist and
    alcoholic
Reekings from the night before. Both Catestants and
    Protholics,

We were tarry-breeked and pig-tailed, and sailed beneath
    the White Ensign;
We loved each other nautically, though most landlubbers
    thought we were insane.

We were full-rigged like the *Beagle*, piston-driven like
    the *Enterprise*
Express; each system was a back-up for the other, auxiliarizing
    verse with prose.

Our engines ticked and tacked us up the Lough, cranks and
    link-pins, cross-rods
Working ninety to the dozen; our shrouds and ratlines rattled
    like a cross-roads

Dance, while swivels, hook blocks, cleats, and fiddles jigged
    their semi-colons
On the staves. We staggered up the rigging like a bunch
    of demi-golems,

Tipsy still, and dreamed of underdecks — state-rooms, crystal
    chandeliers,
And saloon bars — until we got to gulp the ozone; then we
    swayed like gondoliers

Above the aqua. We gazed at imperceptible horizons, where
    amethyst

Dims into blue, and pondered them again that night, before the
mast.

Some sang of Zanzibar and Montalban, and others of the lands
unascertained
On maps; we entertained the Phoenix and the Unicorn, till we
were grogged and concertina'ed.

We've been immersed, since then, in cruises to the Podes and
Antipodes;
The dolphin and the flying fish would chaperone us like
aquatic aunties

In their second, mermaid childhood, till we ourselves felt
neither fish nor flesh, but
Breathed through gills of rum and brandy. We'd flounder
on the randy decks like halibut.

Then our Captain would emerge to scold us from his three
days' incommunicado
And promenaded on the poop-deck, sashed and epauletted
like a grand Mikado

To bribe us with the Future: new Empires, Realms of Gold,
and precious ore
Unheard-of since the days of Homer: we'd boldly go where
none had gone before.

Ice to Archangel, tea to China, coals to Tyne: such would
be our cargo.
We'd confound the speculators' markets and their exchequered,
logical embargo.

Then were we like the *Nautilus*, that trawls the vast and purple
catacomb
For cloudy shipwrecks, settled in their off-the-beam,
intractable aplomb.

Electric denizens glide through the Pisan masts, flickering
their Pisces' *lumière*;
We regard them with a Cyclops eye, from our bathyscope
beneath *la mer*.

Scattered cutlery and dinner-services lie, hugger-mugger,
on the murky floor.
An empty deckchair yawns and undulates its awning like
a semaphore.

Our rising bubble then went *bloop, bloop* till it burst
the swaying windowpane;
Unfathomed from the cobalt deep, we breathed the broad
Pacific once again.

Kon-Tiki-like, we'd drift for days, abandoning ourselves
to all the elements,
Guided only by the aromatic coconut, till the wind brought
us the scent of lemons —

Then we'd disembark at Vallambroso or Gibraltar to explore
the bars;
Adorned in sequin-scales, we glimmered phosphorescently
like stars

That crowd innumerably in midnight harbours. O olive-dark
interior,
All splashed with salt and wine! Havana gloom within
the humidor!

The atmosphere dripped heavy with the oil of anchovies,
tobacco-smoke, and chaw;
We grew languorous with grass and opium and *kif*, the very
best of draw,

And sprawled in urinous piazzas; slept until the fog-horn
trump of Gabriel.

We woke, and rubbed our eyes, half-gargled still with
    braggadocio and garble.

And then the smell of docks and ropeworks. Horse-dung. The
    tolling of the Albert clock.
Its Pisan slant. The whirring of its ratchets. Then everything
    began to click:

I lay bound in iron chains, alone, my *aisling* gone, my sentence
    passed.
Grey Belfast dawn illuminated me, on board the prison ship
    Belfast.

FROM

OPERA ET CETERA

(1996)

for Manus, Gerard and Mary

Eesti

*I wandered homesick-lonely through that Saturday of silent
Tallinn*
*When a carillon impinged a thousand raining quavers on my
ear, tumbling*

*Dimly from immeasurable heights into imaginary brazen gong-
space, trembling*
*Dimpled in their puddled, rain-drop halo-pools, concentrically
assembling.*

*I glimpsed the far-off, weeping onion-domes. I was inveigled
towards the church*
*Through an aural labyrinth of streets until I sheltered in its
porch.*

I thumbed the warm brass worn thumb-scoop of the latch.
Tock. *I entered into bronze*
*Dark, shrines and niches lit by beeswax tapers and the sheen
of icons.*

*Their eyes and the holes in their hands were nailed into my
gaze,* quod erat demonstrandum:
*Digits poised and pointed towards their hearts. They are
beautiful Panjandrums*

*Invoked by murmuring and incense, hymns that father passes
on to father,*
The patina of faces under painted faces. They evoke another

*Time, where I am going with you, father, to first Mass. We
walked*
*The starry frozen pavement, holding hands to stop ourselves
from falling. There was no talk,*

*Nor need for it. Our incense-breath was words enough as we
approached the Gothic,*
Shivering in top-coats, on the verge of sliding off the metronomic

Azure-gradual dawn, as nave and transept summoned us with
  beaded, thumbed
And fingered whispering. Silk-tasselled missals. Rosaries.
  Statues stricken dumb

Beneath their rustling purple shrouds, as candles wavered in
  the holy smoke.
The mosaic chapel echoed with a clinking, chinking censer-
  music.

This red-letter day would not be written, had I not wandered
  through the land of Eesti.
I asked my father how he thought it went. He said to me in
  Irish, Listen: Éist.

LETTERS FROM THE ALPHABET

for Leon McAuley

A

Invisible to radar, *Stealth* glided through their retina of sweep
    and dot.
No bleep appeared to register its Alpha wing. The watchers
    were asleep, or not.

An Ampoule-bomb lay Ampere-wired-up in it, waiting for its
    primal sec-
Ond, like its embryonic *A* becoming *Be*. It wanted flash and
    Instamatic.

Its crew is snorkelled into oxygen, and getting high as kites. Its
    eagle eye
Zooms in and out across the infra-red. Its map is virtual reality:

O porcelain metropolis, inlaid with palaces of majuscule
    Baroque
And Trojan *equus* statues; fountains, spices, frozen music,
    gardens, oranges from Maroc!

I put my feet into the crew's shoes, my hands into their gloves,
    and felt the chill
Of borrowed armour. My *a priori* gauntlet twitched and hit the
    button: *Kill*.

B

I buzzed on to the screen invisibly, like *the second hypothetical Person or example*, like I was a tab of mescaline, heretical.

Like an aspirin dot I flitted through the frames of twenty-four-
a-second *noir*;
Through amber fog and urban streets I drove a minuscule of
scarab-armoured car.

I crawled, blue-bottle-green, across the drive-in windowpane.
I dithered on
Its glass. I was a sound like 78s or engines revving off,
diminuendo on.

Then His Master flipped the Twenties record over on its second
shellac back
And listened to the hiss of bumbled opera, revolving from the
archaic black.

Fluffy was the needle-dust. He scraped it with the callus of his
thumb.
He grooved it in again. The clockwork clucked and tutted. The
orchestra went dumb.

C

We have this plan because, if all else fails, we will rehearse its
    contemplated moves
Again, as argent beings of the horse-men are contingent on
    their hooves

Plunged into a fully-moonlit destination. It's the crescent
Elvis paring of the King's big toenail, like a snipped-off tense
    of present.

It's the belle who found it, hoovering on hands and knees
    behind the Cadillac-
Sized king bed-head. It's the overpowering smell of diapers
    and lilac.

So I stuck another candle in the purblind cataract of wax;
I pronounced the little *see* in *incense* as I said a prayer for *pax*.

I felt like the clunk of the coin as it dropped through the slot
    of the box: dark
Reliquary, from which I glimpsed the moon, the fingernail,
    the scimitar.

D

Whoever takes an arrow to this bow will really feel the slippery
  sap
Of the freshly-peeled salley-rod and the tensile spring of the
  future slap

Of the string, all imaginary targets riddled through with past
  plu-
Perfect hits and misses; the lucky shot of two birds skewered
  in the perfect blue.

All thumbs and fingers tweezerlike, I unbarbed his fletcher's
  herringbone,
Like I unstuck the hoops and loops of the Velcro Celtic
  Twilight Zone.

I unzipped it open, and so witnessed the opposing oars of
  quinquereme
And decked-out trireme, how they rowed majestically into
  Byzantium:

A shower of arrows welcomed them like needles to a magnet,
  like the whole
Assault of future into present, the way that the South attracts
  the North pole.

E

E is the teeth of the bit on the end of the shank of a key
Which Carter fits into the keyhole ankh of Tutankhamun's
    reliquary.

It's like he put the *ka* in *karaoke*, or his A-side met his doppel-
Gänger B and shook hands with himself, saying, *Sorry for your
    trouble.*

The stylus ticked and ticked like it was stuck in one groove of
    eternity. The disc-
Warp wobbled, river-dark and vinyl-shiny. Dust was in its
    Lethe dusk.

The noiseless E-type black Felucca came for him across the
    water.
It was automatic. The back door opened up. The other Carter
    sat beside his mater.

Carter joined Carter. It was a crux of matter. She handed him
    the hip flask.
He drank. *Where are we going, mater?* She drew her veil. She
    sealed his lips. *Don't ask.*

F

F stands for forceps, or rather a wrench with adjustable jaws.
  I rubbed
The milled-edge Zippo callus on my thumb, and felt that
  everything was dubbed:

The *mise en scène*, the plot, the lines, the jokey thumb-and-
  finger 'money' signs,
The way a lucifer flared up, illuminating dark conspirators'
  designs,

Who are mostly Trojan shadows, adumbrated in the lens of
  infra-red,
Or bugs reverberating with the buzz of what was overheard
  and said.

He switched it off. *This is the spanner in the works? The word?
  The horse's mouth?*
I said it was ineffable. I'd bought the dope from guys who
  knew its worth.

Hector looked into its larynx and agreed the tapes had been
  secreted.
The forceps president resigned. His oratorical expletives were
  deleted.

G

His hand had been clamped in a G-clamp to the Black &
Decker workbench.
Claw-head hammers, pincers, lost-head nails: they said it was
the work of *Untermensch*.

Meanwhile, G-men trawled the underworld with darkened
retinas and double-
Breasted trench coats. Shook hands at funerals, saying, *Sorry
for your trouble.*

Meanwhile, bugs proliferated all across the city: gnats, gads,
gargle-flies and gall-flies
Spawned from entomology of *G*; they laid their eggs in gigabits
in databanks and files of lies.

Meanwhile, they took in the buzz in the bar through the radio-
blue-bottle-lens,
As 'Black' told 'Decker' what had really *sotto voce* happened.
The bits they got made sense:

*Meanwhile, his hand has been clamped in the jaws of a vice to
the workbench.*
*X and Y are dissecting the best approach to the work. X picks
up a wrench.*

H

The Powers-that-Be decreed that from the — of ——
   the sausage rolls, for reasons
Of security, would be contracted to a different firm. They gave
   the prisoners no reasons.

The prisoners complained. We cannot reproduce his actual
   words here, since their spokesman is alleged
To be a sub-commander of a movement deemed to be illegal.

An actor spoke for him in almost-perfect lip-synch: *It's not the
   quality*
We're giving off about. Just that it seems they're getting smaller.
We're talking quantity.

His 'Belfast' accent wasn't West enough. Is the *H* in H-Block
   aitch or *haitch* ?
Does it matter? *What we have we hold? Our day will come?*
   Give or take an inch?

Well, give an inch and someone takes an effing mile. Every
   thing is in the ways
You say them. Like, the prison that we call Long Kesh is to the
   Powers-that-Be *The Maze*.

I

I is the vertical, the virtual reality. I tell it slant.
I am leaning into you to nudge you. I am Immanuel, and you
    are Kant.

I have been around so long, I have the memory of an elephant;
Although I think that I deserve some praise, I hope you're not
    a sycophant.

I am Sherlock Holmes and you are Watson. And if you're not,
    you are my client.
You are cocaine, I am the nose. You walk straight and narrow.
    I am deviant.

I be the bow and you be the fiddle. You will always be
    compliant.
I am the hinge of language, you its door. I think you under-
    stand my cant.

I am karaoke, you the guy with the mike. I am plainchant,
    you are descant.
When I think, I think I am. But when I have you, what do I
    want?

J

The calligraphic 1 of 19— is close to it, as I transcribed it in
the ring-
Bound half-morocco stamp album in my early teens. It's not
the *Ding*

An sich, for everything is *ad hoc*: what was I doing writing
this, all those aeons
Ago — *13 Nov 1941, Centenary of Announcement of
Discovery of Quaternions?*

Or, *5 Dec 1949, 100th Anniversary of J C Mangan's Death*
I took it out of catalogues, of course, the way that Aleph
leads to Beth.

Or, two musicians are cutting turf. *A* asks the other, *B*, for a
reel he half-
Remembers. The other takes his J-spade. In the bank of turf
he cuts a staff.

Then the notes. O'Keeffe was one of them. I think the other
was a Murph.
Of course the notes are not the tune. The tune itself they
called 'The Bank of Turf'.

K

K is the leader of the empty orchestra of karaoke.
K is the conductor on the wrong bus that you took today and
    landed you in yesterday

Where everything was skew. The rainbow colours were all
    out of kilter,
Like oil had leaked out all over the road from a dropped and
    broken philtre.

There, no one wanted to be recognized, and walked around in
    wrap-round
Polaroids. There was Semtex in the Maxwell House, and
    twenty shillings in the pound.

K came into it again, with the sidelong, armed stance of
    a Pharaoh.
He took my kopek, docked it with two holes, and told me it
    was time to go.

All the motor cars were black. I got behind the wheel of one.
    It worked OK.
Welder's sparks zipped from the trolley. The radio was playing
    karaoke.

L

I'm always sitting in the wrong corner of the room or in the
    wrong angle,
So that part of it is hidden from me always. Like you are in
    the ingle-

Nook and I am not, or you are upstairs ironing. I can nearly
    hear the hiss
As the Sunbeam hits the aromatic damp of cloth. It's like
    a breathy kiss,

The warm snog of a freshly-pressed cotton shirt I put on for
    the interview.
Like, I don't know who's upright, who is horizontal. But the
    L is me and you.

As the ironing board remembers it, it bears a burnt sienna
    scorch
Of memory. For all its *this* and *that* and *is* and *was* it carries
    a torch.

I felt like the girl in a hairdresser's, flicking backwards through
    an issue of *Elle*,
As it gets dark outside. A momentary train passed by with
    lighted windows on the El.

M

When *M* is amplified among the gongs and incense it becomes
    an *om*
Resounding in the saffron gloom. Smoke rises up as if from
    meerschaum.

It's a sort of unusual Vermeer, with pewter mugs and dogs
    drunk under
The table. Hanging from the ceiling is a caged *macaco* monkey,
    ponder-

Ing the digits of her basic American Sign Language for *nuts*.
    They bring
Her beer instead. Outside, on the icy mere, the families are
    skating.

It is beautiful to breathe the civic, clean, cold-stone-sober air
    after all that smoke,
To see the skated babies slithering around in Babygros under
    older folk,

While in the artist's backyard, drawers and bras and shirts
    and pinafores are fro-
Zen on a line; stiffened overnight, they're creaking to and fro.

N

I am a dash or a void. It's up to you to make me up. Wake up,
    You, the reader! I have some tales to tell you, and the night is
    but a pup.

I was Nemo once, a kind of Prospero. When I imbibed a bit
    of Bob,
My Nameless One became His Nibs, an eponymous proper
    Nabob.

Of course, my nadirs have been various: *Electric Ray the
    Numbfish*,
For example. He was really nesh. Those jokes about the actress
    and the Bish?

Still, I am a nebula: my lives illuminate their dazzling
    firmament;
Innumerable stars gaze down at you, as if they really meant.

You mean you smoked a bit of dope? The names of things
    have gone all AWOL?
Listen to me. Nemo is not a nobody. And *Nautilus* is not
    a narwhal.

O

The tea-cup stain on the white damask tablecloth was not
    quite perfect. Never-
Theless, I'd set my cup exactly on it, like it was a stain-
    remover.

I sipped the rim with palatable lip. I drank the steaming
    liquor up.
My granny then would read my future from the tea leaves'
    leavings in the cup.

I stared into enormous china O and saw its every centrifugal
    flaw,
The tiny bobbles glazed in its interior of Delphic oracle.
    I yawned

Into its incandescent blaze of vowel like the cool of dudes
    in black fedoras
At high noon; trigger-fingered, shadowless, they walked
    beneath sombreros.

They stopped me inadvertently and asked for my identity.
    I did not know
Until the mouth of a gun was pressed against my forehead,
    and I felt its O.

P

Let *p* be a logical palabra, opposing itself to *q*,
Thus: a Pyrex bowl is not the Christmas pudding steaming in
   it; *pea* is not a *cue*.

You can imagine the scene: Holmes and Watson, Pee and
   Queue, have disembarked
From the dog-cart. They have gone into the gloomy Hall.
   Inside is a time-warp.

The statues were all wrapped and swaddled. A log fire bubbles,
   spits and cracks;
The rattled Pyrex is an intermittent dither in the background.
   It's the crux

Of why Lord ——— was beaten to death in the billiard room
   with a snooker cue,
Of how he lay petrified, undiscovered until Boxing Day, of
   why the statue

Of himself had been removed. Holmes sucked his meerschaum.
   Puffs of shaggy smoke
Were intermittent as he said, *The proof is in the pudding*. Then
   Watson spoke:

Q

Q is useless without its *u* except in narcotic cases like qat.
You stick a bunch of leaves in your cheek and chew: it's an
    elaborate

Social ritual too. The French gunrunner Arthur Rimbaud is
    said to have par-
Taken of it, especially when he felt a little bit under par:

I am an ephemeral and not at all too-discontented citizen
Of a metropolis where hashish has pacified the wild assassin . . .

The dope, the grass, the speed, the smack, the junk, the weed,
    the blow, the crack
Illuminated him. His *O* was blue, his *I* was red, his *A* was
    black:

Then a little daughter put a squiggly *o* on top of Q to make
    a cat;
She looked at it, then put a pair of wings on it, and said, *That's*
    bat.

R

I love the shape of an *R*: its curve, its upright and its flying
  buttress.
When it is amplified it is the warble-thunder of a Flying
  Fortress.

I saw it crissed and crossed by ack-ack battery torches in the
  war theatre.
I'd assembled it from Airfix. High on glue, I was its aviator

Or the tiny gunner in the Perspex bubble swivel turret, trigger-
Fingered. Below us lay the woven Persian contoured abstract
  Paisley figures.

The sky was an unreachable ceiling, where Spitfire-flies
  buzzed lazily
Around the sun. The ocean was brown lino, imagined into
  lapis lazuli.

Sometimes I'd curl into an armchair continent and gaze at my
  creations:
Heinkel, Stuka, Messerschmitt, like words an orator resounds
  in empty amphitheatres.

S

The train slowed to a halt with a sigh like *Schweppes*. I see
    you now, Miranda,
Through the glassed-in cloudy steam of yesteryear. Do you
    remember, Miranda,

The archaic of when I met you first, that time when all
    the motor cars were black?
My heartache? I did not stand out from the crowd, I was
    a stand-in in a claque.

And you were Carmen, Miranda, you were Madama Butterfly.
    You were prox-
Opera, the roles that you insinuated into. And you knew you
    were it. Those parox-

Ysms of grief! Those swooning cadences! Those rolling eyes
    and *R*s! The spotlight
Kissed you as the claque went crazy, hurling flowers and lire
    at you. It was out of sight.

And I was there, Miranda, in the empty theatre, picking up
    your petals. I walked on plush.
I felt I was the silent *s* in *aisle*. And where were you, Miranda?
    Hush.

T

T is *tea*, which is what they used to call grass or dope or smoke
or blow.
It's the junction of minor and major roads. Its amber's neither
stop nor go.

It's the bitten amber mouthpiece of the unsmoked meerschaum
in the pipe-rack.
It's the tin of Mick McQuaid tobacco, the *psst* as you prise its
blue lid and the vac-

Uum escapes; it's the pungent, urgent, aromatic whiff of
nicotine.
I unblossomed it and rubbed it. I tamped it down into
the bowl. I lit it with a Mezzanine —

You remember those old-fashioned lucifers that came in
a yellow matchwood box?
The sulphur, bulbous, rose-bud red of their tips? You know,
the equinox

Of when we talked, and you were smoking Passing Clouds?
That *dim sum* place, whatever
It was called? The silly names we gave each other? No? 'The
Twelfth of Never'?

U

The urchin is a hedgehog, hence its corallaceous spines. It's
    made its *U*
Into a balled-up Erinacean *O* of Rimbaud green or blue,
    depending how you

See it. It is a self-protective device, like the independent eye
Of the chameleon, or the stripes on a zebra crossing. It's
    the amber eye

Of the traffic lights. It's a corona — not Havana, but
    the sound-horn
Of a daffodil, emitting blue stars from its halo crown of
    thorns.

If you drive over one it gets squashed, so you often come
    across
Them flattened, parchment-like on rural roads, especially in
    poems like this.

Their *Zeitgeist* is reverse, if *verse* means *the turn at the end
    of a furrow.*
They propagate themselves by not eating their own farrow.

V

To gouge out, as the eye with the thumb. To signal *Victory*,
    or *Up yours*.
To take a detour to the Vee-Dub rally, where Beetles droned
    around for hours.

To puff through the valley. To listen to the murmuring inversion
    of its stream
In mill wheels. To appreciate its Alpine air and rack-and-pinion
    antiquated steam

Train. To feel the locomotive cinder in your eye, to smell
    the coal-smoke.
To be soaring on the cranky ski-lift. To see the snow as white
    as coke.

Like an avalanche, infinitive comes into it and buries me
Diurnally beneath itself in wave of verb and rock and stone
    and tree.

I ended up embodied in the glacier: my frozen outstretched *I*
Stared out at me, like the *v* in *Balaklava*, all wool and mouth
    and eyes.

W

I call you Double You. You, you wouldn't know your *yin*
    from *yang*, nor one side
Of a doppelgänger baseball from the other. You think your
    curve's a slide.

Well, I'm willing to believe you, for I think I know ambivalence,
    the double
Vale of Tears where cataracts plunge into pools of logo-bubble.

The iridescent globe is frail: you blow it, then I touch it and
    it van-
Ishes, all its wobbly gliding gone, an instant after it began.

Or I see you in some gondola, slowly soaring, slung beneath
    your air balloon,
Your buoyant gas that takes my vision to the stratosphere,
    the hunter's moon

Which you're a drifting speck against, like something in my
    eye. I rubbed it
And I saw the constellation *W*; or Cassiopeia, as some
    astronomer has dubbed it.

X

I dipped my fingertips into the font of stone-cold, heavy
    water
And felt a volt of tingle up my spine. She asked what was
    the Ampère matter.

It froze me to the bone, her lapidary, *volte-face*-like Marian
    blue
Becoming flesh. She unstoned her mummy lips and spoke
    unlike a statue.

Of Nobel and of Molotov she drawled, of atom bombs and
    Coulomb
Interactions. She broached the suture of the future with
    aplomb.

She ripped the bandage off my eyes. Elastoplast, it made
    a Velcro
Kind of zip. What before was monochrome and mezzotint
    was Day-Glo.

She thrust my fontanelle into the font of stone-cold-sober
    imprimatur.
Stet. She crossed me out. She left me with the empty ampoule
    of Lourdes water.

Y

It's only now that I recall the catapult I cut from the ash tree,
How I bound with wire to the tangs of its fork an elastic strip
    snipped out free-

Hand from a long-deflated inner tube. Not to forget the
    leather thing-
Amajig for holding the stone or whatever. I guess you call it
    the sling.

But the sling is, I think, the elastic too. There must be
    a language of slang,
Some children's twang where words hit home, dit-dah,
    to the Auld Lang

Syne of what they were, and why. As if the marble shot had
    boomeranged
And got you right between the teeth, just to remind you it
    was no meringue.

Still, I try to bite into it. Then I did. Nothing happened.
    I thought on,
A thong of stretched elastic swish. Then I hit the recall button.

Z

The ultimate buzz is the sound of sleep or of bees, or
    the slalom I'll
Make through the dark pines of a little-known Alp on my
    snowmobile.

You will hear me fading and droning towards you from
    the valley next
To one, for I have miles to go: when I deliver all the letters,
    that's the text.

The canvas sack on my back reminds me I am in the archaic
    footprints
Of my postman father. I criss and cross the zig-zag precedents.

Snow is falling fast, my parallels already blurring on
    the mountainside,
But I am flying towards you through the stars on skis of
    Astroglide.

In the morning you will open up the envelope. You will get
    whatever
Message is inside. It is for all time. Its postmark is 'The Twelfth
    of Never'.

ET CETERA

Auditque Vocatus Apollo

We were climbing Parnassus. My guide kept asking me 'how
   a man can
Penetrate through the lyre's strings'. I tried to think of a silly
   answer, and a can-

Can dancer's disembodied legs sprang to mind, or the patent
   ostrich-egg-
Slicer of a harp. *Our mind*, he said, *is split*. Too true. Like he
   was Quee and I was Queg —

One of those guys. Orpheus. Apollo. Rilke. Ahab. Dick. And
   climbing Mount
Olympia is like that: enquiring for the whale that disappears
   beneath its fount-

Ain spray. You think you've reached the summit when another
   distant crest
Appears to challenge you. *Quo vadis?* Something like that.
   I asked if we could rest.

I don't know why I started this. One summer doesn't make
   a swallow.
Suddenly, the jangling of a lyre. I cried, *Who's there?* He says,
   It's me. Apollo.

Solvitur Ambulando

The verse he spoke was like the way he was: those bruised
    blue eyes, the gringo moustache
Flecked with grey, the flat-topped hat, the black cheroot with
    its eternal inch of ash.

The haiku scar in his knee only partly accounted for his bow-
    legged walk;
The rest was many horses, and the monosyllables in which he
    talked

Of nothing much. No one knew his age, nor dared to guess
    his provenance.
He waltzed in black alpaca jacket through the swing doors of
    The Last Chance;

He unbuttoned it and hitched it, showing his two hands full
    of Colts,
Then holstered them again, all this in the noon-struck space
    of two greased lightning bolts.

I was the barkeep under the counter, so I can tell you that
    the story of the song
Is true: *The inch of ash was first to go. The bar was seventeen
steps long.*

Vox et Praeterea Nihil

It sounded right and wet outside, if you believed the off-beat
    windscreen wiper
Swish-swash variously beyond the drawn blinds, the melancholic
    dim Scotch piper

Tuning-up noise of the far-off traffic jam. I was trying to
    decode
Whatever they'd rehearsed from arbitrary parps in Morris
    Minor mode.

Like the wedding-carillon of limousine and honking entourage,
    the notes
Are always different, though the tune remains the same;
    the 'quotes' are really 'unquotes',

As the campanologists — invariably — are out of synch on
    dangling long
Elastic ropes, though all are trying hard to tell their *Ding an
sich* from *dong.*

It's not so much the pull, I'm told, but letting go that matters,
    like Sagittarius
With eyes closed, aiming for the bull. That's why the same
    refrain is always various.

Graecum Est: Non Legitur

The fly made an audible syzygy as it dive-bombed through
    the dormer
And made a rendezvous with this, the page I'm writing on.
    It was its karma.

This tsetse was a Greek to me, making wishy-washy gestures
    with its hands
And feet. I made to brush it off, before it vaulted off into
    a handstand

Ceiling-corner of the room. It dithered over to the chandelier-
    flex
And buzzed around it upside down in a stunt-plane Camel
    helix.

The landing-page approached my craft as I began to think
    again. The candle guttered.
My enormous hand was writing on the wall. The words began
    to stutter

As the quill ran out. *Syzygy*: His dizzy Nibs was back.
    I took on board more ink.
He staggered horse-like towards the blue blot I'd just
    dropped. Then he began to drink.

Par Nobile Fratrum

I found George hiding in an angle of his language, studying
    the badge agenda.
'You have to see it through Estonian, with its eighteen cases
    and no gender.'

He had on a gold ring stickpin signifying Irish, plus
    the Esperanto green star.
He had had the Thoughts of Chairman Mao given to him by
    some Jolly Roving Tar

Who'd learned the lingo in Beijing when it was called Peking.
    For years they
Corresponded. George sent him missionary tracts and all
    the Good News hearsay.

Then the other died. I think his name was Chi or Chang.
    At any rate, the widow
Sent George Chang's green star. Or was it Eng? George
    stared out the window:

'If one parent is bilingual, it is absolutely crucial not to break
The language bond. I did once, and found it was extremely
    fragile. I have learned by my mistake.'

Jacta Est Alea

It was one of those puzzling necks of the wood where
    the South was in the North, the way
The double cross in a jigsaw loops into its matrix, like
    the border was a *clef*

With arbitrary teeth indented in it. Here, it cut clean across
    the plastic
Lounge of The Half-Way House; my heart lay in the Republic

While my head was in the Six, or so I was inclined. You know
    that drinker's
Angle, elbow-propped, knuckles to his brow like one of
    the Great Thinkers?

He's staring at my throat in the Power's mirror, debating
    whether
He should open up a lexicon with me: the price of beer or
    steers, the weather.

We end up talking about talk. We stagger on the frontier.
    He is pro. I am con.
Siamese-like, drunken, inextricable, we wade into the Rubicon.

Aquila Non Capit Muscas

Nor does the angel condescend to share our cheese and wine,
but trapezes
In a daddy-long-legs ceiling-angle: not aloof, not partizan,

But mindful of the sacrosanct occasion, *rouge* glugged from
the neck into our
Necks. The holey Emmental. The drooling Brie. The varicose
in Roquefort.

It's that picnic weather where we'd wandered from the cool
of the cathedral
As the Angelus grew dim behind us. We found this spot without
the city wall

And we were prostrate in a galaxy of buttercups. Principalities
and Powers
Of flies buzzed round us as we opened up the basket. We ate.
We dozed for hours.

I dreamt I stalked on yonder far-off blue plateau with bullets,
gun and beagle,
Abroad for days, enquiring for the Lesser-Spotted Fly-catching
Eagle.

Cave Quid Dicis, Quando, et Cui

You will recognize them by their Polaroids that make
    the span between their eyes
Immeasurable. Beware their digital watches; they are bugged
    with microscopic batteries.

Make sure you know your left from right and which side of
    the road you walk on.
If one stops beside you and invites you in, do not enter
    the pantechnicon.

You'd be participating in another's house removal. You could
    become
A part of the furniture, slumped in some old armchair. That
    would be unwelcome.

Welcome is the mat that does not spell itself. Words don't
    speak as loud as deeds,
Especially when the safety is off. Watch it if they write in
    screeds,

For everything you say is never lost, but hangs on in the starry
    void
In ghosted thumb-whorl spiral galaxies. Your fingerprints are
    everywhere. *Be paranoid.*

Labuntur et Imputantur

It was overcast. No hour at all was indicated by the gnomon.
With difficulty I made out the slogan, *Time and tide wait for
no man.*

I had been waiting for you, Daphne, underneath the dripping
laurels, near
The sundial glade where first we met. I felt like Hamlet on
the parapets of Elsinore,

Alerted to the ectoplasmic moment, when Luna rends her
shroud of cloud
And sails into a starry archipelago. Then your revenant
appeared and spake aloud:

*I am not who you think I am. For what we used to be is gone.
The moment's over,*
*Whatever years you thought we spent together. You don't
know the story. And moreover,*

You mistook the drinking-fountain for a sundial. I put my lips
to its whatever,
And with difficulty I made out the slogan, *Drink from me
and you shall live forever.*

Quod Erat Demonstrandum

She was putting together her Cinderella outfit in the usual
    sequin
Sequence she'd bought as pocket galaxies. The headless
    armless mannequin

Was on her mind from yesterday's shop window, as she
    approached her
Doppelgänger in the glass. Suddenly no sisters, as the
    pumpkin coached her

To the ball, drawn by the equine mice. The palace floor was
    disco-glitter stars
She polished, gliding in her fur-soled slippers. The Prince,
    just back from the wars —

Whatever wars they were — escorted her, unscarred by his
    experience.
'He'll make an extremely good king, whatever "being a good
    king" means',

The door-mouse whispered to me through his epaulette.
    'Things will evolve. You see,
I knew him as a frog, and she's no tailor's dummy. QED.'

Omne Vivum ex Ovo

Like seconds hatching out of minutes from a marbled Easter
   craquelure,
The embryonic beak is inside pecking, nodding like an
   agitated raconteur

Who tells strange tales of mocking-birds and ostriches,
   envelopes and sealing-wax
That warms your thumb impressed on it, the whorly
   autograph that no one asked

You for: the files contained the fingerprints already. Your
   identity was known
To Principalities and Powers by the guardian reconnaissance
   angel flown

In from God knows where, to hover at your shoulder. And
   the story is about
To break, however garbled, from whatever source, however
   roundabout:

Nothing comes from nothing, and we know that every living
   thing comes from an egg.
The prisoners are standing firm. *Delete.* The renegades will
   not renege.

OPERA

*for Marlyn Beck
and Philip Hammond*

Alpha

Our Camel squadron took off in an *A* formation so as not to be
Confused with a skein of geese. We raised our hands in signs
    of *V* for Victory

And honked our rubber bulb-horns in a parped anticipation
    of our recon-
Naissance. Goggled, snorkled, gauntletted, we ran the gamut
    of *sine qua non.*

Baron von Richthofen swooped out of the sun in his red
    Fokker tri-plane,
Writing cursive loops and firing hyphen-guns. Three of us
    made up a quatrain

Dog-fight, till our airy armies swam together like an alphabet
    in soup,
Or stars embroidered on the blue veil of Our Lady of
    Guadaloupe;

Remote among the clouds above, we sparred like Montagues
    and Capulets.
They shot blank verse at us. We answered with a shower of
    rhyming couplets.

Bravo

A major-domo barred the door, all false-teeth epaulettes and
    braid,
Uniform fire-engine red. I tipped a nod and wink to him,
    and left the rest unsaid.

He swept off his hat. The big vermilion heart of him engrossed
    his body, till its core
Became him, though he still maintained his hands, with which
    he opened up himself — cantor

Of the ventricles and arteries — and sang my entrance.
    I stepped into the atrium.
Above me, the sky of the mouth. Below, the floor of the
    tongue. Then, Byzantium

Of vocal chords and larynx. Bee-loud glades of business.
    Trojan horses
Whinnying, yet reined in by their constables. Words of
    retribution and remorse

Buzzed across the city. Video advertisements for peace. Talk
    about the futures
Of uninfibulated lips, how they would take a scissors to our
    sutures.

Charlie

'Oscar the Dog' had 'gone out for a walk', so it was up to
    Charlie to stand in.
Loaded Lüger by his side, he lay upon a gold-black bale of
    cannabin.

Since this was in the Southern hemisphere the stars were all
    the wrong way round.
There, water gurgled into unplugged plug-holes with an anti-
    clockwise sound.

The pre-War pick-up truck drove up and stopped and
    shuddered till its lights went off.
Car doors creaked. Men got out. The radio was playing
    Rimsky-Korsakov.

The twin volcanoes — Balalaika, Karaoke — rumbled
    grumpily.
Stars poured down in bucketsful. Chuck reacted rather
    jumpily,

And shot before shot at. He was cut into a thousand by
    a Triad
In a hemisemidemiquaver, while the wireless played
    Schéhérazade.

Delta

The blues they make down there come out of Mason jars and
    sinsemilla cigarettes,
The hollers of the whippoorwill, the clicking of cicadas'
    castanets.

They have sold their souls to many devils. They're the alcohol
    in syllabub.
They phrase their wired-up twelve-bar syllables with accents
    of Beelzebub.

Broken bottle-necks are popular for stabbing, or for sliding
    on steel strings.
A knife would do as well, as, hunched over his azure guitar,
    the blind man sings

Of doom and gloom, of snakes in rooms, the various uses of
    a coffee-spoon,
Of sugar, tea, and locks, and keys, how everything goes
    mostly to this tune:

Woke up this morning, blues were on my mind. I put
    the record on. It wouldn't go.
I pulled up the blind. The sunlight was too loud. I put on
    shades of indigo.

Echo

Baffled by the earphones stereoed into my labyrinthine
    intervention,
I cupped them to me for what seemed like an infinitely long
    span of attention.

Trying to skat along with it, my tongue got tied in knots —
    Thumb Knots, Marlin Spikes
And Sheepshanks — and it struck me that the jazz had been
    recorded on two mono mikes.

It struck me like a bell that Charlie Parker often parked his
    saxophone
In pawn-shops while he mained the 'horse' into his veins
    while sitting on the 'throne'.

The sax's bell was beaten gold, like some enormously
    expensive lavatory bowl;
Ensconced in Caesar's 'Little Palace', he shot the bop into
    the heart of Soul.

Diminishing thirteenths cascaded by. The faulty springs were
    tautened by elastic bands.
My fingers were all ears and thumbs. I listened to the span of
    Charlie Parker's hands.

Foxtrot

Syncopated like a panto horse's hooves when changing down
    from trot to walk,
I undertook the delicate negotiations, talking rot instead of
    talk.

I played my cards, and kept the guns below the table in their
    make-believe;
We were not playing with the full deck, since the Ace of
    Spades was up a sleeve.

I saw its black heart pinned to a barn door, drilled through by
    a single bullet
In some imaginary marksman showdown, commemorated in
    this ballad

Where the hero is your two-track hood, who robs to give the
    poor some *Tuck*.
Robin's Zeno's arrow hit the Zen-spot. The Sheriff thought it
    was a spot of luck.

Not so. It was on the cards. They didn't even spot the polka-
    dotted horse.
I shuffled hands and footsteps as the wireless played a minuet
    of Morse.

Golf

But really, Xanadu is something else, I was drawling at the
  nineteenth hole:
We were drinking 'Milk of Paradise'. The jukebox pumped
  us full of rock 'n' roll.

I gnawed my green olive to its stone and spat the pip into
  a fingerbowl,
Into the stubbed-out crisps and cigarette-butts. We spoke
  a rigmarole

Of lakes, putts, troughs, fairways, bunkers, greens, trees,
  hazards, tees, the principles
Of golf-ball aeronautics, the difference between the various
  dimples and pimples,

Bogeys, eagles, albatrosses. Alf complained about his handicap,
That he'd been born eighteen drinks ahead. He shakily
  unscrewed a hub-cap

Of cocaine. Suddenly, we both took short. He followed me
  into the Gents.
We snorted it like three Wise Men whose brains were shot
  with gold, and myrrh, and frankincense.

Hotel

I jiggled the jiggery-pokery key in the lock of Room 207.
The bed was unmade. Six Silk Cut butts in the ashtray. A
    Seventh Heaven

This was not. I crashed out anyway. The nylon-sheeted
    mirror aura of my pre-
Decessor wrapped me in its Turin shroud. Everything seemed
    redolent of Brie.

I dozed until the chambermaid's annunciation. She badly
    wanted to 'make
Up' my room. She simply had to change the unused towels.
    I got showered wide awake

And strolled down to the bar into the wall-to-wall, cool-
    filtered muzak.
It was packed with businessmen, gesticulating in their bookies'
    tic-tac.

Much later — six or so night-porter's miniatures beneath my
    belt — I loomed
Upstairs. Unlocked a door. A suit lay on the bed. Not mine.
    Whose was this room?

India

Larger than life, the Empress of India sat enthroned in
    the stoned foyer
Of the Royal Victoria Hospital. I was looking for the 'X-Ray

Department', and the Empress didn't have the answer, though
    she had a handy
Way with orb and sceptre. And her green bronze gaze did not
    include Mahatma Gandhi.

I stubbed out my cigarette-butt on her plinth and walked
    right through the heavy-duty
Blasted-polythene swing doors. There sat Mahatma in
    a nappy dhoti,

Holding his two arms at one arm's length apart, as if a mother
    wound a skein
Of wool on them. *You want to talk?* I answered, *Can you
bring me to Sinn Féin?*

The volunteer lay on the bed. His dark glasses still on. His
    Armalite beside.
I just about made out his skeleton. I tried to prise some peace
    from him. Then he died.

Juliet

I met him in Verona Market, fingering the oranges and the
  greens.
He seemed interested in local produce. We were into Kings
  and Queens.

I bought a bunch of thyme. He bought rue. Our hands
  touched. I was contagious to a Montague,
And the grand piazza was pizzaz with heraldry emblazoned
  in a rendezvous

Of factions: oriflammes and banderoles, standards, swallow-
  tails and bannerettes,
All fluttering with shamrocks, roses, thistles, high above
  the parapets

Where guzzling trumpeters tilted trumpets to their lips like
  bottles full of Coke
Or dope-imbibers gazing at the ceiling, relishing their sky-
  writing smoke.

We called the song they played 'Our Song'. I thought together
  we would be, perhaps.
But the Montagues put on their cloaks, the Capulets put on
  their caps.

Kilo

The *Sûreté* had guaranteed the operation would be covert,
   low-key,
Hunky-dory, under wraps, each detail okey-dokey as
   synecdoche;

You recognize the Citröen by its wheels? That's what I mean:
   the part
Denotes the smoky whole, especially when played by
   Humphrey Bogart.

A car-klaxon blew a foggy Gauloise note of pianissimo
   accordion bass
Droned out across an empty ballroom floor; the dancers
   were in hyperspace.

The foreign freighter creaked its starry moorings. Frogmen
   swam up through a galaxy,
Synchronized like watches. The rendezvous would happen in
   a Falls Road taxi.

Paki Black, Red Leb, and Acupulco Gold: dogs sniffed the
   aromatic rainbow.
Maigret blew a cloud of briar smoke and spoke: *Lo-Ki? Kilo?
   OK! KO!*

Lima

By covert way of bugs in bags, and cameras in mikes and
    lapel butt-
On holes, through scam and zoom in hotel rooms, the case
    was open and shut.

Editing it, we put a lot of jump cuts in. Otherwise, you
    would be watching
Paint dry, so to speak. With reconnaissance slice and splice,
    what we're about is catching

Someone in an icon act of giving or receiving. We move in
    on that,
Especially when llama trains descend the Andes and emerge
    in Laundromat.

We've got their bleats all taped, explaining to each other how
    the 'Lima beans'
Turn into rocks of crack or coke. If you ask me, they're a
    bunch of hashasheens.

From his black alpaca coat Inspector Morse took out his
    Baedeker and fount-
Ain pen. He unscrewed the mosaic tortoiseshell. Then he
    wrote this skewed account.

Mike

The trump or jew's harp is a great 'accomplishment', especially
    when fed
Into the jaws of a Mike, who twangs and amplifies it with his
    knucklehead.

It buzzes from the cavern of the mouth, and resonates its bit
    between the teeth:
Didgeridoo, parlante, intermezzo, pizzicato, it reminds me of
    Pádraig O'Keeffe,

Who used to phrase his fiddling of 'Rocking the Cradle' with
    a latch-key
Clenched between his non-existent dentures; more often than
    not, he'd be on the spree.

It sounded like a doll's cry, emanating from the sound-box in
    its back,
As you bed it down and watch its eyes roll shut into their
    cul-de-sac . . .

Just now I heard an elephant trump some two miles down the
    road from Belfast Zoo,
And it struck me with the force of logic, that a jaw's harp is a
    much superior kazoo.

November

Yellow fog converged implacably against the cold damp
    windowpane. Sherlock
Had just shot up and was fiddling with a languid fantasia on
    a Bartok

Theme. Watson tried to do the crossword, but the clues were
    fiendishly difficult.
The fog was Wordsmith's 'Daffodils', or saffron as the garments
    of a cult.

The great sleuth stuffed his big blow-pipe full of the aromatic
    acrid black shag mix
And puffed a fug across the upstairs room in Morse of nicotine
    and hieroglyphics.

Jaundice, mustard, amber was the smog. The doctor dug into
    a pot of Mrs Hudson's marmalade,
Perusing out the wisps of rind. He hummed a few bars of
    'The White Cockade'.

The detective measured up his hypodermic for a second jag,
    and found a vein.
Watson turned to the 'Agony' column. *I say, Holmes!* he said.
    But Holmes was entering Cockaigne.

Oscar

I held the figurine aloft, revelling in my actor's gravestone
    smile;
I boldly faced an orchestra of flash, as paparazzi packed
    the aisle.

I thanked everyone: all those who'd made it possible for me
    to be,
Down to the midwife and my grade-school teacher; my
    analyst; the Committee;

Not forgetting William Shakespeare, who had writ the script
    on vellum,
Nor the born anachronist director, who had set it in the *ante
    bellum* —

The way he saw it, Hamlet was a kind of Southern dude who
    chewed cheroots.
He wanted Vivien to play Ophelia Leigh. The uncle was a *putz*.

So, everybody, give a big hand to *All Our Yesterdays*, this
    apron weft
And warp of life we strut upon a brief while, till *All exeunt,
    stage left.*

Papa

Emerging from *La Traviata*, the Princess was surrounded by
     a pack of pap-
Arazzi, zapping her with antiquated flashbacks. In a chromium
     hub-cap

Of the limousine I saw it all reflected, the fisheye lens distort-
Ed by her Bambi look, her handbag's patent *noir*, her skirt of
     ultra-short.

Bespoke aides engaged each others' walkie-talkies, quacking
     to the marksmen on their roof-
Top high. The windows of the cabriolet whirred up their
     smoked-glass bulletproof.

A suddenly-jumped-up, up-braided major-domo opened the
     car door.
She jack-knifed herself in. There sat the other Princess with
     her mobile semaphore.

Hands in gloves, they yakked of *l'ancien règime*, when they
     had often asked what they would be,
And Papa'd snorted in his Mafioso way, *We'll see, Kay. Sara,
     we'll see.*

Quebec

We were to recognize each other by a known code of button-
hole
And that day's copy of *Le Monde*. They'd flown me straight
in from out of Charles de Gaulle.

But then, he doesn't show. It's two hours later and I'm
standing with the oxblood
Briefcase at my feet, attached to me by mental leash, when
this black hood

Appears from nowhere on his cool-dude blades. He's got
a yellow Walkman on.
He passes me this folded Rizla, then glides off like he was
made of teflon.

I opened it to see the message was in mirror, so I took it to
the Gents.
Briefcase at my feet, I peed, then read the paper's looking-
glass intelligence:

Names, numbers, sources, drachms, minims, scruples.
Methadone and moonstone.
I got into a booth to contact them, and opened up the book
of Anglophone.

Romeo

Romeo was not built in a day, not to speak of Romulus or
    Remus —
Cain and Abel — why Protestants are called Billy — and
    Catholics are Seamus.

It took a school lab labyrinth of history to produce these
    garbled notes
In careful fountain-pen. The arrowed maps of North and
    South, the essays filled with quotes:

The emptied jam-jar full of frogspawn, blooping on the
    window sill;
The tapioca of school meals; the sandwiches of squashed
    Norwegian sild;

John West in his sou'wester; Vesta matches in their yellow
    box, the Swift in blue;
The Orange lily and the Shamrock green; shades of Capulet
    and Montague —

It's all a tangled tagliatelle linguini Veronese that I'm trying
    to unravel
From its strands of DNA and language. Perhaps I need a
    spirit level.

Sierra

The Great American Bald-headed Reconnaissance Eagle
    dwindled in its spiral
High above, as we macheted through the Alpine jungle,
    speaking doggerel

To fool the bugs. The glades buzzed loud with sounds of
    killer bees and coffee-beans;
Squawk-box parrots flitted in and out like cunningly-
    constructed gold machines;

Cappuccino monkeys abounded in the trees, high on
    intravenous caffeine.
Ever upwards, through the chaparral, till we attained a peak
    in Darien,

We struggled. Then we rubbed our eyes: a whole Pacific-
    ful of stars lay spread
Beneath our feet. We tried to read its horoscope, till Cortez,
    like a pot-head,

Spoke out loud and bold: 'I hereby name the various dopes
    of Mexico —
Chimborazo, Cotopaxi, Acapulco and *Sierra del Fuego.*'

Tango

It's all long steps and pauses, where the woman uses the man
    as a crutch;
Ironically, it is unlikely that it comes from the Latin verb 'to
    touch'.

It is not the foxtrot nor the frug, still less the polka-dot or
    rigadoon;
Zapateado, tarantella, rhumba, mambo, allemande, it's not. It
    is a swoon

Of music, castanetted by the clicking silver buttons of
    the square bandoneon,
Which is its instrument, bass-and-treble toned like
    the chameleon:

Beautiful gloomy levity of camouflage, like when the girl's
    bolero
Creaks against the moustachioed starched shirt, as he struts
    and pansies in torero

Mode. He leans into her quickstep jitterbug. Her legs are all
    akimbo
As he shimmies lower, lower, entering the possibility of
    limbo.

Uniform

I've just put on this borrowed armour: second-hand cold
  freezes my bones — but
Really, I feel cool when putting on the company kit. It makes
  me want to strut.

It straightens up my spine. And you have to get the right fit:
  uniforms do not look good
Loose. Tight is what you want, like body-builders' biro veins
  of condom nude,

Statuesque in stances. Geared, belted, buckled, studded,
  epauletted, butt-
Oned-up, I touch my holster-flap and contemplate my
  regulation gun-butt.

It's matt black as the Ace of Spades. I feel I am its Jack; I am
  its suit,
Elaborate as Kama Sutra in my thigh-high, shiny, leather girl-
  shaped boots.

I like especially to guard the homes of opera stars and
  marchionesses,
To feel emblazoned on my serge the twin lightning zig-zags
  of the *SS.*

Victor

Before a trumpet clarion brings the panoply of war to mind,
the fine duet
Of cor anglais and flute takes on an Alpine clarity. The theme
is 'L'Alouette'.

Slowly, we get to the core of the matter: the Gruyère peasants
were revolting.
The Emperor wore iron gloves; theirs was a fragile dynasty
of Ming

And cuckoo clocks that kept calling at the wrong times; the
outspoken bird
Was wont to contradict its cogs and ratchets. *Tell*, not *Klee*,
was The Word.

Will took up his cross-bow like he would a fiddle. Tuned her
to the cuckoo —
'S two time-worn notes, and played 'La Marseillaise' until the
cockadoodledoo.

Then he put the first bolt in his belt. The second fitted to his
string. He shot.
In less time than it takes to tell he hit the pip; afterwards, he
overthrew the despot.

Whisky

Of how the life of water is distilled to liquid gold; how
    the water of
The Liffey becomes Guinness; how explosive cocktails take
    the name of Molotov;

How the wild mountain thyme blows around the blooming
    heather, and the perfumed smoke
Of poteen rises high into the azure sky; how turf is the
    conducive agent, and not coke;

How coke is crack, not heroin, nor smack; how marijuana is
    La Cucuracha,
Maryjane, or blow; how many States of mind there are in
    Appalachia;

How you turn into an insect overnight, or after-hours, from
    eating
Magic mushrooms; how the psilocybin got your brain and led
    to some 'Strange Meeting';

How the tongue gets twisted, how 'barbarian' is everyone who
    is not Greek;
How things are named by any other name except themselves,
    thereof I meant to speak.

X-Ray

The faces of the disappeared in blown-up, blurred wedding
    photographs;
The bombing of the Opera House; my lost wall map of
    Belfast; the pikestaffs

Spiked with rebels' decomposing heads; the long-since rotted
    hempen rope;
The razor-wire; the Confidential Telephone; the walls that
    talk of FUCK THE POPE;

The dragons' teeth; the look-out towers; the body politic
    surveillances;
The terrorist, the might-have-been of half-forgotten, long-
    abandoned chances:

All these are nothing to the blinks and blanks of night's
    inscrutable eternity, which stars
The Northern sky with camp fire palimpsests of ancient wars;

Or these are nothing to the cerebral activity of any one of us
    who sets in train
These zig-zags, or the brain-cells decomposing in some rebel
    brain.

Yankee

I doodled on my flute: some phrases from a half-remembered
    marching-tune étude
Which summoned up a panoply of orange and purple
    oriflammes, the rectitude

Of gleaming ceremonial swords and bowler-hatted cohorts,
    insignia of compasses
And pyramids, all shimmered in the July heat. I wore my
    new dark glasses'

Incognito, being from the other side. I kept my mouth shut,
    so to speak;
I feared my syllables of shibboleth would be interpreted as
    Greek.

Pickpocketlike, I mingled with the crowd and felt its huge
    identity
Of Ulster crush around me. I became a pocket of an absolute
    nonentity . . .

I ran into this guy last night who knew the tune. He played it
    on his Cordovox.
Its name? According to Melodeonman, 'The Battle of
    Appomattox'.

Zulu

At last, I remember the half-broomstick assegai with which
    I used to kill
Imaginary soldiers. I danced around them like a hound of
    Baskerville.

I faced the typecast phalanxes of English, shielded only by
    a dustbin-
Lid; sometimes, I'd *sotto voce* whistle 'The Dragoons of
    Inniskillin',

Till an Agincourt of arrows overwhelm'd me, shot by Milton,
    Keats and Shakespeare,
And I became a redskin, foraging behind the alphabetic
    frontier.

Pale boldface wagons drew themselves into a hurried O
    of barricade;
Mounted on my hobby-horse, I whooped so much, I had
    to take a slug of orangeade.

I loved its cold-jolt glug and fizz, tilted bottle upheld like
    a trumpet
To the sun; or so it might be, in the gargled doggerel of this
    dumb poet.

THE TWELFTH OF NEVER

(1998)

for Paula Meehan and Theo Dorgan

St Tib's Eve. *Never. A corruption of St Ubes. There is no such saint in the calendar as St Ubes, and therefore her eve falls on the 'Greek Kalends', neither before Christmas Day nor after it.*
    — Brewer's Dictionary of Phrase and Fable

Tib's Eve

There is a green hill far away, without a city wall,
Where cows have longer horns than any that we know;
Where daylight hours behold a moon of indigo,
And fairy cobblers operate without an awl.

There, ghostly galleons plough the shady Woods of True,
And schools of fishes fly among the spars and shrouds;
Rivers run uphill to spill into the starry clouds,
And beds of strawberries grow in the ocean blue.

This is the land of the green rose and the lion lily,
Ruled by Zeno's eternal tortoises and hares,
Where everything is metaphor and simile:

Somnambulists, we stumble through this paradise
From time to time, like words repeated in our prayers,
Or storytellers who convince themselves that truths are lies.

The Poppy Battle

She wore the bit of the poppy between her teeth
Like a wound or a salve, while the ritual salt
Was spilled. The Civic Guards performed a somersault,
Then cleared their throats in salvo as she laid the wreath.

The former puppet languished in an unmarked grave.
I'd read about it in a powder magazine.
Light glittered on a detail of the architrave
In military hospitals that reeked of gangrene.

Red crepe fake felt paper poppy petals with their dot
Of laudanum in everybody's buttonhole
Exuded empty perfumes of Forget-me-not.

I dreamed they had inhabited the planet Mars
With shell-shocked, pockmarked soldiers on a long parole:
Poppy the emblem of Peace and the Opium Wars.

The Tobacco and Salt Museum

The Professor drove me into smoggy Tokyo
From the far-off airport in her unmarked Datsun car.
Acid rain hissed down. She wore a green kimono.
Coded neon glimmered in a game of rouge et noir.

You took a certain exit out of Shinjuku,
And found the Russian Bar the smallest in the world.
You filled the seven seats and stuck to them like glue,
And drank a measured amplitude of vodka, swirled

In momentary clarity. I smoked the Peace
You'd given me as broken token of the city.
Tobacco leaved and tumbled like a Golden Fleece,

I peered into a microscope to see the salt
In pyramids of Ptolemaic eternity,
Whereupon we stopped at this short, temporary halt.

Adelaide Halt

There is a smell of coal and iron. Black lumps
Of ballast gleam between the rained-on parallels.
I hear a blast of steam. Smoke floats across the dumps.
The platform trembles with the far-off decibels

Emitted by the almost imminent express.
Seventeen long coaches shimmered by to Dublin:
A blur of diners, drinkers, couples playing chess.
A sudden interim, then nitroglycerin

Booms from the quarry where they're mining basalt.
A gable wall says FUCK THE POPE. I feel exposed,
As fragile as a model galleon carved from salt.

Overhead, the adenoidal honking of wild geese.
Adelaide? The name? A city or a girl, who knows?
There is a drink called Hope, a cigarette called Peace.

Salt of the Earth

'Nodding buds with four crumpled petals, showy red,
Orange or white flowers, exuding milky juice' —
Was this the Soldier, Red-rag, Cusk, or Poppy-head?
The Sleepy-pap, or Fire-flout, Ceasefire or Truce?

STC gazed at the page illuminated
By a candle as he sprinkled his thesaurus
Over it to see the words hallucinated
Into sentences. He felt like Saul at Tarsus.

Whole fields in Flanders and Kent are salted with them.
Good farmers do not like to see them in the corn,
And call them cankers, whose growth they find difficult
        to stem.

Children's eyes are dazzled by these Thunder-flowers;
Crumpled Coleridge took an age to be re-born —
Poppy the emblem of Death and the Special Powers.

Nine Hostages

I cut my hand off at the wrist and threw it at the shore.
The goblin spilled a bag of red gold in my lap.
He wore emerald boots and a bloody fine cap.
Let Erin remember the days of yore.

I'd been riding the piebald mushroom for some time,
Following the Admiral's vermilion cruise.
He wore a blue cocked hat and tattered tartan trews.
We were both implicated in the crime of rhyme.

Up in the deep blue like a red balloon I flew,
Following the sickle grin of Old Man Moon.
Gun-metal gunships sailed in through the foggy dew.

In Creggan churchyard last night I fell into a dream
Confronted by a red dragoon, a green gossoon.
The red hand played the harp with oars of quinquereme.

The Rising of the Moon

As down by the glenside I met an old colleen,
She stung me with the gaze of her nettle-green eyes.
She urged me to go out and revolutionize
Hibernia, and not to fear the guillotine.

She spread the madder red skirts of her liberty
About my head so I was disembodied.
I fell among the People of No Property,
Who gave me bread and salt, and pipes of fragrant weed.

The pale moon was rising above the green mountain,
The red sun declining beneath the blue sea,
When I saw her again by yon clear crystal fountain,

Where poppies, not potatoes, grew in contraband.
She said, *You might have loved me for eternity.*
I kissed her grass-green lips, and shook her bloodless hand.

The Rising Sun

As I was driven into smoky Tokyo
The yen declined again. It had been going down
All day against the buoyant Hibernian Pound.
Black rain descended like a harp arpeggio.

The Professor took me to a bonsai garden
To imbibe some thimblefuls of Japanese poteen.
We wandered through the forest of the books of Arden.
The number of their syllables was seventeen.

I met a maiden of Hiroshima who played
The hammer dulcimer like psychedelic rain.
The rising sun was hid behind a cloud of jade.

She sang to me of Fujiyama and of Zen,
Of yin and yang, and politics, and crack cocaine,
And Plato's caverns, which are measureless to men.

Fairground Music

I plunged my head into the laudanum-black pall
And gazed into the crystal lens of yesteryear:
A tang of Woodbine cigarettes and Phoenix beer,
Of bread and salt and cabbages, held me in thrall.

I knew it was a faery trick to take me from
The imminent republic of the future,
For the ballot-box contained a condom time-bomb,
And the red hand still remained without a suture.

I plunged my head into the lion's open jaws
And took the Ghost Train to Imperial Japan.
The tiny cabin smelt of alcohol and gauze.

Then everything was over in about a sec:
I glimpsed a skeleton or two, a Caliban;
I felt a damp hand fondle the nape of my neck.

Green Tea

I saw a magnified red dot on a white field.
I saw the terraces and pyramids of salt.
I saw a towering mushroom cloud of cobalt.
I made sure my papers had been signed and sealed.

The writing everywhere on walls illegible to me.
The faces in the crowds unrecognizable.
The labyrinth to which I hadn't got the key.
Investing in the Zen is inadvisable.

Zeno made a gesture with his disembodied hand.
A landscape wafted into being from his brush.
The flow of water is represented by sand.

If anything, I think I drank too much green tea.
The snows of Fujiyama had all turned to slush.
Hibernia beckoned from across the blue sea.

Sod of Death

'Tis well I remember the old Kerry dances
Under Astarte's ghostly light at the cross,
Where we'd jig each other's partners into trances
Fuelled by Japanese poteen and sticks of joss.

Then the Pooka would appear, to lead us o'er the moss
Into the realm of the Metamorphoses,
Whose shapes are as innumerable as Chaos
Ever burgeoning with versions of our species.

I was the wolf. She was the bear. I was the fly.
She was the salmon. I was the pig. She was the mud.
Then Cynthia herself joined in our revelry —

Her anorexic face, the craters of her eyes!
We saw that all Hibernia was drained of blood.
So we went with the flow, and entered Paradise.

Lir

Next to Poppy in the Herbal is Potato
Whose stalks and leaves and berries, like the Nightshades,
Are narcotic as the hemlock brewed by Plato;
Mashed-up, they make a pottage fit for renegades.

The tubers are not poisonous because they grow
Uninfluenced by light, which toxins seem to need.
Why, then, do I wander like a scarecrow
Blown by the autumn wind, like dandelion seed?

Our green fields have been sown with these Lion's Teeth,
Whose broken stems exude a bitter milky juice;
All Ireland has been turned into a blasted heath,

And coffins sail off daily for Amerikay,
As I do now, becoming this wild phantom goose,
Defeated by the wolfbane dawning into day.

Wolf Hill

Bring me my bow, my arrows tipped with aconite,
And I'll negotiate the border mountains high,
Protected by my sword and shield of samurai,
Which gleam beneath the wintry skies like selenite.

The moon shines like a globe of solid crystal salt,
A ghostly galleon ploughing through the tattered clouds;
I stalk the gloomy bog below which fog enshrouds,
And gird my loins that I might suffer no assault.

The haughty moon maintains her foreign silver coin,
And I have tracked the rough beast to his last retreat.
I slit him open from the gullet to the groin:

Therein lay little Erin, like one of the Undead,
A pair of bloody dancing shoes upon her feet,
Her gown a shamrock green, her cloak a poppy red.

Belladonna

I paid my passage with a coin of Spanish gold
And soared across the ocean to the promised shore,
Wherein I met a Caliban of ancient mould.
His eye was blue, his face was pocked like old Roquefort.

His running sores were patched with rags of Rebel grey,
His Phoenix talons bitten to their scaly quick;
He told me he had soldiered in the late affray
As double agent for the imminent republic.

Chameleon, he'd flitted back and forth between
Their shifting lines, being paid by some, by others not.
The pupil of his eye was bright with atropine;

He stared at me and asked, *O Death, where is thy sting?*
I answered, 'They have shot you with Forget-me-not,
And that is why you're neither man, nor beast, nor thing.'

Wallop the Spot

One morning in May as I carelessly did stray
Across the wild Slieve Gallon braes, I met with Captain Rock,
Who did salute me on the banks of sweet Lough Neagh.
He wore a wig, stilettos, and a poppy frock.

He opened up his Chinese box and offered me
A pinch of salt, some rare tobacco from his powder-horn.
Then he engaged me with the future history
Of Ireland free, where beauties waited to be born.

He wore a spot upon his cheek, an earring in his nose.
The pupil of his eye was black with laudanum.
The last I seen of him was hanging on a gallows

At a crossroads, with two other deviant brutes.
The next I heard of him, his skin was someone's drum,
His tibiae and humeri were Orange flutes.

The Lily Rally

The Papists stole me then and tried to make me play
Their Fenian music, but my loyal embouchure
Resisted them, and all the Melodies of Moore.
I threw their Roman legions into disarray.

My cardinal inquisitors were robed in red.
They touched their foxglove fingers to my breathless holes.
They murmured prayers for the saving of their souls.
They read their Riot Act at me from A to Z.

So then they built a bonefire for to burn me in,
Of broom, and brush, and willow, and potato flowers.
They bore me towards it on a purple palanquin.

As the flames roared around me they heard a strange noise
Through all their chanting from their scarlet Book of Hours —
'Twas my ould self still whistlin' 'The Protestant Boys'.

The Irish Exile Michael Hinds

Your air mail had a border like the Tricolor.
I slit it open with a knife of Damask steel,
As it exuded perfumes of a humidor
Replete with odorous tobacco and smoked eel.

Included was a Russian doll, a crystal rock
Of salt, a miniature of Japanese poteen,
A pack of cigarettes called Peace, a single sock,
A plan of ancient Tokyo, a sprig of green.

I took it I'd to meet you in the Vodka Bar
Beneath the rising moon of Gorgonzola cheese,
From whence you'd drive me in your toy Toyota car

Through intersections where the stop and go are garbled,
Where fluent crowds converge in milling Japanese,
In sequences of poppy, amber, emerald.

Wrap the Green Flag Round Me

At the Presidential ordination, Erin
Wore a silver wolfskin coat and gloves of kid.
Her bodyguard, a bearskin. All the knights were kilted,
The doublebreasted-suited dignatories foreign.

Above, the moon maintained her realm of a sixpence.
Dim bronze temple gongs resounded through the noon.
The courtiers performed a stately rigadoon,
While wheeling dealers made a ritual obeisance.

I felt the embouchure of trumpets in my bones,
The Sumo drumming palpable upon my skin,
The rattling of the chains below, and martyrs' groans.

I donned the magic mantle of the green gossoon
To spread myself into a fifth dimension.
I pocketed their Starry Plough, their pockmarked moon.

Dark Rosaleen

The songlines were proceeding at a daily pace
Like invisible barbed wire or whitethorn fences,
Running through the Monday of the market-place,
Where fellows mongered ballads under false pretences.

The port was packed with mountebanks and picketpocks,
Highwaymen on holiday, and soldiers on the spree.
Female sailors festered in the feisty docks,
And ragged rascals played the Game without a Referee.

I caught one by his buttonhole, and asked him plain
And proud, if ever dear old Ireland would be free,
Or would our forces be forever split in twain?

Could we expect the promised help from Papal Spain?
He caught my eye, and answered me quite candidly,
The only freedom that you'll find is in the dead domain.

The Wind that Shakes the Barley

Once down by the Liberties I met with Captain Wilde,
Resplendent in a dogskin coat and rabbit stole.
He wore a green carnation in his buttonhole,
And looked the very image of a fairy child.

I took him in my arms and set him in the lap
Of my kimono, all the better for to see him,
And I kissed his bonsai hands, I felt his wooden limb.
Then I undid myself, and offered him my pap.

He peeped at me from underneath his bicorn hat,
And murmured, with the voice of a ventriloquist,
Just read my lips: the Eagle does not hunt the Gnat.

He bit the good side of my neck. I snapped at him
With quadrupedal scissors of the Tailor's Twist,
And made of him a disembodied interim.

The Tailor's Twist

It was clear the cluricaune had taken my bitch
Again last night for a ride, from her tattered pelt
And her poor ribs ranged in patches like a bacon flitch.
He did not reckon on the cunning of the Celt.

I stitched her back together with a spider's thread
And, with my foxglove thimble, gave her magic powers.
Next night, I laid out dribs of poteen, salt, and bread.
The cluricaune came for them in the early hours.

I watched him feed his face with food and salt and drink
Till, satisfied, he tried to jump my canine chum.
She twitched, and held him fast, and he began to shrink.

Then I put on my jacket of the hunting pink.
I penned his neck between my finger and my thumb,
And stuck the bastard's neb into a well of ink.

Catmint Tea

The cat and I are quite alike, these winter nights:
I consult thesauruses; he forages for mice.
He prowls the darkest corners, while I throw the dice
Of rhyme, and rummage through the OED's delights.

He's all ears and eyes and whiskery antennae
Bristling with the whispered broadcast of the stars,
And I have cruised the ocean of a thousand bars,
And trawled a thousand entries at the dawn of day.

I plucked another goose-quill from the living wing
And opened up my knife, while Cat unsheathed his claws.
Our wild imaginations started to take wing.

We rolled in serendipity upon the mat.
I forged a chapter of the Universal Laws.
Then he became the man, and I became the cat.

Spot the Wallop

The cluricaune, you must know, is a leprechaun
Who's taken to the drink. He also likes the pipe.
You'll never guess his proper name: he's called Anon.
You could mistake him for a naughty guttersnipe.

That's why the bottle of poteen you thought was still
Half-full is always empty in the blight of day.
And why do you think there's salt in the pepper mill?
And why does the morning milk turn sour in your tay?

The cluricaune is wont to get completely pissed,
To stagger through your cat-flap like a cowboy shootist,
Of whose prankish misdemeanours I could make a list.

And it's ding, dong, bell, poor pussy's in the well,
The cluricaune is prinking in the dingly dell:
Scattered petals of the starlit Scarlet Pimpernel.

Let Erin Remember

Today we are celebrating President's Day.
Hence, the rows and the ructions at Lanigan's Ball
Are quite traditional. They dance an Irish Hay.
The gentlemen wear uniforms of tattersall.

The ladies favour emerald and cyanide,
A single glowing bead of amber at their throats.
They orchestrate their movements in a double stride,
One poppy shoe on show beneath their petticoats.

Each glitterata has a snuff-box in her garter,
Each dandiprat a twist of salt beneath his wig.
This night these will be strong media of barter

When they lie down amongst the barley and the rye,
Beneath the moon, to play a round of thimblerig,
By which gambit they resuscitate the ambered fly.

Planxty Miss Dickinson

I've seen a narrow fellow tumbling through the rye —
You could mistake him for a whiskery ear
Of it, such is his camouflage of elfin gear;
And his whispery voice is like a mimicry.

Sometimes I see him casting a gossamer thread
To catch a butterfly and hitch a ride on it,
To waltz about above me like a drunken Zed,
Then vanish in a twinkling from my ambit.

And the drift of his speech is sometimes difficult to get,
Being wavery like blown grass, but I know some things
About its complicated phatic etiquette.

For instance, they've no way of saying yes, nor no,
For all their words and deeds are borne on viewless wings
Into the windblown ambiguity of snow.

The White Devil

I followed his vanishing footprints through the snow,
Beneath the moon, among the calligraphic trees.
Far-off silver temple bells were tinkling in the breeze.
Silhouetted on a branch was one black crow.

I offered it a pinch of salt to make it talk.
It told me of the wolfish fellow's habitat.
I tracked him to Slieve Gullion, just above Dundalk,
And called on him to make his requiescat.

He sprang a curse, and snarled his lupine length at me.
I sliced him four times with my sword of samurai,
And made of him a quadrupedal amputee.

Then I consoled him, saying, *All things have their span.*
He yawned his maw at me. Out flew a butterfly.
Dying, he became the head and torso of a man.

1798

I met her in the garden where the poppies grow,
Quite over-canopied with luscious woodbine,
And her cheeks were like roses, or blood dropped on snow;
Her pallid lips were red with Papal Spanish wine.

Lulled in these wild flowers, with dance and delight,
I took my opportunity, and grasped her hand.
She then disclosed the eyelids of her second sight,
And prophesied that I'd forsake my native land.

Before I could protest she put her mouth to mine
And sucked the broken English from my Gaelic tongue.
She wound me in her briary arms of eglantine.

Two centuries have gone, yet she and I abide
Like emblems of a rebel song no longer sung,
Or snowy blossoms drifting down the mountainside.

1998

In this ceremony the President will eat the host,
Which represents the transubstantiated moon.
Then Her Nibs'll christen the Montgolfier balloon:
Traditionally, it's always called *The Holy Ghost*.

She steps on board the gondola, and borne high
Above the madding crowd, she showers them with beads
Of mistletoe and amber, opium poppy seeds,
And little petalled parasols of madder dye.

Then all of us imbibe the haemoglobin wine
In dribbled sips of intravenous sacrament,
Where we combine in knowing what is yours is mine.

This is why we can commune so easily, I think:
Already, you've partaken of our President.
You ate her bread. You licked her salt. You drank her drink.

Drops of Brandy

I bumped into the fairy host last Hallowe'en.
I'd taken one or quite a few drinks for the road,
And so I thought I'd take the short cut through Glenkeen.
A mist surrounded me. The light was blue as woad.

Then a disembodied hand lifted the thin veil
That separates us, and I saw their dancing throng
Of thousands, all arrayed in colours of the Gael,
Like figurines of jade. I did not stay too long,

Or maybe I abided a Gargantuan age;
But I remember being fed with cowslip cream,
And amber berries of a Lilliputian gauge

That shrank me to a blip in their crystal fishbowl.
Then they loomed through glass like Gullivers. It was no dream:
I swear to God, they left me home through the keyhole.

Mountain Dew

For everything can be contained in anything.
For every drop of rain that falls, there blows a flower.
For there are more then sixty seconds in an hour.
The long and short of it is like a piece of string.

For every line you write are countless thousands not.
For to travel is to go from where you've been.
For the first time that you read these words is sight unseen.
The knotted cord is implicated in the plot.

For fairies are not often seen without their nook.
For every hempen rope is wound of many strands.
For all the lies you told are entered in a book.

For dragons are implicit in the dragonfly.
The hourglass is complicit with its sifting sands.
For all the prophets claim, the end is never nigh.

Saké

The female puppet is legless. To make her walk
You must manipulate the hem of her garment.
Her hair is black as night, her face white as chalk.
Beware: she can turn suddenly violent.

When she is not active you must rest her on her stand.
Don't even think of throwing her down on the bed,
For you're the tool, and she the doppelgänger hand.
To know her inner self will stand you in good stead.

Let the orbit of her eye accommodate you;
Put yourself between her poppy lips to make her speak;
Let her every practised action be your debut.

For once I knew a character like you, my friend,
Who took his puppet drinking seven days a week.
A fortnight past, she took control. You know the end.

Who Ploughed the Lowlands Low

I know a headless corpse, a disembodied hand,
The mode of automatic writing on the wall,
A Cheshire cat, the Banshee's awful caterwaul,
The merrows and the mermaids basking by the strand.

One day, one became a mortal for a spell,
Entranced by a boy she saw fishing off a rock.
She followed him, abandoning her scaly frock,
Although to her the roads glowed like the flags of hell:

For every step she took she felt she walked on knives;
And everywhere her footstep fell the poppies grew.
Her ears were tortured by the keening of fishwives.

She haunted him for years within his rustic bound.
One day he went to sea. He fell into the blue.
She plunged in after him and, saving him, she drowned.

The Hag with the Money

It could be one of those lonesome bits of the road
Where water seems to run uphill, or a blue dell,
Or a pool where a prince might turn into a toad,
Where harebells grow in winter for an untold spell.

Or when you hear the weeping of a stolen child,
Or when the mountain shimmers like a purple cloud,
You hear the pourings of the waters and the wild,
Like chattering of fairies in a windswept crowd —

It's there you might well see a pair of cut-off feet
Come twinkling through the forest in their poppy shoes,
Unstoppable as driven rain or snow or sleet.

I know a woman was away for seven years.
When she returned it seemed she'd little left to lose:
They'd drawn her teeth and danced the toes off her. They'd
    docked her ears.

Digitalis

Since I got my fingers stuck in a Witch's Glove
One night my writing hasn't been the same, I fear;
And something's always whispering within my ear
About the murky underworld of goblin love.

That's when Mr Stump takes over — he who writes these lines
In automatic carabine — and I succumb
To all his left-hand fantasies of fife and drum,
Where soldiers sometimes use their guns as concubines.

Or often he describes a land across the sea
Where all the men are uniformed in sailor blue —
His conversation's like the stumbling of a bee

Within a Fairy's Thimble — blushful Hippocrene —
And then he starts this cuckoo's rumour about you:
That's when I clamp him in my paper-guillotine.

Lord Gregory

There's muskets in the thatch, and pikestaffs in the hay,
And shot in butter barrels buried in the bog,
Extrapolated powder in the tin for tay;
And everything is wrapped in blue-as-gunsmoke fog.

It's that dewy blue of your mantle, Mavourneen,
Cobalt banner of the yet-to-be republic
Which enraptures us, as numerous as grass is green:
We are your unseen agents, growing thin and thick

In every patch of field, and briar, and the mireland.
Creeping through the thistled fields, we are the weed,
That disrespected emblem of old Ireland.

'Three persons grow from but one stalk,' so said St Pat,
'And you will propagate yourselves in thought and deed,
And what will you be then, O Peasant, O Aristocrat?'

The Blue Shamrock

Now they rehearse their ancient music on the harp,
And blow blue music from the bonsai bamboo flute,
The President is talking to the ancient carp
Which swims in green gloom in the Pisces Institute.

Like a ventriloquist she reads its silent lip,
Interpreting the gnomic bubbles of its word,
Which bloop like quavers of a psychedelic trip,
Or nimble foldings of the origami bird.

As a surface of the pool begins to ripple
She undoes the couplets of her blue kimono,
And as King Fish comes up she offers him her nipple.

This, Dear Sir, is when the spirit enters matter
Or, as a master summarized it long ago,
Old pond: a frog jumps in: the sound of water.

Sayers, or, Both Saw Wonders

We lay down in the Forest of Forget-me-not;
You slept, and from your open lips an Admiral
Emerged as if out for a daily ramble,
Quivering its wings as vivid as a Rorschach blot.

It crept down you, over a stream and through the rye
Into an open socket of an equine skull,
To wander for a lull within that Trojan hull,
Before it crawled out from the other empty eye.

Then it returned into your mouth the way it went.
You woke, and told me of your labyrinthine dream:
The highway — river — palace — rooms of vast extent —

'It looks as if the soul's a butterfly,' I said,
'Yet many who've elaborated on this theme
Have never seen the inside of a horse's head.'

Dancers

The Charlemont Arms was packed with twisters, quacks,
    and sailors,
Fawney-riggers, saltimbancos, jerks and twangmen,
Hog-rubbers, slobber-swingers, double-jointed men,
And knackered horses flogged by croppy tinker tailors.

Come night, they congregate to dance a langolee
Above the horse's skull below the flagstoned floor,
With nugging-dresses, quiffs, and other sorts of whore,
And pockmarked dandies wielding canes of ivory.

I met a Captain Cutter, as he styled himself,
As I went out again to plough the Rocks of Bawn.
He buttonholed my earlobe like a vampish elf,

And asked me would I ride the headless horse at dawn.
I shook him off, and hid myself within a stook
Of corn. He followed and took out his reaping-hook.

Clonmel Jail

My name is Captain Nicholas Hanley Caravat.
I'm famous throughout Ireland for my blunderbuss,
My brace of pistols, and my sword, for I'm a democrat:
These are my fellows of the agriculturus.

Who disregards us will be given warnings three:
The digging of a grave, the killing of a sheep,
The burning of a house. For all men are born free:
A naked fact that's feared by landlords, when they sleep.

Every dark or so, we'd come out in our women's clothes,
And work away until the crowing of the cock,
Till one of you betrayed me for an English rose.

And now they are about to hang me like a rat,
I blow a kiss, and throw to them my silken stock,
And help them fit me with their hempen caravat.

Milk of Paradise

I fell to drinking with a Doctor Tom de Quincey,
Who claimed he'd found the one and true catholicon
For palsy, gout, apoplexy, rabies, quinsy,
And every other ailment in the lexicon.

His compatriot, a Saxon rhymer of renown,
Had sipped this elixir to summon up the Muse,
Who blew him poetry like floating thistledown,
Spontaneous as the dandelion's milky ooze.

He drew an azure naggin from his shanavest,
And he exchanged it for my Irish two-pound note.
I downed it in three slugs of rhythmic anapaest,

And this is why you must beware my flashing eyes,
My floating hair, my pupils black as creosote,
With which I saw through Doctor Ecstasy's disguise.

Planxty Patrick Connors

The buttons of his vest were buds of opium,
The vest itself of tattered Oriental silk,
Embroidered with a riot of geranium
And emerald, and curlicues of Dragon's Milk.

Its pockets, fobs and slits were manifold capacious,
Holding in their depths the many sundry item:
Salt, tobacco, ballads, manifestos spacious,
Guns, pens, flint, steel, bone dice, coin ad infinitum.

His wounds were ponceau red, his face as white as milk.
He lay expiring on the kitchen floor, for we
Had tracked him to his lair, like others of his ilk.

He had a crossbow bolt embedded in each limb.
With claymores broad we made of him an amputee.
We decapitated him. Then we divested him.

Crack

This Fortnight Market last I fell in with these Keogh boys
Who plied me liberally with brandywine and snuff.
They showed me upstairs and took off my corduroys,
And dressed me in a raffish crinoline and ruff.

Next they walked me downstairs to their Captain's wake.
He lay trussed in his shanavest and caravat,
His sword and blunderbuss beside. He looked like William
    Blake.
Thirteen candles signified the sabbat.

The Locals then produced a rock of crystallite,
And short clay pipes, and crumbled leaves of Widow's Weed,
With which we chased the burning tiger through the night.

Come dawn, they asked me to fulfil my woman's role.
I breathed smoke into him, and said the Backwards Creed.
His eyes sprang open, and I saw his very soul.

Jarrow

I found him lying where they'd raked him with a harrow.
I kissed his wounds and thrust my bloodied lips to his
To breathe life into him, that we might see tomorrow.
I felt him pulsing as his *was* became an *is*.

I took him home and put him in my marriage bed,
And staunched him with a thousand leaves of Soldier's
    Woundwort,
And I bandaged him, and stitched him with a linen thread,
Then draped his body in my madder underskirt.

I left him dreaming for a month of Sundays, till
He woke one Easter, and unveiled his second life.
The iris of his eye was green as chlorophyll,

His pupil pansy-black. He glittered like a knife.
He spoke: 'Take me to that Saxon field tomorrow,
There to lie, and propagate our seeds of yarrow.'

Yellow

They made these four fields one, and planted it with rape,
Except the fairy thorn tree, which they left alone.
I'd often hide myself within its flowery cape
To contemplate the dreadful state of Ireland's Own.

A blackbird scraked a lyric with his yellow bill
From deep within the complicated maze of gorse;
I heard the wailing of a baby in a crib,
A passing tumbril drawn by the headless horse.

One morning I woke to find the mustard meadow
Had been mown into a burnished hieroglyph of gold
That spoke of harvest bows, and lover's knots, and Easter
    snow.

I summoned up my ornaments of yesteryear:
Volatile rebel Easter lily, Orange bold:
Rotted buttonholes of triumph, peace, war, and fear.

Twelfth Day

Drunk as a bee that bumbles from deep in the bell
Of a Fairy's Thimble, in a heat-dazed summer meadow,
We sprawled as if we listened to a radio
Which broadcast nothing except insect decibel.

The volume of the field was many atmospheres
Of crawling, chittering, tiny Arcadians,
To whom teeming minutes might be days, and hours years.
In this vast universe we were the aliens.

Every flower we saw, each stalk, was colonized
By troops of little fellows marching up and down
In perfect harmony, as if transistorized.

I went to pinch one 'twixt my index and my thumb
When someone turned the volume up in Portadown,
And then I heard the whole field pulsing like an Orange drum.

The Ay O'Haitch

We march the road like regular quaternions
In jackets of the froggy green, and Paddy hats.
Our socks are gartered and our hair in Croppy plaits:
We are the Ancient Order of Hibernians.

Our silken banners waver in the dewy breeze
With emblematic gold embroidery of Ireland:
Wolfhound, Shamrock, Harp, the Plough in Hyades —
Five provinces not fingered by a severed hand.

We blow a fife tune on our red accordions
And thrum the goatskins of our borrowed Lambeg drums,
For we're the Noble Order of Hibernians.

We are pedestrians, we're not equestrians;
We will outbreed the others; we have done our sums.
Will you, Sir, join our Union of Hibernians?

Centaur

Today the President reviews her regiments
Of troop and horse, resplendent in their uniform
Of Prussian blue. They are her true communicants.
Cherry blossom rains down on them like a snowstorm.

She reviews the veterans tomorrow fortnight,
Whose gorgeous tattered raiments are now badged with red;
And some have one eye; one stoops like a troglodyte;
And some with three eyes couldn't make it here; they're dead.

Some others share three legs, and some have none at all,
And most have digits missing, or a bit of brain;
As for the knackered steeds, their canter is a crawl.

She gazed into her globe memento of Japan,
And shook its bubble world of contraband cocaine.
Bonsai monster: horse's temple, torso of a man.

The Londonderry Air

Snow falls eternally within my souvenir
Of him, who wore the suit of Lincoln corduroy.
He was my noble pikeman, and my pioneer;
Snow falls eternally upon my Danny Boy.

I used to see him at the rising of the moon
With other fellows, exercising in the field,
For they'd refused to take the Saxon gold doubloon —
Indomitable hearts of steel, who'd never yield!

One Sunday, coming home from Mass, from him I stole
A kiss; he left on Monday for to join the war;
I never saw him more, yet he resides within my soul

Like some strange seedling of the plant of Liberty,
That breeds eternally beneath the Northern Star,
Returning as the blossom on the whitethorn tree.

No Tengo Mas Que Dar Te*

This salamander pendant is a dragoneen
Of ruby-studded, modelled gold, with pearls for eyes,
Which divers salvaged from the forty depths of green,
Where lay the wreckage of a former enterprise.

Survivor both of fire and water, noble gremlin,
Someone pinned you to a navigator's doublet
As an emblem to be borne through thick and thin,
So that their love might read forever like a couplet.

I think of her whose hand once held this wingèd thing,
Which I now clasp in mine; I feel an aftershock
As if our fingers touched; *O Death, where is thy sting?*

And now her sailor's long since made his final voyage,
He's been stripped of all appurtenants of wedlock,
Since they plucked the salamander from his ribcage.

*I have nothing more to give thee.

Found

Agnus Dei reliquary, arquebuses,
Awls and astrolabes; beads, bellows, buckles, breech-blocks;
Candle holders, collars, cords and crucifixes;
Dagger hilts and dishes; ewers, esmerils and flintlocks.

Gaiters, goatskins, goblets, gunner's rules and glasses;
Heddles, holsters; ingots, jug-spouts, keys; a lion mask;
Mallets, Ming, muskets; nails; an oriflamme of damask;
Pearls, pellets; querns; ramrods, rings, and silver tasses.

Spokes, shoes, shot, steelyards, shackles; two escudo pieces;
Toggles, tweezers, tambourines and taper-sticks;
Urns and ukeleles; vices, yokes, axes, adzes —

Not to mention the admiral's medallion,
Nor the golden chalice, nor the Eucharistic pyx:
All these were found on board the foundered Spanish galleon.

Manifest

I saw the ghostly galleon late this Hallowe'en,
Its rigging cobweb-rimmed with filigree of salt,
Where wraithlike sailors flitted like so many shades of green
Within deep woods they sailed beneath the starry vault.

It seemed the vessel brought its stormy ambit with it,
Slow tornado crackling through the atmosphere
Of windswept branches amid sparks of moonlit violet,
Its steersman at the tiller like a gondolier.

A ladder was let down for me; I climbed on board.
Seized by disembodied hands, I was transported to
Their eerie captain. He unscabbarded his sword.

He asked me plain, what I had thought or done or said
To make Old Ireland free, or had I fought at Waterloo?
I had no answer for him. He chopped off my head.

The Horse's Mouth

I got that story from the Pooka, who appeared
To me last night. He stepped out from the wardrobe door,
Shimmering in its deteriorating mirror,
Shivering the fringes of his ectoplasmic beard.

I saw my breath as visible to him as nebulae
Of chalky sentences he'd drawn with a hook
From deep within me. Then he read me like a book.
I tried to speak, but there was nothing I could say.

I travelled through an hourglass of Saharan time
To universes unexplored by Star Trek,
Where monsters gyred and gimbled in primordial slime;

'And here,' he said, 'the worms devoured your eyes, and here,
The vultures scrabbed your heart, the vampires lanced your
        neck —
All this,' quoth he, 'to teach you necessary fear.'

Fear

I fear the vast dimensions of eternity.
I fear the gap between the platform and the train.
I fear the onset of a murderous campaign.
I fear the palpitations caused by too much tea.

I fear the drawn pistol of a rapparee.
I fear the books will not survive the acid rain.
I fear the ruler and the blackboard and the cane.
I fear the Jabberwock, whatever it might be.

I fear the bad decisions of a referee.
I fear the only recourse is to plead insane.
I fear the implications of a lawyer's fee.

I fear the gremlins that have colonized my brain.
I fear to read the small print of the guarantee.
And what else do I fear? Let me begin again.

Fuji Film

I feared the yen was starting to decline again,
Devaluing my take-home honorarium.
I joined the crowd that swarmed beneath the acid rain
Like schools of fishes in a vast aquarium.

Some wore sharkskin suits that shimmered like a rainbow;
Some were surgeons, with a white mask where their mouth
    should be;
Some bore barracuda grins, and some wore minnow;
One fat businessman swam like a manatee.

I saw two lobster samurai produce their swords
Of infinitely hammered folded Zeno steel
That glittered like the icy blue of Northern fjords.

I snapped them slashing floating dollar bills in half
Beneath the signs for Coke, the giant neon roulette wheel,
The money index pulsing like a cardiograph.

Con Script

Had I all the money that I left in your store,
Hard-hearted landlady, I'd not bide here tonight,
But I'd ride on my horse in the silvery light,
And buy myself an élite military corps.

For I have had enough of drinking in the dawn,
And tinkering and labouring for beer and bed.
But I will be resplendent in my jacket red
As I parade my soldiers on the Royal lawn.

Her Majesty will draw me to her side, and ask
For my advice on how she might promote the war.
She'll offer me a sip of cordial from her hip flask.

'Give me six Irishmen like me, and we will make
A constellation pointing at the Northern Star;
Our swords of light will ravage Ulster, for your sake.'

Picador

We swept through Austerlitz and Friedland like a plough
Through bloodied water, and all Europe cowered.
But when we came to Moscow we were overpowered
By snow; our horses wallowed in the wintry slough.

Up to the stirrups in it, they plunged this way and that,
Slowly scattering across the moonlit landscape.
The Cossack dogs snapped at our heels. We'd no escape.
The huge stars glittered in their frozen concordat.

We found ourselves alone on the edge of a wood,
My horse and I, where wolves howled like a hundred banshees.
My bullets were all spent. I had no food.

I carved the horse's belly open and I crawled
Inside. I ate her flesh for weeks, expiring by degrees.
Some day you'll find us where her bones and mine are sprawled.

Mustard

Populated by poppies, these fields of '14.
The dreams of warriors blow through the summer grass.
Remember the dead by this pane of stained glass.
The bluebells represent their lips of cyanine.

The statues of the saints are draped at Passiontide.
Please take the transubstantiated wine and bread.
The drunken soldiery had taken to the bed.
You'll get a whiff of ethylene and sulphur chloride.

Then came the Angels, with their flaming swords of light.
Church bells doomed and gonged above the town of Mons.
The Tommies rallied, and the Huns were put to flight.

Do you want to try the demonstration gas-mask?
The campaign included many oxymorons.
You want to know how many yards we gained? Don't ask.

Banana Tree

The President is bringing many things to mind
By gazing at the cherry blossom as it blooms:
Dead young samurai; the harvest moon; a drawn blind;
Stiletto tilt of footsteps in deserted rooms.

This road: no going-person on it; twilight falls:
The President is listening for the temple bell,
And as she hears the frog splash in the holy well,
June rain's still falling through the roofs of marble halls.

And now the cherry blossom's blown from the bough —
Snow that we two looked at, did it fall again this year? —
The President divests herself of here and now

And transubstantiates herself into a swan,
Which disappears into a higher atmosphere:
Full moon: a walk around the pond; the night is gone.

1795

Lodgings for the night! Threw down his sword. Snow
    swirled in.
We made the circle wider round the blazing fire,
And dared not say aloud, *Look what the wind blew in,*
For he was someone; we could tell by his attire.

He opened up his jacket of the Arden green
To show two pistols hanging from a bandoleer,
His gorgeous waistcoat fit for any queen,
All in the highest fashion of a Volunteer.

A year or three went by, but still we minded him
Who'd staggered in that night, and every word he spoke,
For rebel armies rose up in the interim.

And now I'm standing in Downpatrick Jail, I stare
At him they're going to dangle from their tree of oak,
And know him from his dying words, the Man-from-
    god-knows-where.

Spenser's Ireland

Rakehelly horseboys, kernes, gallowglasses, carrows,
Bards, captains, rapparees, their forward womenfolk,
Swords, dice, whiskey, chess, harps, word-hoards, bows
    and arrows:
All are hid within the foldings of their Irish cloak.

Fit house for an outlaw, meet bed for a rebel,
This whore's wardrobe is convenient for a thief;
And when it freezes it becomes his tabernacle,
In whose snug he finds Hibernian relief.

Then there is this big thick bush of hair hanging down
Over their eyes — a *glib*, they call it in their spake;
They do not recognize the power of the Crown.

At the drop of a hat they are wont to vanish
Into deep dark woods. Forever on the make,
They drink and talk too much. Not all of it is gibberish.

Sunderland and Spencer

Here's Sunderland, resplendent in a foppish wig,
And Spencer in his doublebreasted overcoat:
You'll see them wheel round Phoenix in their horse and gig,
Reciting rather graphic Latin verse by rote.

Come glim of night, they flit to rakish gambling-clubs,
Or candle-lit bordellos, as the mood would take them,
Rooms in private houses that were fangled pubs —
That garter in the mirror, that uplifted hem!

Then both were smitten by the lovely Erin, who'd
Seduced them by her words of faery glamour,
And her eyes a double-glimmer 'neath her riding-hood.

There was nothing for it but a duel. Fencer
Stuck the other with his point of Latin grammar.
'I think,' said Sunderland, 'we can dispense with Spencer.'

The Display Case

Last night Hibernia appeared to me in regal frame,
In Creggan churchyard where I lay near dead from drink.
'Take down these words,' she said, 'that all might know
    my claim.'
I opened up a vein and drew my blood for ink —

I'd no accoutrements of writing, save the knife;
The pen she gave me was a feather from her plumage,
And my arm the parchment where I'd sign away my life.
'You seem,' she says, 'to have a problem with the language,

'Since you've abandoned it for lisping English,
Scribbling poems in it exclusively, or so I'm told.
Turncoat interpreter, you wonder why I languish?'

Her full speech is tattooed for all time on my mummied arm,
A relic some girl salvaged from the scaffold
Where they quartered me. *God keep the Irish from all harm!*

February Fourteen

Meanwhile, back in Japan, it is Valentine's Day.
The love hotels are fully booked as Bethlehem,
As, canted like a drunken boulevardier,
My soul roams Tokyo holding one rose by its stem.

Snow is falling in the print by Hiroshige
That I gaze at in a hundred TV screens;
Bronze temple-gongs reverberate their cloisonée;
The light is orange-syncopated reds and greens.

Then I met you, Irish exiles, in The Fish Bar,
Where we staggered between three wobbly shamrock stools
Eyed by prismed species pouting in their glazed bazaar.

Fourteen Bloody Marys later you lisped of home.
We then discovered we had come from different schools,
Yet thought the same, like mutants of one chromosome.

Hippocrene

Tomato juice, black pepper, Worcester Sauce — a dash —
Tabasco, salt, the vodka measured to your taste.
Ice-cubes, ditto. Then sip this freezing balderdash;
Think about it. It is not to be consumed in haste.

Immediately ensanguined, your lips tremble and burn,
As if they'd got a massive intravenous shot
Of haemoglobin, and you're drinking from a Grecian urn;
The bar you understand you're in is called The Elfin Grot.

Karaoke singers mouth their lip-synch rhymes.
Tape-loop music tinkles harp arpeggios of ice.
The videos are showing scenes of ancient times:

Here is Moscow burning, horses led to slaughter,
Wandering the snowy waste of martial sacrifice,
Trails of blood emblazoned in the frozen water.

The Arterial Route

The sedge is withered from the lake, and no birds sing.
Above the dark pines, dim sun like a paper moon.
Leading his starved horse, a samurai's returning
From an ancient war. Cold, this early afternoon.

I noted his dented armour and his rusty sword,
His visage lily-white and scarred with starry eyes.
I then approached and boldly asked him for his word
About the last campaign, and was it truth or lies?

'I met a Lady once,' he said, 'a fairy's child.
I sat her on my steed. She showed me everything.
She fed me Milk of Paradise and honey wild.

'I saw pale warriors assembled in the Hall.
They kissed me with their starvèd lips. You feel the sting?
You cannot leave me now. You too are in her thrall.'

The Groves of Blarney

If you ever go across the sea to Ireland
You'll find they speak a language that you do not know,
And all their time's a grand divertimento,
Dancing jigs and reels to McNamara's Band.

'Tis there you'll find the woods of shamrock and shillelagh.
And the pratie gardens full of Easter snow;
You'll hear the blackbird sing a gay risorgimento,
And see Venus rising at the dawning of the day.

Here they'll feed you hot mugs of buttered poteen,
Salty rashers, gander eggs, and soda bread,
And funny cutty pipes of blissful nicotine.

You'll find you will succumb to their endearing charms,
For sometimes they cohabit with the living dead,
And often wake in strange beds, and another's arms.

Finding the Ox

A Zen warrior searches for inner peace.
His bow is like a harp, that he might twang its string
In lonely combat with himself, and so release
The arrow of desire. An archer should want nothing.

His is the blue music of what is happening.
His sword rings true. Its many lives of hammered steel
Were there before him, and he trusts its weighty swing.
He knows the rallentando of a roulette wheel,

Or red leaves floating in a stream of eau de nil,
Bisected by a showy rival blade, while his
The leaves avoided. He's the opposite of zeal.

When he aims at the bull he closes his eyes.
Sometimes he hits it dead-on with a mighty whizz.
Sometimes he's way off target, which is no surprise.

Eau de Nil

That gorgeous warrior of Egypt, the Mameluke,
Habitually carries all his worldly goods about
His person like a most capacious pocketbook.
If not so burdened with gear he could swim like a trout.

Snuff-box, tobacco-pouch, salt-cellar, worry-beads,
Bouzouki, waterbottle, reliquaries, amulets,
Bejewelled scimitar, papyrus property deeds,
Three four-foot lances, fistfuls of pistols, bullets.

Come that July, he faced Napoleon Bonaparte
Beneath the pyramids of forty centuries.
He pranced about like he was Bony's counterpart.

Shot down or drowned in the Nile were the Mamelukes;
For a fortnight the French pillaged their laden bodies
With bayonets they'd beaten into fishing-hooks.

Trooping the Colours

Breeches, gaiters, busbies, turnbacks, epaulettes, and plumes;
Dolmans, girdles, cloaks of tiger-skin, valises;
Jackets, waistcoats, frocks, the fruit of many looms;
Bicorns, sashes, shakos, piping, braid, pelisses —

Carmine, pike-grey, crab-red, drab, philemot-yellow;
Yolk, parrot- popinjay- or rifle-green, and buff;
Garter-blue and amaranth, raspberry, tobacco;
Cornflower, chamois, madder, pompadour, and snuff —

So we paraded in our catwalk carapace.
Light flittered round us from our lances and swords.
A bugle call, a drum-roll, and off we marched to face

The enemy. Our motto was, *In God We Trust.*
See me now in my tattered petticoat and cords,
Blackened by powder and blood, and raddled with rust.

The Year of the French

Come nightfall, drugged with honied cakes of opium,
We'd hear the droning of innumerable bees,
The calls of owls and crocodiles within the cranium:
Visitations, some said, of Egyptian deities.

Hieroglyphic forms flitted between the low camp fires,
Past dozing sentries, as if orchestrated by
The distant strumming of innumerable lyres;
To pass the time we would count the stars in the sky —

Galactic battalions of those fallen in war.
We'd hear the footsteps of their walking mummied dead
Retreating into the shifting interior.

Murmuring the names of our selves, that they might be known,
We'd carve them with our bayonets on a Pharaoh's head.
Let you trace them in a future black as the Rosetta Stone.

Legions of the Dead

The key to Hieroglyphic and Demotic was the Greek —
Timeless rolling syllables of stout Achilles —
Indomitable body carved by Praxiteles —
Metamorphoses of martial words we speak.

My Irish is corrupted by the English tongue —
Emperor or Pharaoh in a Trojan horse —
Rape-and-pillage dragon-boats of Ancient Norse —
The now-forgotten lyrics of a rebel song —

The hand cut off and thrown to the Ulster shore —
The harp that once resounded in the High King's hall —
The indecipherable babble of days of yore.

Their armies were composed of hieroglyphic men
Like us, who marched through history, and saw kings fall.
Opposing soldiers are at one within our regimen.

Banners

For all that died from shot and sword, more died of disease:
Plagues, dysentery, miasmas, suppurating grot
Beyond the non-existent doctors' expertise.
Some were given military burials, others not.

Starved with cold, *La Grande Armée*, like dots in domino,
Stumbled through Borovsk and Vereya to Mojaisk,
To recross the battlefield of Borodino:
For this enormous freezing tomb, no obelisk,

But the ground ploughed by cannonballs, harrowed by lances,
Littered with cuirasses, wheels, rags, and thirty thousand
Bodies with no eyes who devoured our glances.

As we passed them we almost took them for our foes,
And for a moment I thought of dear old Ireland:
Fields of corpses plentiful as dug potatoes.

Spraying the Potatoes

Knapsack-sprayer on my back, I marched the drills
Of blossoming potatoes — Kerr's Pinks in a frivelled blue,
The Arran Banners wearing white. July was due,
A haze of copper sulphate on the far-off hills.

The bronze noon air was drowsy, unguent as glue.
As I bent over the big oil-drum for a refill
I heard the axle-roll of a rut-locked tumbril.
It might have come from God-knows-where, or out of the blue.

A verdant man was cuffed and shackled to its bed.
Fourteen troopers rode beside, all dressed in red.
It took them a minute to string him up from the oak tree.

I watched him swing in his Derry green for hours and hours,
His popping eyes of apoplectic liberty
That blindly scanned the blue and white potato flowers.

Paddy's Knapsack

One day, raw swedes, potatoes, turnips, barley-seed
And rye — the forage of whatever plundered country —
On another, cheeses, apples, pheasants, jugs of mead,
And honeycombs, blood puddings, fat charcuterie.

Sometimes, the contents of a German butcher's shop,
A Russian prince's cellar, or a Spanish bar;
At times, so much to drink we didn't know when to stop;
At times, so parched we dreamt of water in the jar.

As I open my old knapsack all comes back to me:
That whiff of Parma ham, gunpowder-tea and snuff,
Aroma of red herrings, phantoms of the liberty

That we enjoyed as fellows of the Harlequin.
I don the mask again, and scent, among the other stuff,
The perfume of a girl whose cloak I pillaged in Turin.

The Ambassadors

Here, let me take you down to the Poppy Fields.
You scent them? They are almost bended for picking.
Here strut the soldiers in their ceremonial shields.
You list them? They are all alive and ticking.

As you can see, the shields are furnished like mirrors
To reflect and shimmer the wavery poppies,
Like bandaged veterans of former bloody wars
For, as you know, all businesses need copies.

I hope I'm not being indiscreet when I reveal
That our President has many body-doubles:
Who knows what is what within the car of armoured steel?

You know, our two states could stand in each other's stead.
Excuse me, Sir, I am sorry for your troubles.
It seems you've got a poppy bullet in your head.

Heart of Oak

Coming to in the Twelfth Meadow, I was still
Woozy with whatever it was had happened me.
I felt like Ahab's Herman Melville,
Regurgitated by a monster of cetacean pedigree.

It'd seemed I'd swum into my own enormous maw
Some months ago. I'd made the ribcage my abode:
Vaulted hall wherein a swallowed galleon creaked and yawed,
And labyrinths of gloomy light were blue as woad.

In this realm, everything was fitted to my needs:
The Captain's library, his map and compasses,
His davenport, at which I wrote these many screeds,

His microscope, his grand *pianoforte* —
Only the guns and shot were completely useless.
I left them there to rust when I regained my liberty.

Envoy

Now you've travelled through the Land of Nod and Wink,
And sucked the pap of *papaver somniferum*,
In fields abounding in high cockelorum,
You'll find that everything is slightly out of synch.

These words the ink is written in is not indelible
And every fairy story has its variorum;
For there are many shades of pigment in the spectrum,
And the printed news is always unreliable.

Of maidens, soldiers, presidents and plants I've sung;
Of fairies, fishes, horses, and of headless men;
Of beings from the lowest to the highest rung —

With their long ladder propped against the gates of Heaven,
They're queued up to be rewarded for their grand endeavour,
And receive their campaign haloes on the Twelfth of Never.

BREAKING NEWS

(2003)

in memoriam
William Howard Russell
1820–1907

Belfast

east

beyond the yellow
shipyard cranes

a blackbird whistles
in a whin bush

west

beside the motorway
a black taxi

rusts in a field
of blue thistles

Home

hurtling from
the airport down
the mountain road

past barbed wire
snagged with
plastic bags

fields of scrap
and thistle
farmyards

from the edge
of the plateau
my eye zooms

into the clarity
of Belfast
streets

shipyards
domes
theatres

British Army
helicopter
poised

motionless
at last

I see everything

The Gladstone Bar circa 1954

two men are
unloading beer

you can smell
the hops and yeast

the smouldering
heap of dung

just dropped by
one

of the great
blinkered drayhorses

Trap

backpack radio
antenna

twitching
rifle

headphones
cocked

I don't
read you

what the

over

Breaking

red alert
car parked

in a red
zone

about to

disintegrate
it's

oh

so quiet

you can
almost

hear it rust

News

alarms
shrill

lights
flash

as dust
clears

above
the paper

shop

The Belfast Telegraph
sign reads

     fast   *rap*

Horse at Balaklava, 1854

one minute

muscles rippling
glossy flank

flowing mane
the picture of life

the next

ripped open by
a shell

from chest
to loin

as by a
surgeon's knife

remark

·   the glaring eyeball
and distended nostril

gnashed teeth

next year rotting
harness

a debris of skin
and leather

straps
cloth and buckles

collapsed about
the skeleton

Russia

after Isaac Babel

the knife
glitters

as she slits
fish

guts slithering
into a

zinc bucket

more drink
the soldiers cry

warts blaze
on the faces

of the serving-men

Shop Fronts

cheek by jowl

chemist
tobacconist

Wilkinson Sword
razor-blades

Warhorse
plug

Wire

I met him
in a bar

he shook

my hand

spoke
of coffee-grinders

this

and that

time
and place

by now

he'd lit

a cigarette

he reeked of
explosive

Breath

watching
helicopter

gone

there's a
clear blue

space

above
my head

I feel

rinsed

clean

you know
that quiet

when the
washing-machine

stops
shuddering

Blink

everyone is
watching everybody

in the grey light
of surveillance

people hurtle
through shop

windows or are
sucked back

at a touch of the
rewind button

everyone eyes
everyone

down to the cut
and colour

of their clothes
the pattern

of the retina
the fingerprint

the bits
and pieces

being matched
as everyone

identifies
with this or that

their whereabouts
being watched

War

Sergeant Talbot
had his head

swept off
by a

round-shot

yet for half
a furlong

more

the body kept
the saddle

horse and rider
charging on

regardless

The Indian Mutiny

There I was
looking down the muzzle
of a hostile gun

with a spyglass —
I think, said I, they're
going to fire at us,

and as I spoke, *pluff*
came a spurt of smoke
with a red tongue in it —

a second of
suspense, when *whi-s-s-h*, right
for us came the round-shot

within a foot
of our heads, and plumped
into the ground a storm

of dust and grit
with which we upped and away
and into the courtyard.

No one asked us
for our passes
as we climbed the staircase

to the upper room through
heaps of glass and broken mirrors,
tapestries and beds of silk,

to stare into the blue beyond
of palaces and azure minarets,
domes, temples, colonnades

and long façades
of fair perspective. Look for miles
away, and still

the ocean spreads,
the towers of the city
gleam amidst it,

spires of gold
and constellated spheres
so bright

I had to rub my eyes
before this vision
vaster and more beautiful

than Paris; down
another staircase then,
into a courtyard

large as Temple Gardens
bounded by a range of palaces
of gilt and stucco:

green shutters
and Venetian blinds occlude
the apertures which pierce

the walls in double rows,
and there are statues, fountains,
orange-groves, aqueducts

and kiosks, burnished domes
of metal, fresco paintings
on the blind-windows.

Through all these
the soldiery run riot,
forcing their way

into the long corridors —
you hear the crack
of musketry, the crash

of glass, as little jets
of smoke curl out from
the closed lattices.

The orange-groves
are strewn with dead
and dying sepoys,

the white statues
drenched with red.
Against a smiling Venus

a British soldier shot
through the neck
pumps gouts of blood

and soldiers drunk
with plunder pour out
from the broken portals

bearing china vases,
teapots, lamp-shades, mirrors,
which they dash to pieces,

others busy gouging
the precious stones
from stems of pipes,

from saddle-cloths, from
hilts of swords, from pistol-butts,
their bodies swathed

in gem-encrusted stuffs:
court after court
connected by arched passageways

where lie the dead sepoys,
clothes smouldering
on their flesh.

One who had his brains
dashed out by round-shot
made me think —

minutes telescoped
into each other — twelve inches
lower and I'd not

be here to write
nor would you read
this news of how

we freed Lucknow.

Some Uses of a Dead Horse

the bones give
buttons

snuff-boxes
and knife-handles

the hooves
yield

a beautiful
Prussian blue

the shoes
shot

Detail

men and horses
fell

in swathes
like grass before

a scythe
but I was saved

by this

he opened
the Bible

to reveal
the bullet

stopped
at Revelation

Waste Not

birds flock
above the field

near
dark

women with shears
attend

the dead
harvesting

gold braid
and buttons

In St Patrick's Cathedral, Dublin

British Army
regimental

colours
flown

in this
campaign

or that

now

hang

tattered by
the moth

or shot

Skip

I'm writing
this

in a black flip-
top police

notebook
I gleaned

from the
bomb-

damage
of Her Majesty's

Stationery Office

Fragment

from a piece of
the Tupperware
lunchbox that held

the wiring

they could tell
the bombmaker wore
Marigold rubber gloves

Campaign

shot
the horse fell

a crow
plucked the eyes

time passed

from a socket
crept

a butterfly

Spin Cycle

here it comes
again I said

I couldn't
hear

myself
speak for the

thug-thug

helicopter
overhead

I put in
the ear-plugs

everything went
centrifugal

Spin Cycle 2

gun-gun

ear-plugs in

blank-blank

Harvest

a swathe
of honeyed light

cuts through
the gunsmoke

swarms
of men and horses

crawl
all over

the wheat
and barley fields

like mutilated
bees

Théodore Géricault: Farrier's Signboard, *1814*

he holds
the reins

of the massive
straining draught

horse in one
fist hammer

in the other
man and horse

deadlocked
raked by light

before the red
glow of the forge

this

painted in oil
directly on to

roughly carpentered
gap-jointed

boards
a door

or shutter
wood

and nail heads
showing through

this the year
before Waterloo

The Forgotten City

after William Carlos Williams, 'The Forgotten City'

When on a day of the last disturbances
I was returning from the country, trees
were across the road, thoroughfares and side streets
barricaded: burning trucks and buses, walls
of ripped-up paving-stones, sheets of corrugated
iron fencing, storm-gratings, brown torrents
gushing from a broken water main.
I had to take what road I could to find
my way back to the city. My bike hissed
over crisp wet tarmac as I cycled through
extraordinary places: long deserted avenues
and driveways leading to apartment blocks,
car-ports, neo-Tudor churches, cenotaphs,
and in one place an acre or more of
rusting Nissen huts left over from the War. Parks.
It was so quiet that at one gatekeeper's lodge
I could hear coffee perking. I passed
a crematorium called Roselawn, pleasant
cul-de-sacs and roundabouts with names
I never knew existed. Knots of men and women
gathered here and there at intersections
wearing hats and overcoats, talking
to themselves, gesticulating quietly.
I had no idea where I was and promised myself
I would go back some day and study this
grave people. How did they achieve
such equilibrium? How did they get
cut off in this way from the stream of
bulletins, so under-represented
in our parliaments and media when so near
the troubled zone, so closely surrounded
and almost touched by the famous and familiar?

Minus

no
helicopter

noise
this hour

gone by
the room

still
dark

I raise
the blind

on
a moon

so bright
it hurts

and oh
so cold

my breath
sounds

like frost

Francisco Goya: The Third of May 1808, *1814*

behold
the man

who faces
the stream

of light
white-shirted

arms
flung

open
to receive

the volley
offering

the firing-squad
his ghost

he is not
blindfolded

Last Effect

take
the watch

feel
the weight

of its bullet-
dented case

the Braille

of its
glassless dial

hands
arrested

at the minute
and the hour

of his salvation
death

postponed
for years

until that
yesterday

he failed
to see

O what is time
my friend

when faced with
eternity

Siege

the road
to Sevastopol

is paved
with round-shot

the road
from Sevastopol

with boots
that lack feet

Exile

night
after night

I walk

the smouldering
dark streets

Sevastopol
Crimea

Inkerman
Odessa

Balkan
Lucknow

Belfast
is many

places then
as now

all lie
in ruins

and
it is

as much
as I can do

to save
even one

from oblivion

Wake

near dawn

boom

the window
trembled

bomb

I thought

then in
the lull

a blackbird
whistled in

a chink
of light

between
that world

and this

Edward Hopper: Early Sunday Morning, *1930*

clear
blue sky above

upper storey
blinds half-drawn

not a soul about
the strip

of shop fronts
only a red

white and blue
barber's pole

and a fire
hydrant

casting
shadows

on the sidewalk
from the east

beyond
the frame

immeasurably
long

another shadow
falls

from what
we cannot see

to what
we cannot see

dawn
before the War

The War Correspondent

1

Gallipoli

Take sheds and stalls from Billingsgate,
glittering with scaling-knives and fish,
the tumbledown outhouses of English farmers' yards
that reek of dung and straw, and horses
cantering the mewsy lanes of Dublin;

take an Irish landlord's ruinous estate,
elaborate pagodas from a Chinese Delftware dish
where fishes fly through shrouds and sails and yards
of leaking ballast-laden junks bound for Benares
in search of bucket-loads of tea as black as tin;

take a dirty gutter from a backstreet in Boulogne,
where shops and houses teeter so their pitched roofs meet,
some chimney stacks as tall as those in Sheffield
or Irish round towers,
smoking like a fleet of British ironclad destroyers;

take the garlic-oregano-tainted arcades of Bologna,
linguini-twists of souks and smells of rotten meat,
as labyrinthine as the rifle-factories of Springfield,
or the tenements deployed by bad employers
who sit in parlours doing business drinking Power's;

then populate this slum with Cypriot and Turk,
Armenians and Arabs, British riflemen
and French Zouaves, camel-drivers, officers, and sailors,
sappers, miners, Nubian slaves, Greek money-changers,
plus interpreters who do not know the lingo;

dress them in turbans, shawls of fancy needlework,
fedoras, fezzes, sashes, shirts of fine Valenciennes,
boleros, pantaloons designed by jobbing tailors,

knickerbockers of the ostrich and the pink flamingo,
sans-culottes, and outfits even stranger;

requisition slaughter-houses for the troops,
and stalls with sherbet, lemonade, and rancid lard for sale,
a temporary hospital or two, a jail,
a stagnant harbour redolent with cholera,
and open sewers running down the streets;

let the staple diet be green cantaloupes
swarming with flies washed down with sour wine,
accompanied by the Byzantine
jangly music of the cithara
and the multi-lingual squawks of parakeets —

O landscape riddled with the diamond mines of Kimberley,
and all the oubliettes of Trebizond,
where opium-smokers doze among the Persian rugs,
and spies and whores in dim-lit snugs
discuss the failing prowess of the Allied powers,

where prowling dogs sniff for offal beyond
the stench of pulped plums and apricots,
from which is distilled the brandy they call 'grape-shot',
and soldiers lie dead or drunk among the crushed flowers —
I have not even begun to describe Gallipoli.

2

Varna

On the night of August 10th, a great fire broke out,
destroying utterly a quarter of the town.
A stiff breeze fanned the flames along the tumbledown
wooden streets. Things were not helped by the current drought.

It began in the spirit store of the French commissariat.
The officers in charge immediately broached the main vat,
but, as the liquid spouted down the streets, a Greek
was seen to set fire to it in a fit of drunken pique.

He was cut down to the chin by a French lieutenant,
and fell into the blazing torrent. The howls of the inhabitants,
the clamour of women, horses, children, dogs, the yells
of prisoners trapped in their cells,

were appalling. Marshal St Arnaud displayed great coolness
in supervising the operations of the troops;
but both the French and we were dispossessed
of immense quantities of goods —

barrels of biscuit, nails, butter, and bullets,
carpenters' tool-boxes, hat-boxes, cages of live pullets,
polo-sticks, Lord Raglan's portable library of books,
and 19,000 pairs of soldiers' boots.

A consignment of cavalry sabres was found
amid the ruins, fused into the most fantastic shapes,
looking like an opium-smoker's cityscape
or a crazy oriental fairground —

minarets, cathedral spires of twisted blades, blades
wrought into galleries and elevated switchbacks,

railroad sidings, cul-de-sacs, trolleyways, and racing tracks,
gazebos, pergolas, trellises, and colonnades.

Such were the effects of the great fire of Varna.
Next day the cholera broke out in the British fleets
anchored in the bay, then spread into the streets,
and for weeks thousands of souls sailed into Nirvana.

3

Dvno

Once I gazed on these meadows
incandescent with poppies,
buttercups and cornflowers
surrounded by verdant hills

in which lay deep shady dells,
dripping ferns shower-dappled
under the green canopy
of live oaks and wild apples,

aspens, weeping-willow, ash,
maple, plane, rhododendron,
sweet chestnut, spruce, Douglas fir,
and Cedar of Lebanon,

round which vines and acacias
vied with wild clematises
to climb ever on and up
to twine the trunks of the trees,

and I thought I was in Eden,
happily stumbling about
in a green Irish garden
knee-deep in potato flowers.

But at night a fog descends,
as these woods breed miasmas,
and slithering through the brush
are snakes thick as a man's arm;

the vapours rise and fatten
on the damp air, becoming

palpable as mummy shrouds,
creeping up from the valleys

fold after fold in the dark,
to steal into a man's tent,
and wrap him, as he's sleeping,
in their deadly cerements.

One day, down by the sea-shore,
I scraped my name with a stick
on the sand, and discovered
the rotting face of a corpse;

and by night in the harbour
phosphorescent bodies float
up from the murky bottom
to drift moonward past the fleet

like old wooden figureheads,
bobbing torsos bolt upright.
Tiger, Wasp, Bellerophon,
Niger, Arrow, Terrible,

Vulture, Viper, Albion,
Britannia, Trafalgar,
Spitfire, Triton, Oberon:
these are vessels I remember.

As for the choleraic dead,
their names have been unravelled
like their bones, whose whereabouts
remain unknown.

4

Balaklava

The Turks marched in dense columns, bristling with steel.
Sunlight flashed on the polished barrels of their firelocks
and on their bayonets, relieving their sombre hue,
for their dark blue uniforms looked quite black
when viewed *en masse*. The Chasseurs d'Afrique,
in light powder-blue jackets, with white cartouche belts, scarlet
pantaloons, mounted on white Arabs, caught the eye
like a bed of flowers scattered over the valley floor.

Some, indeed, wore poppies red as cochineal,
plucked from the rich soil, which bore an abundance of
        hollyhocks,
dahlias, anemones, wild parsley, mint, whitethorn, rue,
sage, thyme, and countless other plants whose names I lack.
As the Turkish infantry advanced, their boots creaked
and crushed the springy flowers, and delicate
perfumes wafted into the air beneath the April sky:
the smell of sweating men and horses smothered by flora.

Waving high above the more natural green
of the meadow were phalanxes of rank grass, marking the
        mounds
where the slain of October 25th had found their last repose,
and the snorting horses refused to eat those deadly shoots.
As the force moved on, more evidences of that fatal day
came to light. The skeleton of an English horseman
had tatters of scarlet cloth hanging to the bones of his arms;
all the buttons had been cut off the jacket.

Round as shot, the bullet-skull had been picked clean
save for two swatches of red hair. The remains of a wolfhound
sprawled at his feet. From many graves the uncovered bones
of the tenants had started up, all of them lacking boots.

Tangled with rotted trappings, half-decayed horses lay
where they'd fallen. Fifes and drums struck up a rataplan;
so we swept on over our fellow men-at-arms
under the noon sun in our buttoned-up jackets.

5

Kertch

A row of half a mile
across the tideless sea
brought us to a beautiful beach

edged by a green sward
dotted with whitewashed houses
through which the French

were running riot, swords
in hand, breaking in windows
and doors, pursuing hens:

every house we entered
ransacked, every cupboard
with a pair of red breeches

sticking out of it, and a blue
coat inside of it; barrels of lard,
bags of sour bread, mattress feathers,

old boots, statues, icons, strewn
on the floors, the furniture
broken to kindling —

such an awful stench
from the broken jars of fish oil
and the rancid butter,

the hens and ducks cackling,
bundled by the feet
by Zouaves and Chasseurs,

who, fancied up in old calico
dresses, pranced about
the gardens like princesses.

I was reminded of Palmyra
after we had sacked it:
along the quay a long line

of walls, which once
were the fronts of storehouses,
magazines, mansions, and palaces —

now empty shells,
hollow and roofless, lit from within
by lurid fires,

as clouds of incense
rose from the battered domes
and ruined spires,

all deadly silent
save for the infernal noise
of soldiers playing on pianos

with their boot-heels,
and the flames crackling
within the walls

and glassless windows,
the great iconostasis
of the Orthodox cathedral

shot to bits, the golden
images and holy books ablaze
amid the crashed candelabras

and broken votive lamps,
while the Byzantine mosaics
were daubed with excrement.

Thus did we force the straits
of Kertch, and break the Russian forts.
Corn, oil, naval stores,

prodigious quantities of guns,
bullets, grape-shot, brandy of a high degree —
all fell into our hands.

And we spread terror and havoc
along the peaceful seaboard
of that tideless sea.

6

Tchernaya

After only two or three days, the soil
erupted with multitudes of snowdrops,
crocuses, hyacinths, gladioli,
marigolds, daffodils, and buttercups.

Finches and larks congregated in little flocks.
Buntings, gold-crested wrens, yellowhammers,
linnets, wrens, and tomtits formed little claques,
piping and twittering and shimmering.

Strange to hear them sing about the bushes
in the lulls between the thud of the bombs,
or to see between the cannon-flashes
the whole peninsula ignite with blooms,

spring flowers bursting through the crevices
of piles of rusted shot, and peering out
from under the shells and heavy ordnance.
A geranium waved from an old boot.

The insides of our huts became gardens.
Grapes sprouted from the earth in the sills,
the floors, and the fireplace. As in a trance,
we watched the vines crawl slowly up the walls.

Albatrosses, cranes, pelicans, and gulls
haunted the harbour. Eagles, vultures, kites
and hawks wheeled over the plateau in squalls,
vanishing for two or three days at a time.

Then they'd return, regular as clockwork,
after feeding behind the Russian lines.

I know, for I remember my watch stopped,
and we made a sundial with white stones.

The Tchernaya abounded with wildfowl.
Some of the officers had little hides
of their own where they went at night to kill
time. This was deemed highly exciting sport,

for the Russian batteries at Inkerman,
if their sentries were properly alert,
would send two or three shells at the sportsmen,
who took short odds on escaping unhurt.

In the daytime, they'd take two or three French
soldiers down with them to act as decoys,
who were only too glad of the break. Hence
we coined the old saying, 'dead as a duck'.

Then there was betting on how many flies
would fill a jar in which lay a dead dove,
and the two-or-three-legged dog races —
little to do? There was never enough.

Thus we spent the time by the Tchernaya,
making it up as we went along, till
long before the battle of Tchernaya,
we each had two or three life-stories to tell.

7

Sedan

Cavalry men asleep
on their horses' necks.
In the fields, heaps

of sodden troops,
the countryside charming,
covered with rich crops,

but trampled
underfoot, vines and hops
swept aside by the flood

of battle, the apples blasted
from the trees, scattered
like grape-shot.

Gutted knapsacks, boots,
cavalry caps, jackets, swords,
mess-tins, bayonets,

canteens, firelocks, tunics,
sabres, epaulettes,
overturned baggage cars,

dead horses
with their legs in the air,
scattered everywhere,

dead bodies,
mostly of Turcos and Zouaves,
picked over by pickpockets,

one of them staggering
under a huge load of gold
watches and teeth.

Hands hanging in the trees
in lieu of fruit,
trunkless legs at their feet.

I will never forget one man
whose head rested
on a heap of apples,

his knees drawn up
to his chin, his eyes wide
open, seeming to inspect

the head of a Turco or Zouave
which, blown clean off,
lay like a cannonball in his lap.

What debris a ruined empire
leaves behind it!
By the time I reached Sedan

with my crippled horse,
it was almost impossible
to ride through the streets

without treading on
bayonets and sabres, heaps
of shakos, thousands

of imperial eagles
torn off infantry caps,
or knocking into stooks

of musketry and pikes.
I thought of Sevastopol,
mirrors in fragments

on the floors, beds
ripped open, feathers
in the rooms a foot deep,

chairs, sofas, bedsteads,
bookcases, picture-frames,
images of saints, shoes, boots,

bottles, physic jars,
the walls and doors
hacked with swords,

even the bomb-shelters
ransacked, though in one dug-out
I found a music-book

with a woman's name
in it, and a canary bird,
and a vase of wild flowers.

FOR ALL WE KNOW

(2008)

for Deirdre
comme toujours

La nuit s'approche et mon village
S'endort là-bas silencieux
La cloche sonne, et son langage
Annonce le fin des adieux

Quand vient le soir après l'orage
Fuyons, prenons le droit sentier
Adieu les rêves de jeune âge
Anges, gardez notre foyer

[Night approaches and my village/Slumbers over there in silence/
The bell rings, and its language/Announces the end of farewells//
When evening comes after storm/Let us flee, let us take the right path/
Farewell the dreams of youthful days/Angels, watch over our hearth]

— OLD SONG

Fugue must perform its frequently stealthy work with continuously shifting melodic fragments that remain, in the 'tune' sense, perpetually unfinished.

— Glenn Gould
'So You Want to Write a Fugue'

PART ONE

Second Time Round

Ce n'est pas comme le pain de Paris. There's no stretch in it,
you said. It was our anniversary, whether first or last.

It's the matter of the texture. Elasticity.
The crust should crackle when you break the *baton*. Then
   you pull

the crumb apart to make skeins full of holes. I was grappling
with your language over the wreck of the dining table.

The maitre d' was looking at us in a funny way
as if he caught the drift I sought between the lines you spoke.

For one word never came across as just itself, but you
would put it over as insinuating something else.

Then slowly, slowly we would draw in on one another
until everything was implicated like wool spooled

from my yawning hands as you wound the yarn into a ball.
For how many seasons have we circled round each other

like this? Was it because you came from there and I from
   here?
That said, before we were a gleam in someone else's eye?

Behind the screen of reasons, how much further back we go.
La nuit s'approche, you said, and then I saw the parish church

below the Alps of those three words, and snow falling, a bell
tolling as their farewells dimmed into the gathering dusk.

Our two candles were guttering by now. We climbed the stair
and found ourselves spreadeagled on the patchwork double
   quilt

following the dips and gradients of the staggered repeats
four widow aunts had stitched into it fifty years before

the last war, one of them your ancestor. So they told you
as you told me that day in Paris we two first ventured

under it, into the future we would make together
there and then, the bread you bought that morning not
    yet broken.

Hotel del Mar

Sound of waves without. You were abroad and ignorant in
the tongue you heard whispering from a dinner table more

than one remove away from you, two pairs of lips closing
in on one another in the flickering candlelight —

murmuring of sweet nothings, you surmised, since it was
    Greek
to you. Waves on the beach. Did we two, you wondered,
    ever

come across like that? Some lonely traveller to overhear
words not understood, a shadow on the periphery?

Whatever window opened then, moonlight shivered on you,
the gold crushed velvet curtains stirred in the breeze off
    the sea.

The couple spoke more boldly now, as if you were not there.
So you told it that I might fathom the deep of its sound,

we two seas foundering into one another over
the neck of a peninsula, making it an island.

On the Contrary

It's because we were brought up to lead double lives, you said.
You were lying next to me, both of us verging on sleep.

We always had to withhold ourselves from the other side,
guarding our tongues lest we answer to their outspoken laws.

And so we lost ourselves in the dark forest of language
believing in nothing which might not be governed by touch

or taste, the apple bursting indescribably with juice
against the roof of the mouth, or the clean cold smell of skin.

As our promise was never to be betrayed by our words
so we became our own shadowy police watching us,

as loaded the long goods train clanks slowly towards Dublin,
we hear the shriek in the night from across the trip-wired
         fields,

as the searchlight trawls across the bedroom window you turn
towards me speechlessly and we look into each other's eyes.

Treaty

It's like putting yourself in someone else's shoes, you said,
or checking into a hotel under another name

except back home you need them to believe in the fiction.
For this is not a strange country where you are free to be

whosoever you like, to bask in the equable sun
in happy ignorance of the language. There you are not.

Remember those radiating pathways of Versailles where
you confessed yourself happy to be known to none but me?

Whereas here the insignia are all too familiar
and country roads are walked in circumspection to music

in order to encompass the other's territory —
this story we've been over so many times, inventing

that which we might have been had we been born as another,
as truly we tell them a name that sounds like one of theirs.

Redoubt

If only because in another country you are free
to renegotiate yourself or what you thought you were,

I found myself this night approached by a man in a suit.
When he asked me what I was drinking I didn't demur.

French was a lingua franca. He showed me a worn photo,
wife and children smiling at us from some Polish city.

We'd already exchanged names, whatever they were. So what
did I do? I told him I was a writer, not well known.

Me? I'm a salesman, he said, I travel in fountain pens.
He represented all the big companies like Mont Blanc.

It was the coming back-to-the-future thing in the East,
though back where I come from, he said, they'd never gone
    away.

But what they desired now was 'Western exclusivity'.
And what sort of thing do you write, would you like to try
    mine?

Even before he proffered it I knew it was a fake.
He'd filled it with fancy ink. *De l'encre violette.*

So I wrote I was a writer of fiction and poems,
and if you're about to ask me what they're about, I said,

that's for the reader to say, whose guess is as good as mine.
He smiled. And how did it all end up? I said, picturing

the scene, bottles with strange labels glinting in the back-
    ground,
the bartender pretending to polish a glass, and you

looking the Mont Blanc man in the eye. I imagined snow
outside, the footsteps that brought you there already erased

as were his that crossed yours at the threshold if not before,
as we two were strangers to each other when we first met.

I stared at my face for an age in the en suite mirror.
Then I must have crawled into bed before my mind went
    blank.

The Assignation

I think I must have told him my name was Juliette,
with four syllables, you said, to go with *violette*.

I envisaged the violet air that presages snow,
the dark campaniles of a city beginning to blur

a malfunctioning violet neon pharmacy sign
jittering away all night through the dimity curtains.

Near dawn you opened them to a deep fall and discovered
a line of solitary footprints leading to a porch:

a smell of candle-wax and frankincense; the dim murmur
of a liturgy you knew but whose language you did not.

The statues were shrouded in Lenten violet, save one,
a Virgin in a cope of voile so white as to be blue.

As was the custom there, your host informed you
        afterwards —
the church was dedicated to Our Lady of the Snows.

Revolution

Then I would try to separate the grain from the chaff of
helicopter noise as it hovered above on my house.

This was back in the late Sixties, I didn't know you then.
Later I'd picture you in an apartment in Paris.

You'd be watching riot police and students on TV,
banners and barbed wire unfurling across the boulevards

and the air thick with stones. The helicopters came later
within earshot grinding the sound bites into vocables.

I felt I had a malfunctioning cochlear implant,
that someone I didn't know was watching me from on high.

The picture would break up into unreadable pixels.
I'd imagine putting my lips to the door of your ear

as I held the conch you brought back from Ithaca to mine,
listening to shells becoming shingle, and shingle sand.

Through

Irrevocable? Never irrevocable, you said,
picking me up wrong through the din of the coffee machine.

We were in the Ulster Milk Bar I think they blew up back
in the Seventies. We must have been barely acquainted.

Noise is what surrounds us, I'd said earlier, gesturing
to the wider world of disinformation, the dizzy

spells that come when someone you know might have been
    in a bomb
as the toll has not yet been reckoned except by hearsay.

I'd have my ear glued to the radio, waiting for what
passed for the truth to come out, men picking through
    the rubble.

Some of the victims would appear in wedding photographs
blinded by a light forever gone. Graveside by graveside

I shake hands with men I have not shaken hands with for
    years,
trying to make out their faces through what they have become.

Pas de Deux

It all began in Take Two, what with us looking at clothes.
You'd brushed against me as I stepped aside from the mirror

to let you size yourself up against a blue pencil skirt,
pinching its waistband to your waist with your arms akimbo.

I caught you taking me in from the corner of your eye
as I fingered the nap on a Donegal tweed jacket.

Nice jacket, you said. Yes? I said. Yes, you said, I love that
Harris tweed, the heathery feel of the handwoven wool.

You're not from around here, I said. No, from elsewhere,
        you said.
As from another language, I might have said, but did not.

Though your English was perfect I couldn't place the accent
and you'd put things in such a way no native would have done.

N'a pas fait qui commence, you came to say later, only
begun is not done. And so it was we got acquainted,

as with the glow of our cigarettes we'd scrawl neon signs
to each other on the dark, the words fading instantly

as written, comprehended by the eye in retrospect
as over us a helicopter drowned conversation.

That was the kind of spin that passed for dialogue back then,
one side revolving the other's words for other meanings,

or sidestepping the issue, demanding actions instead.
It took us some time to establish our identity,

for you'd learned where you came from to choose your words
        carefully.
And often you'd seal my lips with a kiss as silently

under a blanket we'd struggle into one another
to end up sleeping like two naked spoons or back to back,

the second-hand pencil skirt on your side of the wardrobe,
the second-hand tweed jacket brushing against it on mine.

Second Hand

Nice watch, I said. Yes, you said, Omega. White gold bezel
with black guilloche enamel inlay. Porcelain dial.

Arabic numerals, alpha hands. Seventeen jewel
movement. Pre-War, all original — look, it's even got

the original black silk ribbon band. Butterfly clasp.
You turned your wrist to show me as you spoke. How
    long ago

was that? I knew you a matter of minutes back then; now
it's years. As it turned out your uncle collected watches.

This one had been your aunt's. He'd take off the back of
    a watch
to show how it worked, levers, gears, bearings, wheels, screws
    and springs

registering elapsed time with a dispassionate tick.
You held it to my ear. I listened to the seconds pass

as now I listen to the wind on this cold starry night,
and I wonder if your Omega watch is working still.

Le Mot Juste

Still the interminable wrestle with words and meanings?
you said. I'd an idea you were quoting from something.

But from what? Rather than answer, I put my pen aside
and poured the miniature jug of milk into my coffee.

You watched over it quizzically as it became *au lait*.
Wouldn't you rather talk about your day? I said at length.

I practised a little Well-Tempered Clavier, you said,
and I envisioned your nimble fingers on the keyboard.

The C-minor prelude and the B-minor fugue, you said,
the two ends of the book as it were. I've often wondered

how many quills Bach went through over those twenty-two
    years.
Do you know that Bach had twenty children? I do, I said.

You reached suddenly across the table to put your mouth
to mine, murmuring what I took for a fugue on my lips.

Proposal

You were one of the first to go for an Apple, when they
first came out, you said, it must have been the year whenever,

1984? Stuck, you'd click on the Option button
whereupon up popped a menu of possible answers

through which you dropped down until it took your mind
  to the end
you so desired, the Tree of Knowledge looming within reach.

All too soon you were plucking data from the air, making
documents, files and spreadsheets, putting your life in order.

We'd climb into bed to the noise of a helicopter
to bury our selves under the clothes to muffle the beat

with the beat of our synchronized hearts. When all was done
  but
not said, you'd speak temptingly of the serendipity

of the Apple, how it seemed to put words into your mouth
to say what you wanted to say but could not until then.

The Shadow

You know how you know when someone's telling lies?
    you said. They
get their story right every time, down to the last word.

Whereas when they tell the truth it's never the same twice.
    They
reformulate. The day in question and whatever passed

between them and the other can be seen so many ways,
the way they sometimes ask themselves if it happened at all.

All this was *à propos* of your first time in East Berlin.
The Wall was not long down. It was Easter 1990,

you found yourself in a place in Herman-Hesse-Strasse.
You were alone in the dining room one evening, reading

The Glass Bead Game over *Bierwurst*, sauerkraut and a draught
    beer,
when the middle-aged waiter approached you from
    the shadows.

Bitte, he said; may I? You gestured towards an empty chair.
You wouldn't remember how the talk took the turn it did,

but however it happened his life began to come out.
He'd set up two schnapps by then. He'd been in the Stasi
    once.

The lie is memorized, the truth is remembered, he said.
I learned that early on in their school before I became

interrogator. That was after I learned to listen
in. They played many tapes of many stories, some true, some

false. I was asked to identify which was which, and where
the conversations might have taken place, whatever time.

And the ones who sobbed over and over, I am telling
the truth, never changed their story, he said. End of story.

You've told me this story more than once, more than once
    telling
me something I never heard before until then, telling

it so well I could almost believe I was there myself,
for all that I was at the time so many miles away.

The Fetch

To see one's own doppelgänger is an omen of death.
The doppelgänger casts no reflection in a mirror.

Shelley saw himself swimming towards himself before he
    drowned.
Lincoln met his fetch at the stage door before he was shot.

It puts me in mind of prisoners interrogated,
of one telling his story so well he could see himself

performing in it, speaking the very words he spoke now,
seeing the face of the accomplice he had invented.

When all is said and done there is nothing more to be said.
No need for handcuffs, or any other restraint. They take

a swab of his sweat from the vinyl chair in which he sat.
Should he ever escape his prison the dogs shall be loosed.

Your death stands always in the background, but don't
    be afraid.
For he will only come to fetch you when your time has come.

Second Take

Most of the witnesses we knew then are dead if not gone,
sequestered in havens to become shadows of themselves.

Take Carrick, whose name was a byword for integrity,
bundled into an unmarked car to vanish without trace:

whatever he'd borne witness to must have been worth
      knowing,
so much so they say he arranged his own disappearance.

Take McCloud, a man notoriously hard of hearing,
whose earpiece was tuned to every whisper in the city:

he fell foul of a so-called cancer of the inner ear,
a steady creep of secrets invading the labyrinth.

Take the others who were given a new identity,
not that we could say for sure who they were in the first
      place.

Take me, you said, the first time ever you set eyes on me:
for all that I told you then, you took me for what I was.

Corrigendum

I put what you call a bug in all of the light switches,
said the Stasi man, to entrap the couple by their words.

Their names had been put forward as what you call
    dissenters,
so I listened to all they had to say to each other.

There were long periods of silence but for the TV
and I won't say what they did when all was dark and silent,

and for all that they quarrelled they never raised their voices,
which by itself might be construed as evidence of guilt.

So many schnapps later the Stasi man was on the verge
of oblivion. His last words were, Do you believe me?

I nodded as if I did. I reached a loose-leaf notebook
from my handbag and asked if he would write his name.
    He did.

When I came to the next day and tried to make sense of it
all the pages were blank and I never saw him again.

Fall

So what do you do? I said. We'd just exchanged names. I do
what you might call cultural *journalisme*, you replied.

It was windy that day and when it rained the sun came out.
Raindrops, leaf-shadow dappled and spattered the blue cobbles.

Two pigeons clucked. The butcher's lay at the end of the block.
We were standing some seven doors down. You're not covering

the Troubles? I said. I watched your lips frame a silent No
as the bomb went off at the end of the block and drowned all

conversation. All the more difficult to find the words
for what things have been disrupted by aftershock and shock,

a fall of glass still toppling from the astonished windows,
difficult to ponder how we met, if it was for this.

From this we averted our eyes as we skirted the crowd,
the sirens dwindling into silence as we walked away.

L'Air du Temps

Nice perfume, I said. Thank you, you said. It was our first
    date.
I've always wondered about perfumes, I said, what is it?

L'Air du Temps by Nina Ricci, you said, she made it up
just after the War. Spirit of the Times, it was supposed

to evoke the era, the girls in Pompadour hairstyles
blowing kisses everywhere, garlanding the tank turrets.

Lalique designed the flacon later, 1951,
the frosted glass stopper a pair of intertwining doves.

As for the scent, it opens with luminous bergamot
and rosewood, developing a bouquet of gardenia,

violet, jasmine and ylang ylang. Wraiths of green moss
and sandalwood give *L'Air du Temps* its gentle persistence.

The base is powdery orris, cool woods, musk and resins,
permeated with a faint radiant heat of amber.

They say it goes well with pastels and purples, the latter
in every shade from palest lavender to heliotrope.

Fabrics should be near transparent, or crisp and clean, you
    said.
You were wearing a 1950s blouse of pastel blue.

So what shade would you call that? I said, looking at your
    blouse.
You looked down at yourself. It's a very, very pale French

blue, you said. It puts me in mind of winters in Paris.
It is frosty, and if you stand in Montmartre you can

see for miles. I'm looking at the patchwork quilt of Paris:
parks, avenues, cemeteries, temples, impasses, arcades.

I can see the house where I was raised, and my mother's house.
I am in her boudoir looking at her in the mirror

as she, pouting, not looking, puts on *L'Air du Temps*, a spurt
of perfume on each wrist before she puts her wristwatch on.

Never Never

You were telling me a story of your great-grandmother's
over a bottle of Burgundy by a bubbling fire.

Deep in the Forest of Language there dwelt a manikin
not called Rumpelstiltskin. His name was not that important.

One day a riderless mare came trotting up to his door.
The manikin brought her to stable and fed her some hay.

He was surprised when the mare upped and spoke in the
  King's French.
I am not a mare, she said, but the King's daughter bewitched.

And because you have fed and stabled me I shall become
princess again. And she changed as she spoke before his eyes.

In return you have three wishes. I only want one wish,
said the manikin. I'm a manikin. Make me a man.

The by now fully-formed beautiful woman blinked at him
and in the blank and pupil of her eye he became man.

You took a long sip of wine. And what happened then? I said.
The princess summoned a horse from nowhere and galloped
  home.

The man walked to a great city. He became a joiner.
He grew skilled at his trade and his heart was in all he made.

He grew justly famous for his miniature chests of drawers,
each crafted from a plank of his oak house in the forest.

But still he pined for the day that he'd set the princess free.
He never looked at a woman until the day he died,

his last wish to be buried in the Forest of Language,
his body to be laid in a box of his own device.

To this day if you happen to pass that shadowy glade
you may see a ghostly rider riding a ghostly mare.

You lit a cigarette. And as for the princess? I said.
She married an English prince, you said, and got beheaded.

Birthright

Again you are trapped in the smouldering streets. Knots
    of men
armed with axes, files and chisels guard the intersections.

For all that you avert your gaze you know they know your
    kind.
The city wards have long been sealed and there is no escape.

For all that you assumed a sevenfold identity
the mark of your people's people blazes on your forehead.

You will be questioned by the black stream of the shibboleth,
your story picked like a cheap lock until it comes unstuck.

Whatever happens to you next is nothing personal.
What is written has been written, these the words on the page.

You will be taken down to the ironmonger's cellar
to be stood blindfolded before the splintered deal table

where seven inquisitors prepare a sentence to be
rasped out in the light of your inextinguishable name.

Collaboration

I am being paraded through the streets with my head shaved,
with no memory of what I have done to deserve this.

I run a gauntlet of women who call me slut and whore,
staggering under their fusillade of accusation:

What stories did I tell, what lies? What names did I reveal?
What men did I sleep with? What did I do? For what reward?

Or in a catacomb deep under Paris they press gloves
of barbed wire onto my bare hands, and when the wounds
    have healed

they point to the brambles left on my palms, saying, Surely
these lines of head and heart and mind are those of a traitor.

When you wake I hold you tight, saying, It's only a dream,
the language of dream has nothing to do with that of life.

And as eventually you sink back into the deep well
of sleep, I wonder if by my words I have betrayed you.

From Your Notebook

Dresden evening, then dusk. Linnets exploding over
the ruins of the *Frauenkirche*. They are building it

back stone by stone, the stones blackened as if in a coal fire,
every one of them numbered. This is all done according

to the still extant blueprints. The *Frauenkirche* will rise
from the ashes and be restored to its former glory.

Now I remember church music murmured in the background,
the muted hum of an organ playing under stained glass.

My glass of red wine flickers in the candlelight. It's dark
by now, the other tables empty. A waiter stands by.

I will finish this postcard in the hotel. Now I am
in my room writing this by the light of a Dresden lamp

whose base I take to be a Dresden figurine of Hope,
holding her bright orb aloft under a parchment lampshade.

Prelude and Fugue

They took me to a *Bierkeller* and fed me a ham hock.
I washed it down with cold Pilsener. Boisterous music

on the go, a man with a trombone in a pork-pie hat.
My host is sketching me a Bach prelude on a napkin.

He wrote this while in Dresden. Would you like somewhere
    quiet?
So we go upstairs to the ground floor where we find a snug.

The fugue that follows has some interesting dissonances.
I found myself gazing at the optics in the mirror.

Something else was going on. There was a jukebox in back.
You know this song? I nodded that I did in time to it.

He nodded back. There is something of the carol in it.
Then he told me how the candle-flares were like Christmas
    trees,

and so to the zoo where a keeper was running amok
among the burning monkeys and the teetering giraffes.

The Story of the Chevalier

I was walking away from the war across a white plain.
No one on the road behind me, nor on the road before.

A mare galloped out of nowhere with her reins trailing blood.
She halted beside me and nodded for me to get on.

We travelled towards the dark forest and reached it by
    nightfall.
Snow was in the air, but not here where no stars could
    be seen.

Her hooves picked out a meticulous path under the trees.
By happenstance she led me to the woodcutter's cottage.

I was just about to open the door when it opened.
I walked into the dark until my eyes got used to it.

When I looked back into the dark outside the mare had gone.
I turned into the other dark and saw you standing there.

Your dark hair was as it is now, tumbled to your shoulder,
and bore two scarlet ribbons I had never seen before.

To

Remember the fountain pen rep you met in wherever?
I said. Dresden, you said. I thought it was Berlin, I said.

I'd just come from there, you said. The Wall was not that
    long down.
For all that I dressed the part, a grey Eastern suit with skirt —

I wore a hat — I felt people were looking through me to
the *Ausländer* I was. But I safely boarded the train.

I'd exchanged no words with anyone bar the ticket clerk.
The dining-car said *Speisewagen* in Black Letter script.

I looked it up and found that *Speise* meant fare, as in food.
The carriages were all compartments and side corridors,

and the passengers did a lot of walking up and down,
so much so I thought I might draw attention to myself.

So I put the dictionary away and ventured to
the *Speisewagen*, door after sliding door. That was when

I first saw him. He was faring on dark bread and blond beer.
A book with a German title lay face down before him.

I sat down two tables away somewhat unsteadily.
I thought for a split second I'd seen your *Doppelgänger*.

As it were. For when he glanced up and met my eye, his face
was unreadable. It was as if he had just come to

as you had gone away. What is it in us that makes us
see another in another? All the way to Dresden

I could see you when I shut my eyes, remembering you
as you were — this wordless annunciation of yourself

clothed momentarily in the body of another,
thinking in another language had you been spoken to —

as strange to me as when I first saw you in your own flesh,
as we go with each other as we have done, fro and to.

Rue Daguerre

I turned to where your mouth should have been but you
    were not there.
The dream I'd found you in faded like breath from a mirror.

I must be in your former apartment in Montparnasse,
I thought, abed on the uppermost floor under the eaves.

Chestnut candles were flickering at the dormer window.
Light dappled the parterres and borders of the patchwork
    quilt,

and I remembered how you once thought the quilt was Paris,
the *quartiers* demarcated by pattern and colour.

You had it all mapped out. October was a crisp apple
bitten, with that nip in the air you walked straight out into.

We would meet in the yellowed light of a daguerreotype
of Paris, by the silent fountain in the empty square,

our rendezvous untroubled by any living presence,
since the camera fails to capture anything that moves.

The Story of Madame Chevalier

The swallow flew to my ear from her nest under the eaves.
She told me a stranger was approaching through the forest.

So I climbed to the top of my tall tower and looked out
to see if it was you returning after seven years.

I found you in a clearing. You had changed. But not so much
I didn't know you under the ruin of your cocked hat.

It was evident your memory had been shot to pieces
in the war. You didn't know me from Eve. I took you home.

I bandaged you and bedded you until you got better.
It took you a good nine months not to look at me awry.

Only then did you see the quilt I'd wrapped you in aright.
There are bits of me in here, you said. This must be your
        work.

I tore up your old shirts the day you enlisted, I said,
and sewed the scraps back together in this crazy pattern.

Before

You stepped out from the shadows wearing a linen jacket
I'd never seen you in before, buttoned on the wrong side.

A sere-cloth dipped in oak-gall ink with buttons of black jet.
A clasp of ebony on the open book in your hands.

Characters of archaic Hebrew Gothic dazzled the page,
black stars danced in the blank universes between the lines,

your mouth disgorging a stream of language not known
    to me
or any man, for all I knew of what had gone before.

You fingered the stitching of the bespoke jacket and asked
would I like to try it on. But how would it ever fit?

We were not the same dimensions, and of opposite sex.
In this realm every size fits every body, you said.

You put the book away and spoke in a language I knew
from a long time before. We are entering a forest,

you said, whose trees have ears and mouths that listen and
    respond
to every passerby. Everything gets reported back.

And in the forest there is a meadow by a river
that can only be found by someone who has lost their way.

By happenstance we'll go into a little palace there,
the table laid by invisible hands, the rooms prepared.

When what's on the menu is eaten you'll know who you are.
You understand? I nodded not knowing whether I did.

I came to life in a room where a nurse watched over me.
I took her for you when she took off her sere-cloth jacket.

I put it on. It's as if it was made for me, I said.
If so, you said, the pattern was cut before you were born.

It belonged to my grandfather who was shot in the war,
and buried in a cemetery which no longer exists.

The Present

Nice watch, I said. Isn't it? you said, Omega, pre-War.
And still running like a dream after what, fifty-odd years?

Twenty-three jewels. If you open up the back and look
at the movement, you'll see how perfectly it fits its case.

Lovely work: levers, bearings, ratchets, gears, wheels, screws
     and springs
performing their task of intricate synchronicity.

Lovely case: gold bezel, black guilloche enamel inlay.
Original crown. Original black silk ribbon band.

Butterfly clasp. You turned your wrist to show me as you
     spoke.
You know your watches, I said. Everything I know, you said,

I got with the watch. It was a present from my uncle.
He collected watches. He'd make up stories about them

when I came to visit. At least I think he made them up.
One I remember in particular, a pocket watch

with a dent in its case he said had saved a soldier's life.
The hands had seized at the hour and minute the bullet struck.

Then there was the watch that once belonged to an ace pilot,
found still ticking away in the wreckage of his aircraft,

the Seamaster chronograph of a master mariner,
the Longines of a former winner of the Tour de France.

And I'd picture these men with their handsome, smiling faces,
every one of them dead even then. You fell silent then.

And your watch, does it have a story? I said. Yes, you said,
it belonged to my aunt who had died for the Résistance.

But other people whispered of her collaboration.
If watches could speak, he would say, what tales could they
   not tell?

You looked at your watch. Look after this watch for life,
   he said,
and the watch will still be working long after you are gone.

The Anniversary

What a beautiful watch! she said. Yes, he said, Omega,
this year's model. White gold bezel, black guilloche enamel.

At least that's what it said in the Omega catalogue.
Guilloche, that's the inlay, she said, see? It's a vine pattern.

She held it to her ear. It's guaranteed for life, he said.
She draped the black silk ribbon of the strap over her wrist.

She buckled the butterfly clasp and adjusted the case
to the hollow in her wrist, admiring the way it looked.

Then she held it for him to see. Yes, he said, it's lovely.
It sits very well on you. I think you made a good buy,

she said. Well, he said, this make was recommended to me
by a guy who knows watches. It's the last word in watches.

Omega. The gift of a lifetime. Look after it well,
it'll still be working when both of us are gone, he said.

Filling the Blank

I could use that in my piece, I said to him *à propos*
of the Mont Blanc. Take, for instance, the white star on
    the peak.

Did you know there was a church in Dresden called
    Our Lady
of the Snows? And isn't it funny it's snowing tonight?

I envisage some paragraphs on Dresden under snow,
the reconstructed domes and steeples beginning to blur

in the twilight. Then perhaps a *Bierkeller* interior.
I'm drinking a hot schnapps in the heat of a gas-fired stove.

I'm the lady who's deep in small talk with a professor
of music in Dresden the spiritual home of Bach.

She dines that night with the string quartet after the event.
She walks the moonlit esplanade of the Elbe before

retiring to her hotel room where she writes all she has
done that day in her journal with a ladies' Mont Blanc pen.

Peace

Back then you wouldn't know from one day to the next
    what might
happen next. Everything was, as it were, provisional,

slipping from the unforeseeable into tomorrow
even as the jittery present became history.

What kinds of times are these, you'd say, when a conversation
is deemed a crime because it includes so much that is said?

And all the unanswered questions of those dark days come
    back
to haunt us, the disabled guns that still managed to kill,

the witnesses that became ghosts in the blink of an eye.
Whom can we prosecute when no one is left fit to speak?

I read in this morning's paper, you said, of a stables
in England which had been set on fire. An eyewitness spoke

of horses whinnying, of hooves battering on the doors,
doors padlocked and bolted against all possible escape.

In the Dark

Tell me again about your sojourn in Dresden, I said.
On my way to meet the professor I had a feeling

someone was following me, you said, but when I looked
      round
no one was there. I was to get the microfilm that night.

I kept singing into myself to keep my courage up.
You know that song, *La nuit s'approche et mon village* . . . ?

. . . *s'endort là-bas silencieux*, I said. Yes, you said.
And I kept wondering what the canister might contain,

whatever it might be that I was not supposed to know.
I was merely the vehicle, as was the professor.

Though for all I know he might have been a double agent.
Anyway, I sat at the table for hours. No one came.

Just before I reached the hotel I looked back, and I swear
there were footprints in the snow that had not been there
      before.

Je Reviens

Nice perfume, I said. Yes, you said, the last time I saw you.
What is it about it? I said. The House of Worth, you said,

1932. My mother would have been seventeen.
It's the scent GIs in Paris would buy for their girlfriends

as a promise that they would return when demobilized.
That some did not goes without saying. *I come again,*

Je reviens. The overall effect is difficult
to describe, since it seems to develop separately

but simultaneously on two distinct levels, wavelengths
of suggestion and risk as well as definite statement.

One factor is mysterious and woody, with piquant
flashes of herbs, the other a heady rush of flowers.

It is based on *narcissus poeticus,* a native
of the underworld attractive to ghostly reflections.

Iris root is an essential ingredient, Iris
a sister of the Harpies, and messenger of the gods,

who ferries the souls of dead women to the underworld,
who personifies the rainbow, the iris of the eye.

How we got from the scent to the Afghan rug I don't know,
but as we sprawled carelessly on its ground of red madder

we began to enter its arabesques of indigo
and purpurin flecked with yellow larkspur of the desert.

At first the pattern seemed to be a Tree of Life, but then
the warp and weft began to shift and shimmer under us,

becoming now a dragon and phoenix in combat, now
a snarl of vines or snakes. Ensnarled and thinking to escape,

we plunged down through the ages till we landed on a field
of Afghan war rug bright with helicopters, guns and tanks.

Zugzwang

As the negotiators end by drawing up a form
of words which can be claimed by both sides as a victory;

as on a factory floor in the former East Berlin
the puzzle women puzzle together the shredded files;

as the door handle is sprinkled with fingerprint powder
to trace the guilty hand among so many innocent;

as the old chess master cannot say if ever he learned
the game, since each new game blossoms with new
    constellations;

as the choreographer charts out moves on a dance floor
like the chalk marks on a snooker table, play having ceased;

as the mad litigant rummages through his suitcase full
of ancient carbon copies to pursue his dubious suit —

so I write these words to find out what will become of you,
whether you and I will be together in the future.

PART TWO

Second Time Round

La nuit s'approche et mon village s'endort là-bas
silencieux . . . You were singing me that song again,

and I was trying to remember where I'd heard it last.
I could see the little church under the Alps at nightfall,

and snow falling beyond the casement window where you sat
with a vase of blue flowers on the table beside you.

Night was approaching the parlour as it did the village
in the words of the song. The world beyond the glass was
        blurred.

But you had gone elsewhere, back to when I first heard it sung.
It would have been in Paris all of thirty years ago.

It was dusk. *L'heure bleue*, you said, the hour of assignations.
Do you remember how the dim gongs of an Angelus

came booming in from the fog, just as I came to the end?
Echoing the bell in the song? you said. The stroke of six.

It must be that time of the year when it gets dark early,
and I am learning to drive on the wrong side of the road

in your Renault 5 Alpine. I shift the unfamiliar
gears. You should pretend to be me, you say, picture yourself

in my shoes, whereon I begin to imagine the rest,
the *broderie anglaise* bodice and the blue pencil skirt

and the black stockings. I'm wearing one of your vintage hats.
I'm beginning to like this role, I say, as I change up

and find myself on a boulevard which is deserted,
silent save for the swish of our tyres and windscreen wipers.

If I'm you, who are you? I say, whereupon you reply
with a smile I have to take my eyes off the road to catch

when a man looms into the windscreen in a split second,
rain pouring from his glistening black ulster and black
    helmet.

Hotel del Mar

You're lying on top of the quilt in a pane of moonlight.
You've opened the window for the pale voile curtains to stir

in the breeze off the white horses foundering on the shore.
You're thinking of me in a city an ocean away,

reverberations bringing to mind the helicopter
which might hover at my roof as it does on a column

of noise. You can see me lying in our shuttered bedroom.
You think I must be thinking of you, and then of the sound

of the waves. I could be you staring at the blue ceiling
dappled by wavering waves in which — like Leonardo

hearing every possible babble in a peal of bells —
I hear the syllables of your name repeated, Nina,

until the helicopter withdraws its barrage of noise,
the waves receding to a murmur as we fall asleep.

On the Contrary

It's because we were brought up to lead double lives, I said.
Yes, you said, because of the language thing it was one thing

with my father, another with my mother. Father tongue
and mother tongue, all the more so when they separated

irrevocably. It seems they could not live together.
I stayed with my mother and would visit him at weekends.

Yet something else was going on, and I remember times
when the phone would remain unanswered when it rang and
     rang.

I dared not pick it up. I see it gleaming and trembling
on its table in the vestibule beside the ashtray

in which one of my mother's cigarette ends lay crushed,
     tipped
with her red lipstick and still smoking. I go to her room

where I know she will hold me and speak some words
     of English
before lapsing into her mother tongue and mine. She smells

of cigarette smoke, tears and perfume. This is the heirloom,
the quilt we're lying on now that I lay on then with her.

She sings of the little village in the Alps where snow falls
eternally, and friends leave friends in the gathering dusk.

She was never outspoken. You can see how the patchwork
might resemble that country in summer, with its bright fields

and the crooked white seams of its intervening roadways.
I would travel them dreamily before I fell asleep.

And what of your father? I said. Oh, he lived by himself,
though I suspect there was another woman on the go,

you said. Sometimes I thought I could smell a foreign perfume.
I'd think the room would be empty but for him when I'd gone.

And I'd see him at the other end of the phone, staring
at his watch, wondering if it is the right time to ring.

Treaty

I grew up between languages, not knowing which came first.
My mother spoke one tongue to me, my father another.

They used both with each other, sometimes both at the same
        time,
and sometimes I would think this was a language of their own.

With visitors we spoke the language of the visitors,
be they doctors, neighbours, relations, clergy or police.

When I learned to write, that was another language again.
I said the words under my breath as I traced the letters.

So you spoke as if from a long way off and long ago.
Why are you telling me all this? I said. Only because

I remember the first time I spoke to you on the phone.
You told me how glad you were to hear the sound of my
        voice.

Whether I spoke to you in my first language when I said
I loved you, I don't know, but I do know the words were true.

Redoubt

I stared at my face for an age in the en suite mirror.
Then I must have crawled into bed before my mind went
    blank.

The next morning when I went down for breakfast he was
    there.
He asked if he could join me and I could hardly say no.

He looked different in daylight, his face was more open,
though he still wore the two Mont Blanc pens in his breast
    pocket.

He told me over the black coffee, bread rolls, ham and cheese,
that he had found our dialogue last night most interesting.

But was I really from Ireland? That was hard to believe,
my French was so good. Your French is very good too, you
    said,

I'd never have guessed you were from where you said you
    were from.
What would you have taken me for had you not known?
    he said.

Oh, definitely a business man, but what kind of business?
I would have thought from the pens that you were into writing.

But writing what? Manuals, statutes, orders, agendas?
You didn't strike me as a writer of fiction, you said.

You said you thought he looked at you twice but he said
    nothing.
But for the two of us the white dining room was empty.

Knives glittered on the linen. The silence was palpable
before the waiter entered and asked if we had finished.

He began to clear away the remains of our breakfast.
The agent looked at me and I looked back at him, you said.

Yes, you said, and you sat staring at each other across
an empty table. Sunlight glittered on the stained linen.

Your eyes dropped. Still he said nothing. When I looked up,
    he'd gone.
I went to pack and check out. I never saw him again.

I looked at you. I wonder what became of him, you said,
looking into my eyes as you once might have done with him.

The Assignation

Something like that happened to me once abroad, I said. I
had walked the mile to the railway station from the harbour,

my steps seemingly followed by the tolling of a bell
and what sounded like far-off, sporadic bursts of gunfire

through darkening streets where half the shopfronts were
    boarded up.
By the time I entered the buffet I was ravenous.

The menu was written in a language I couldn't read.
I found the serving-girl staring at me questioningly —

she could have been your sister, so familiar were her eyes —
so I pointed to what looked like a baguette with *jambon,*

almost disappointed when it turned out to be just that.
She watched me wash it down with a glass of the local beer.

Vous êtes étranger? she said, sounding Eastern European.
Nodding I told her in school French where I was from and
    where

I might have been. I did not know the right times for the train.
You can depend on them, she said, to run after midnight.

I heard the shriek of a train tearing the darkness apart,
the landscape it moved through a world away from the city,

and I thought you might indeed fulfil the assignation
though I could not remember whose decision it had been

to meet as designated strangers on a bare platform.
Perhaps it was determined in some other waking life.

I became aware of the station clock in the mirror,
and watched the second hand tick inexorably backwards.

When I came to I saw your face in the serving-girl's face
and I looked into her eyes, unquestionably your eyes,

and saw fleeting in their depths a world where we never met,
both of us blind to each other and what we would become.

Revolution

The spinning mills going up in an avalanche of flame.
The vacillating gun-turret of the Saracen tank.

The tick and tack of the Remote Bomb Disposal Unit.
The watch you consult to see what has elapsed of the day.

The untrustworthy public clocks, stopped at various times.
The hands sometimes missing or the face pockmarked by
  shrapnel.

The face-powder compact they discovered in your handbag.
The hands at my spreadeagled body, ankles, hips and groin.

The clicking security cameras watching, watching.
The helicopter trawling the murk with its wand of light.

The public telephone box where I'm trying to get through.
The helicopter hovering on its down-swash of noise.

The way your voice comes over in waves of long-distance call.
The things you tell me of what might become of us for now.

Through

Irrevocable: five syllables like rapid handclaps
or a volley of gunshots. Then I told you he was dead.

How did it happen? I couldn't say what reason they had,
or if indeed it was random, else someone else was meant.

I could see him standing next to me in the school yearbook.
I picture the faces of all those others now absent,

some by cancer, some by heart attack, some by suicide,
some by combatants unknown or known, if not by default —

all of us blind to what would become of what we had been.
What turn did I take that led me to meet you when I did?

Open the yearbook. Pretend you're the camera taking
me in for that shuttered second when I look straight through
    you.

As if you were alive in my eyes then as I am now,
as if I remembered what you looked like before or since.

Pas de Deux

I opened the oak doors of the armoire and stepped inside.
Your clothes still hung there, perfumed with memories of
   perfumes.

The nub of the lavender tweed, the nap of the linen.
The black sheen of a pansy-blue velvet rubbed the wrong way.

The blue pencil skirt you bought in Second Time Round under
the matching blue jacket you bought in Double Exposure.

The boxes of hats from Déjà Vu and Pandora's Chest.
The boxes of gloves from La Belle Époque and New to You.

The blouses of pale blue cotton next to the sheer linens
purchased in Second Début, Turnstyle, or Another Time.

And I remember you in Generations or Good Byes
trying on whatever piece behind a half-draped curtain,

my standing at the pier mirror looking at you askance,
as you watched me admiring the cut of your present clothes.

Second Hand

I have your watch before me, your aunt's pre-War Omega,
thirty, forty years older than me and still running strong.

I'm winding it up as I have every day for a year.
I listen to it closely to hear time ticking away.

I see how it nestles in the hollow between your bones,
how your wrist bears the ghost of a strap when you take
     it off.

It's the first thing you take off. Then you dim the Dresden
     lamp.
I kiss the pale weal left by the buckle on a blue vein.

I remember how you wore your watch when driving, facing
inward for your glance as you manoeuvred the Citroën,

a midnight blue vintage Déesse you'd picked up for a song.
You drove too fast. I'd wonder how long it would be before

they'd pull you from the wreck of the immobilized Déesse,
and know by its sweeping hand that your watch was still
     working.

Le Mot Juste

Still the interminable wrestle with words and meanings.
Flaubert labouring for days over a single sentence.

The deaf Beethoven scribbling over what he's just written
with a blunt quill plucked from the innards of a harpsichord.

The skeins of stuff from which your family history is spun,
and what wheels there are within wheels within your vintage
    watch.

Your widow aunts discussing the quilt at their quilting bee
following the dips and gradients of its staggered repeats.

The way the bread is full of unrepeatable bubbles
when you pull it apart and fathom its interior.

Snow falling interminably, irrevocably on
the little village in a song your mother used to sing.

Still the interminable struggle with words and meanings.
These words foundering for now over a single sentence.

Proposal

It happened over an apple. We were in a market,
sunshine and August showers flickering through the glazed
    roof

over a barrel of apples, green with a blush of red,
the dew still seeming to glisten on them. You picked one up.

Try it and see, Miss, said the vendor. You nodded, and bit
into the crisp flesh. You felt its juice explode in your mouth

as I did when you passed it to me for the second bite.
They're called Discovery, said the vendor, a very good

eating apple. We bought a pound of them, some wine and
    cheese,
and repaired to the country where we picnicked by a stream.

You offered me a Discovery. This time I could taste
your mouth from it through the juice. We took bite for bite
    from it

until we finished it as one. We threw away the core.
Then we asked things of each other we'd never asked before.

The Shadow

The Glass Bead Game? I said. *Das Glasperlenspiel*, if you like,
you said, not that my German is anything to speak of.

Though I remember, as a verb, *perlen* means to bubble,
as in upwardly streaming pearls of water in a pot

just coming to the boil. As for what went on in the book,
I'm at a loss to say what it was all about, or not.

The game itself was difficult to visualize. I thought
of a chess more infinitely complicated than chess,

played in three dimensions, if not four or five, for the game,
as I understood it, could admit of most anything,

though politics was frowned on. The game was above all that.
A Bach motet, or how the prose style of Julius Caesar

mirrors the cadences of some Early Byzantine hymns,
the calligraphic gestures of a flock of birds at dusk:

these were considered subjects for the Glass Bead Game.
        Or not.
There were always those who thought the opposite to be true.

The subject of the book becomes a *Magister Ludi*,
Master of the Game. He is skilled in many disciplines.

With a luminous gold stylus he writes a hieroglyph
on the dark, and so initiates a constellation

from which blossom countless others. Were the Game a music
it would require an organ with an infinite number

of manuals, pedals and stops. If geometry, or not,
Pythagoras never dreamed of it. Plato was not close.

Though it originated in the simple abacus,
the wires representing a musical staff and the beads

of various sizes, shapes and colours of glass the notes,
it grew in time to be a model of the universe.

I gather the glass beads became metaphorical beads,
not to be fingered by hand but tuned to some other sense.

At any rate, a Master is not allowed to marry.
Now I remember this one was called Knecht, which means
   not knight,

but vassal. He is in thrall to the Game. He is assigned
an underling, a Shadow. The Shadow must study him.

It does not do for a Master to have a weak Shadow.
And the Master must be fit to stand up to his Shadow.

Though the Shadow may act in his Master's stead, he may not
lay forward proposals of his own. And though he may wear

the Master's robes when occasion demands he can never
be Master himself. Such are the rules of the Glass Bead Game.

So you must cultivate your Shadow, for there is never
one Master, but another lies waiting in his shadow,

you said. And what has all of this got to do with Berlin,
I said, and your time there? You don't know how much
   I missed you.

I kept wondering where you were and what you were thinking.
As did I of you, you don't know the half of it, you said.

Isn't that the trouble? That I don't know the half of it?
Sometimes I wonder if we speak the same language, I said.

You took a sip of cold coffee and stared out the window.
The sun had just come out. Leaf-shadow dappled the cobbles.

It's like this, you said. Those who play the Glass Bead Game
      don't know
there's a war on they're so wrapped up in themselves and their
      Game.

You know I was in Berlin for a reason. Yes, I chose
to walk that path, as surely as I chose to go with you.

There's no point in going into what else I might have been.
Then you walked out the door and I followed in your shadow.

The Fetch

I woke. You were lying beside me in the double bed,
prone, your long dark hair fanned out over the downy pillow.

I'd been dreaming we stood on a beach an ocean away
watching the waves purl into their troughs and tumble over.

Knit one, purl two, you said. Something in your voice made
    me think
of women knitting by the guillotine. Your eyes met mine.

The fetch of a wave is the distance it travels, you said,
from where it is born at sea to where it founders to shore.

I must go back to where it all began. You waded in
thigh-deep, waist-deep, breast-deep, head-deep, until you
    disappeared.

I lay there and thought how glad I was to find you again.
You stirred in the bed and moaned something. I heard
    a footfall

on the landing, the rasp of a man's cough. He put his head
around the door. He had my face. I woke. You were not there.

Second Take

I remember the first time you telephoned me, you said.
Telephoned, I said, isn't that terribly old-fashioned?

And I pictured myself in a red kiosk, the black phone
crooked to my neck, as, earpiece to ear and mouthpiece to
    mouth,

I drop money into the slot of the clunking coin-box.
I press Button B when I hear you speaking and I say,

Is that you? Yes, you say, it's me, didn't you know my voice?
You know what the voice is? you said. What is the voice?
    I said.

A closed-tube resonator, like the canal of the ear,
you said. The vocal column begins in the vocal folds,

which pucker like lips on the mouthpiece of a saxophone.
Every voice can be voiceprinted like a musical score

and can be used to prove you did a crime of which you spoke.
That's why I knew your voice then. And you're speaking
    in it now.

Corrigendum

Did I say Button B? It should have been A. Button B
was the one you pressed to get your money back when
    no one

lifted the receiver from its cradle. You imagine
a room empty with the instrument's repeated trilling,

sunlight vacillating over an unmade patchwork quilt,
or someone listening under its eaves to the distant noise.

I hate to leave a phone unanswered, but I must attend
to its summons there and then, even if it means climbing

the long stair to the lumber room where the tall pier mirror
reflects a rocking horse and two armies of toy soldiers

facing each other across an Afghan rug which trembles
as I walk on it to the red box and lift the black phone.

Why are you not in the room when you told me you
    would be?
I call three times. There is no answer. I press Button B.

Fall

I'm Miranda, you said, though some people call me Nina.
Gabriel, I said, though some people call me Gabriel.

Why Nina? Why not? you said. A rose by any other
et cetera. You bore the scent of a nameless perfume.

We were sequestered in The Crown after the explosion,
illuminated by the emerald and ruby glass

of its famed windows. You'd never seen anything like it,
carved heraldic beasts gazing at you from the reredos.

You were telling me how you wrote about other places,
places usually more peaceful than this, but with a past.

You remembered a church gable pockmarked with bullet holes,
the celebration of bells that set off an avalanche,

words that put us in mind of the ever-toppling windows,
pigeons rising in a blue and emerald thundercloud

to fill the sky above the newly blasted premises
and turn a city caught unawares into onlookers.

You wanted to know whom I thought might be responsible
in such a way as to intimate you'd been here before.

I was born here, you said. My father travelled in linen.
But when I was seven we removed to his part of France.

He'd tell me stories of the War and the Liberation,
of how he met my mother in a crowd of laughing girls,

girls in high wedge-heeled platform shoes and Pompadour
     hairstyles,
blowing kisses everywhere, garlanding the tank turrets.

By now the gaslight had flickered on in dim pearly globes
and I was about to tell you about my mother's War

when there was a general hush for The News coming on,
all eyes swivelling to watch it again in slow motion.

L'Air du Temps

That whiff of *L'Air du Temps* I got back then in the wardrobe —
I remember when I first registered that primal scent,

whence the symbolism of the pair of intertwining doves,
and the frosted glass bottle that made you think of Paris

under a cloudless winter sky, as I did of your blouse
of pale pastel blue, so crisp and clean and near transparent.

Then it began to develop waves, and I was standing
with you on a beach as we noted how the laps of foam

mouthed upon one another, how the crest of the barrel
doubled and broke into a shrubbery of jumping sprays.

We got soaked with spindrift and spray, our cheeks frosted
    with brine,
but we saw the waves well. In the sunlight they were green-blue,

flinty sharp, and rucked in straight lines by the wind, bottle-
    green
under their forelocks, or the turned-over plait of the crest.

The laps of running comb buffeting the sea wall doubled
on themselves, plied and purled in their folded crash and
    back-swash,

clocking the stones underwater against one another.
We leaned unsteadily into the wind all the way back

to the hotel. We stood and looked at the waves for a while
from the bay window. We switched off the lights to watch TV.

They were showing the latest news from my native city.
It looked like a Sixties newsreel where it always drizzled,

the police wearing glistening black ulsters and gun-holsters.
When it came to the bit with the talking heads we switched
    off.

We must have drifted off to the far-off sound of the waves,
both of us thinking of how, when taking off your jersey

of rib-knitted wool in the dark, with an accidental
stroke of your finger you drew a flash of electric light.

Never Never

Once upon a time there was a little boy, let's call him
Gabriel, you said. The tale begins in a girl's bedroom.

Gabriel flies in the window. He's looking for something.
He rummages in a chest of drawers and finds the shadow

that was snipped from his feet when the window slammed
        shut on him
the last time he ventured there. He's trying to stick it back on

with soap when the girl wakes. Poor boy, you need a
        woman's touch,
she says, and she sews back the shadow with needle and thread.

You may kiss me now, she says. What's a kiss? says the boy. So
she gives him a thimble instead. He gives her an acorn.

He teaches her to fly. Have I heard this story before?
I said. Oh, probably, you said. Let's forget the story.

We drank the last of the good wine and tumbled into bed.
Then you gave me a thimble and I gave you an acorn.

Birthright

You ask what's in a name? Where I come from it tells you
    where
you're from, I said, whether this allegiance or the other.

But you can always change your name, you said. Not where
    I'm from,
I said, that would be considered a collaboration.

Or rather, an apostasy. The act of a turncoat.
In any case, they'll find you out no matter what, for there

are other indicators of identity. Such as?
you said. Colour and cut of clothes, I said, the way you talk

and what you talk about, the way you walk, your stance,
    or how
you look askance, the set and colour of your eyes and hair.

Just look at you, you said, you're talking through your hat.
    Look at
what you're wearing, that good Protestant Harris tweed jacket.

The black serge waistcoat a linen broker might have cast off.
The grandfather shirt no grandfather of yours ever wore.

Collaboration

Eventually you sank back into the deep well of sleep.
You'd been telling me about one of your aunts or great-aunts,

or rather the family whispers you'd heard over the years.
She managed to dress stylishly even during the War.

She wore nylons and seemed to have a secret cache of scent.
Where her airs and graces came from no one ventured to know.

What brought it all to mind was a dream you had woken from.
You were in Paris, disembodied and invisible,

swooping round the Eiffel Tower and down the Invalides.
You glimpsed her walking by the Seine. You glided behind her.

You knew by the cut of her clothes it was 1940.
Before you knew it you entered her clothes and became her.

And you found yourself walking, walking, as the church bells
        tolled
and tolled, announcing the hour of your next assignation.

From Your Notebook

I am waiting for you to call tonight and you do not.
I sit and watch the dumb telephone and will it to ring.

I walked all day through the replicated streets of Dresden
thinking of you just as I walked in the footsteps of Bach.

I'm using the dressing table as a dummy keyboard
as I write. One of his more simple fugues, if you must know.

I follow the curve of one of its recurrent figures
trying to figure out the resolution that is never

there in any proper fugue of Bach's. Melodic fragments,
perpetually unfinished, that seems to have been his style.

If you must know, I'm not writing this with a Mont Blanc pen.
I refused it when the agent took it from his pocket.

He must have thought I was willing enough to begin with.
The telephone rings and I let it ring and ring and ring.

Prelude and Fugue

Regarding the zoo where a keeper was running amok
among the burning monkeys and the teetering giraffes,

I'd read Vonnegut's *Slaughterhouse 5*, so it rang a bell,
I said. And I'd gleaned from my mother's memories of
    the Blitz

how the German aeroplanes would drop magnesium flares,
the whole sky lit up by dozens of ghostly, silver lights

floating down on silk parachutes. They were like Christmas
    trees,
she said. The two opposing persuasions would take refuge

in the fields that lay beyond the city, lying hugger-
mugger under the blossoming hawthorn trees in couples

of each other, until the all-clear, blossoming of smoke
above the city. Then a church bell began to toll, then

another and another, as if keeping to a score
of harmony and dissonance, for thee, for thee, for thee.

The Story of the Chevalier

You wore a red halter dress and a white comb I thought
    bone.
A diminutive whistle hung on a chain from your neck.

You took me by candlelight to a room under the eaves.
I said I thought I'd seen the patchwork quilt somewhere
    before.

It's a very old pattern, you said, Cathedral Windows.
My four aunts made it, having been made widows by the War.

They pieced back together the light of the shattered windows.
They saw themselves walking again down a shimmering aisle.

Before I knew it you were holding me under the quilt.
I found you, my arms around you, even more becoming.

When it was over you turned on a lamp at the window.
You took the little whistle from its chain around your neck.

You asked if I would like to blow on it. I would, and did.
And with that I heard the horse whinnying under the eaves.

To

So engrossed was I by the story of your encounter
I found myself to be looking at the world through your eyes

and pictured the man who looked like me emerge, as he might,
from a mirror at the end of a hotel corridor.

So you will understand I was only an onlooker
in all of this, and not there in my actual body,

the way it happens perchance in dreams. Some nights I'd
    go back
to see my parents before they had contemplated me.

They would look through me to the flowered bedroom wall-
    paper
I remember studying before I could speak, seeing

in its arboured trellises a route to the other world
where things that bore no name looked to each other, as they
    would,

for any hint of a family resemblance, reaching out
to touch each other in lieu of words. Your man my double

was like that. I watched him jiggle the key in the wrong lock
before he made his way to another and opened it.

I glided behind. All was dark beyond the vestibule.
He fumbled for and turned on the light switch from memory.

When he went to sit on the bed with his head in his hands
I sat beside him, making no impression on the quilt.

I watched while he poured a drink at the vanity unit.
He looked at himself in the mirror and began to talk

as if to himself, but really it was I, putting words
into his mouth, for I had been there before long ago.

I knew what it was like to inhabit that strange country.
I knew he longed to speak to you, if only long-distance.

But instead he would dream of his young father and mother
looking briefly through him before turning over to sleep.

Rue Daguerre

Later I'd picture you in the rue Daguerre apartment,
standing at the balcony window gazing at Paris

spread out before you like the parterres of the patchwork quilt.
I'd walk over to you and put my hands around your waist.

I'd look over your shoulder to see what you are seeing
through the blaze of the chestnut trees to the crowded avenues.

Crowds used to mean trouble, you'd say, your back still
        turned to me,
back in the Sixties. *La Révolution.* Then we'd kiss

as we sank to our knees to the floor on a Persian rug,
there to enter its intricate, intimate palaces.

At one of the exits we'd find your dark blue Déesse
awaiting with her engine ticking over like a watch.

We'd drive off into the night to arrive at rue Daguerre
in time to see the couple who make love at the window.

The Story of Madame Chevalier

You remember the Incredible Shrinking Man? I said.
Well, last night I dreamed I was him. It began the same way.

The shirt cuffs were the first thing that came to my attention,
drooping down over my knuckles in the bedroom mirror.

And my waistband and shoes were getting looser by the day.
Within weeks you could perch me on your knee like a male
    doll.

Later you would put me to bed in the empty matchbox.
You failed to watch for the spider that came to explore me.

I fought her with a darning needle, a button my shield.
She retreated from me on a thread. I followed her down

to the cellar. How I made my way back I'll never know.
It took me days to travel over the quilt to your hand.

No longer a hand but an Alpine range of sleeping flesh.
I crawled into an open pore and entered your bloodstream.

Before

Before the War, before my father met my mother, what
went on? you'd say, looking at me as if I had a clue.

Take the jacket I'm wearing, you said, it's 1920s,
it must bear the atmosphere it breathed then, all those perfumes

that beguiled the innocent and the not-so-innocent.
The milliners were in full swing with feathers and velour,

perfumes wafting from perfumeries, and all of Paris
radiant beneath the April blue, flower stalls galore.

No more the horrors of Verdun, the Somme and Passchendaele.
Black Americans are playing jazz in the cabarets.

And the blue hours are full of assignations, though I think
the woman who wore this was a little *sérieuse*.

A very sensible cut, really, for the times, though now
it might be considered *outré*. As for the hat? You shrugged.

That's the problem, you said, most people think you eccentric.
But fashions fade, style is eternal. They made things well then,

even the cheaper garments are of better quality
than you'd get now. I know what you mean, I said. Take
      the hat,

I said. It's still all right for women to wear hats, but men?
Most men wouldn't be seen dead in a hat. Do you know why?

It's all because of Kennedy. The President, I mean.
Before him you could walk down Wall Street on a sea of hats.

When Kennedy burst on to the scene, bareheaded, handsome,
dressed impeccably in a slim two-buttoned suit, smiling

that broad smile, asking what they could do for America, sober men threw off their hats in their hundreds and thousands.

But then Kennedy was shot, you said, remember? And men still won't be seen dead in hats, unless they join an army.

The Present

You were still wearing the watch I'd bought you for your
      birthday —
a 1949 Rolex Oyster Perpetual

in rose gold and stainless steel with luminous numerals
I knew you'd wanted. You wanted a man's watch for a change,

for all that you loved your ladies' Omegas and Longines.
I think men and women run to different times, you'd say.

I'm wondering if I wore a man's watch would I speed up,
perhaps we might become synchronized. But you drive too
      fast,

I'd say, and you often look at your watch as you do so,
as if you could never get fast enough to wherever

you're going. You count the hours in minutes as you would
      miles.
Remember us driving through France as the cocks were
      crowing?

By the time we came to Paris the sun was going down.
We parked by your apartment and we climbed the wooden
      hill.

You opened the door. It seemed we'd been away for a while
as we surveyed the empty rooms. You put a kettle on.

It whistled when its time was up. You looked at your
      Longines,
such a pretty thing on your wrist in its guilloche bezel.

You looked at me. I think we'll have a cup of coffee first,
you said. You poured and we eyed each other through
      the tendrils

of coffee aroma that rose from the cups. The seconds
ticked by in the second hand sweep of your second-hand
    watch.

You must be very tired, I said, after all that driving.
Yes, you said, but not that tired. I have my hidden reserves.

The Oyster is synonymous with its watertight case,
you explained. Perpetual is self-explanatory.

I watched the time go by on your glowing watch as you slept
beside me, not quite as naked as the day you were born.

The Anniversary

Yes, but even an oyster must open from time to time,
I said, don't they feed and breathe? Yes, I suppose so, you said,

but that's not the point. The point is, the world is your Oyster.
And you know to your cost how tightly shut oysters can be.

Then I remembered the oyster knife you stole in Les Halles
from a comprehensively stocked kitchen implement shop.

Then over to rue Montorgueil to ogle the oysters
reclining tight-lipped on their beds of crushed ice and seaweed.

We bought two dozen and some good Sancerre to wash them
        down.
We were celebrating one of our anniversaries.

You opened one with a dab twist. When you gave me the knife
to try my hand slipped and I gashed the knuckle of my thumb.

Before I could protest you put your mouth to the deep cut.
When you raised your head I kissed my blood on your open
        lips.

Filling the Blank

I'm the lady behind the counter of the Mont Blanc shop
who says what a nice hand when you try out one of her pens.

I'm the lady you write to when she's far away from home
though by the time the letter gets there she might have
     moved on.

I'm the lady in charge of the airport lingerie store
who asks you if there is anything she can help you with.

I'm the lady in question whose dimensions you reveal
to the lady in charge of the airport lingerie store.

I'm the lady you bump into unwittingly before
you know her name or age or what she does for a living.

I'm the lady propped up at the bar beside you, who puts
words into your mouth before you even know what they are.

I'm the lady who sleeps in you until death do you part.
I'm the lady you see in your dreams though she be long dead.

Peace

So carefully did you measure your words it seemed to me
you rarely said what first came to mind. You reserved
    judgement.

Everything was in the way you said a thing, your manner
and your mannerisms, even the way you cocked your head

spoke volumes. And lately you'd taken to wearing a veil
of an ethereal blue voile with your blue velour hat,

colours we saw later in the glass of the cathedral.
Blue stands for eternity, its gaze plumbs infinity.

To penetrate the blue is to go through the looking glass.
Sometimes its gravity evokes the idea of death.

Insubstantial itself, blue embodies whatever is
caught in it. Sound and shapes disappear in it, you might say.

You'd make a very good negotiator, I would say.
Well, I'm a Gemini, after all, you said. Geminis

see both sides of the question, so they say. We're good
    at trade.
We're ruled by Mercury, the god of commerce and of thieves.

You know that Mercury was Hermes to the Greeks, the god
of music, messenger to the gods, and the conductor

of dead souls to the underworld. He is the god of sleep
and dreams, and carries a staff of intertwining serpents.

He is the god of roads, of travellers, and of memory.
Whatever you find on the road is a gift of Hermes.

As I remember it, we had just driven to Chartres,
'capital of light and perfume', in your blue Déesse.

And afterwards we drifted away between linen sheets
scented with lavender, rehearsing the momentous day

of our marriage, whenever that might be, empyreal
tomorrow blossoming the more we found each other there.

In the Dark

Irrevocable? Unable to be undone, you said.
Unalterable, in other words, irreversible.

As it turned out, my professor was never seen again.
Perhaps he told me too much, but I was not to know that.

Nothing I could have done would have been any different,
for deeds are irrevocable, if not words. Every time

I remember the words of that song, I think of something
different. *Quand vient le soir après l'orage fuyons* . . .

By now I was in Dresden with you, under the night sky
which seemed to blossom with new constellations as you
    spoke

to me as you might have done to him then, of this and that.
And he did remind me a little bit of you, you said,

I had taken him at his word when he spoke of music.
Bach died blind, he said, and was buried in an unmarked grave

in St John's, Leipzig. I travelled there by train the next day.
They found his coffin a hundred and fifty years later.

St John's was destroyed by Allied forces in World War Two.
His remains were reburied in St Thomas's, Leipzig.

1949, the year that I was born. He lies there
to this day. Fugue, my professor said, is a kind of trance

in which the victim disappears for years on end, until
he comes to himself in a strange town and quits the double

life he led unbeknownst to himself. In musical terms
the fugue must perform its often stealthy work with shifting

melodic fragments that remain perpetually in abeyance, or unconsummated, so to speak, you said.

And I think of the blank darkness that descended on Bach as the music which blazed in his head became forgotten.

Je Reviens

You woke up one morning and said, I must go to Nevers.
You gave me to understand in a manner of speaking

that you'd some longstanding unfinished business in Nevers.
It's like this, you said. You gestured to the Persian carpet

that adorned the floor of your apartment. The Tree of Life
is a family tree. The weavers of carpets are women.

The work is done from memory. Daughter learns from
        mother,
each remembering the subtle flaws that went before them.

I'm still trying to untangle what happened in Nevers.
Perhaps I fear my mother found the pattern in Nevers.

We took a slow train to make the long journey. My father
was elsewhere on some business or other, as he would be.

For seven nights my mother would tuck me into my side
of the bed. I'd watch her making up from under the sheet.

A spurt of *Je Reviens* on both wrists, the hat and veil
adjusted just so. Then the gloves, the clutch handbag, the stole.

When to all intents and purposes I was fast asleep
she'd leave. Late one evening the phone rang. I let it ring.

Nothing was said. I'd no idea what was going on.
Last week I got a letter from Nevers that made me think

more than twice of what might have been going on in Nevers.
You must trust me, I have to do this by myself, you said.

Je reviens, you said, I will return within a week —
your last words to me, as I knew by the end of the week.

The phone rang. I picked it up and I knew from the grave voice they'd found my number in your black notebook. The Déesse

was a write-off. I took the train to Nevers the next day. I looked at you. They let me pull the sheet over your face.

Zugzwang

As you might hear every possible babble of language
in bells that tumble and peal to celebrate victory;

as the quilters make a pattern of their remnants and rags,
and the jersey, unravelled, becomes a new skein of wool;

as the fugue must reiterate its melodic fragments
in continuously unfinished tapestries of sound;

as the police might have trawled the wreck of your Déesse
in search of the twist in the plot, the point of no return;

as the words of the song when remembered each time around
remind us of other occasions at different times;

as the geographer traces the long fetch of the waves
from where they are born at sea to where they founder
     to shore —

so I return to the question of those staggered repeats
as my memories of you recede into the future.

Notes and Acknowledgements

The Irish for No
I am grateful to the late John Campbell of Mullaghbawn whose storytelling suggested some of the narrative procedures of some of these poems; and to Michael Foley for reminding me of what Frank Ifield really sang.

Belfast Confetti
Many sources were consulted in the making of this book. I am especially grateful for Jonathan Bardon's very useful bibliography in his *Belfast: An Illustrated History* (Blackstaff Press, 1982). My versions of *haiku* are much indebted to Harold G Henderson's marvellous anthology, *An Introduction to Haiku* (Doubleday Anchor Books, New York, 1958).

First Language
I am grateful to Michael Hofmann and James Lasdun for guiding me towards Ovid's *Metamorphoses*.

Opera Et Cetera
The following definitions can be found in *Chambers Twentieth Century Dictionary*:

    page 311 Auditque vocatus Apollo: and Apollo hears when invoked — Virgil, *Georg.*, IV. 7

    page 312 Solvitur ambulando: (the problem of the reality of motion) is solved by walking, by practical experiment, by actual performance

    page 313 Vox et praeterea nihil: a voice and nothing more (of a nightingale)

    page 314 Graecum est: non legitur: this is Greek: it is not read (placed against a Greek word in mediaeval MSS., a permission to skip the hard words)

    page 315 Par nobile fratrum: a noble pair of brothers — Horace, *Sat.* II, iii, 243

    page 316 Jacta est alea: the die is cast (quoted as said by Caesar at the crossing of the Rubicon)

    page 317 Aquila non capit muscas: an eagle does not catch flies

    page 318 Cave quid dicis, quando, et cui: beware what you say, when, and to whom

The Twelfth of Never

I am grateful to Junko Matoba and her colleagues in the International Association for the Study of Irish Literature, who made it possible for me to visit Tokyo; also Michael and Christine Hinds, who showed me some good bars there. Some of the 'Japanese' poems include versions of, or references to, *haiku*, particularly those of Bashō. As in *Belfast Confetti* these are much indebted to Harold G Henderson's anthology, *An Introduction to Haiku*.

Some of the details in the 'Napoleonic' poems have been culled from David G Chandler's magisterial account, *The Campaigns of Napoleon* (Macmillan Publishing Co., Inc., New York, 1966); also, Philip J Haythornthwaite, *The Napoleonic Source Book* (Arms and Armour Press, London, 1990), and Philip J Haythornthwaite and Christopher Warner, *Uniforms of the French Revolutionary Wars* (Arms and Armour Press, 1991). Likewise, I have lifted some details from Laurence Flanagan, *Ireland's Armada Legacy* (Gill & Macmillan, Dublin, 1988).

It would be tedious to give a full account of the folk-song influences on the poems, but Colm O Lochlainn's *Irish Street Ballads* and *More Irish Street Ballads* (Three Candles Ltd., Dublin, 1939 and 1965, published in one volume as *Irish Street Ballads* by Pan Books, London, 1984) were constantly referred to in the writing of this book.

I am grateful to Harry Bradley for pointing out to me that the great Sligo flute player Peter Horan customarily follows the jig 'Wallop the Spot' with another which he calls 'Spot the Wallop'; also to Charlie Piggott, for bringing my attention to *The Blue Shamrock*, an album recorded by Alec Finn.

Breaking News

This book owes much to the work of the brilliant Anglo-Irish journalist William Howard Russell (1820-1907), who is generally regarded as the father of the art of war correspondence. His dispatches from the Crimea, published in *The Times*, and collected under the title *The War* (Routledge, London, 1855), were especially influential in shaping public attitudes to the management, and mismanagement, of war. The poems 'The Indian Mutiny' and 'The War Correspondent' are especially indebted to his writing; in many instances I have taken his words *verbatim*, or have changed them only slightly to accommodate rhyme and rhythm. A selection of his work, introduced by Max Hastings and edited by Roger Hudson, is published by The Folio Society (London, 1995).

For All We Know
I want to thank Sinéad Morrissey for her editorial suggestions, and Paul Nolan whose comments on the work in progress were stimulating and provocative.

I learned the French song from my sister Caitlín some forty years ago. She learned it from a Dominican nun, Sister Mary de Lourdes, in St Dominic's High School, Belfast. I have been unable to trace any other source for it. Shortly after finishing the book I checked the words of the song with Caitlín, whereupon I discovered I had misremembered the last line of the first verse, which should read, *Du jour annonce les adieux (Announces the day's farewells)*.

My thanks to Peter Fallon for his meticulous editing of this book.

NOTES TO THE NORTH AMERICAN EDITION

Wake Forest University Press published Ciaran Carson's
first collection, *The New Estate*, in 1976 and has published
all of his subsequent volumes—*The Irish for No* (1987),
Belfast Confetti (1989), *First Language* (1994), *Opera
Et Cetera* (1996), *The Twelfth of Never* (1998), *Breaking
News* (2003) and *For All We Know* (2008). This *Collected
Poems* also includes poems from *The Lost Explorer*,
a pamphlet published in Northern Ireland in 1978, which
were included in *The New Estate and Other Poems*,
published in Ireland in 1988. The arrangement of
poems is based on the published Irish editions.

Wake Forest also published *The Alexandrine Plan*
(1998, bilingual, translations of Rimbaud, Baudelaire and
Mallarmé) and *The Midnight Court* (2006), a translation
of *Cúirt an Mheán Oíche* by Brian Merriman. These are
not included in *Collected Poems*, nor are the versions
of Stefan Augustin Doinas from *Opera Et Cetera*.

Our thanks to Timothy Keane for his eagle eye
and knowledge of New York streets.